STOLEN AMPS & DYNAMITE

Derek Henderson was born in Ipswich, England. He moved to Amsterdam in 1995, where he still lives today. He is a freelance music writer, DJ, father of one and a lifelong Manchester City supporter. This is his first published book.

Devised, written and designed by Derek Henderson.
Artwork and design – Dean Sadikot.

3

Two

Maggie Milne groaned as she ended the call with Domino, grabbed her bag, and pushed away from her desk. She was just thinking about a midmorning snack, and now she was going to have to traipse halfway across London and go to overpriced and snotty Wimbledon. *Home to wombles, tennis, and wolf-shifters.*

"Stan, time to go."

"Now? What's happened?" He was just unwrapping his sandwich, no doubt lovingly packed by his long-suffering wife, because as usual he could never wait to eat it at lunch. Like all police officers, Stan worked unpredictable hours.

"A death at Maverick Hale's club."

Stan whistled, eyebrows raised. "A shifter?"

"Yep. Kane."

"Holy shit. He was a nice guy."

"I know. I don't know what's worse. His death, or the fact that I have to see that swaggering fucking rock star."

Stan sighed, rewrapped his sandwich, put it in the drawer, and stood up. "Maverick is not a rock star."

"He thinks he's one."

"He doesn't really."

Maggie glared at him. "He does so. It's all that knocking about with the bands that he books."

4

This book is dedicated to the international music industry, and especially those that are currently finding life very difficult.

The industry has taken a massive hit in these unprecedented times.

The outpour of love, support and respect for the industry worldwide is wonderful to see.

I sincerely hope all world governments do everything they can to save this monumental scene.

Love, respect and best wishes to you all!

Bring that beat back…

X

Stolenampsanddynamite.com

DISCLAIMER

All interviews were completed before the coronavirus shutdown of 2020.

The views and opinions expressed in this publication are solely those of the author and those who were interviewed.

They do not necessarily represent those of the publisher of this publication.

Photographic material and artwork in this book has been reproduced with the permission of the copyright holders as far as possible. Untraced copyright holders should contact the author, who should also be notified of any unintended omissions and/or attribution errors.

CONTENTS

DISCLAIMER 6

CONTENTS 7

INTRODUCTION 11

THE INTERVIEWS.. 22

DJ PHANTASY 25

TREVOR FUNG 35

DJ SLIPMATT 42

MARK ARCHER / ALTERN-8 47

MICKY FINN... 55

808 STATE 70

JAYDEE... 78

DAVE HASLAM 88

GINO LIGHTNER 100

LOUIS OSBOURNE 112

A GUY CALLED GERALD 124

MONDE.. 132

BUSHWACKA! 140

DR MOTTE 151

DJ ELLIS DEE... 155

JOE SMOOTH 161

ENVOY 167

JAKE THE RAPPER.. 180

DJ DIMITRI 191

JIMPSTER 198

DJ ROMBOUT.. 204

OLIVER KUCERA 210

SAN PROPER 214

VEZTAX 219

TYREE COOPER.. 226

SAYTEK.. 230

VINCE WATSON 235

NATHAN COLES.. 245

DJ JURIAAN 254

LEFTFIELD 262

MC P-PHOLL... 267

BILLY NASTY 275

ARON FRIEDMAN 285

CRAZY SHAUN 298

AWANTO 3.. 306

BORIS WERNER 313

DARREN EMERSON 325

DJ DIABLO 334

PAUL JOHNSON... 344

CARL COX.. 357

DAVE SEAMAN 371

DANSOR 379

DJ JP.. 392

DJ LEVIATHAN 407

GENE FARRIS.. 413

MISS DJAX 422

MELON.. 426

VISION IMPOSSIBLE 440

VALENTINO KANZYANI 450

GERT van VEEN / QUAZAR 463

MR C 475

DJ CELLIE... 482

ADAMSKI.. 500

THANK YOU.. 502

INTRODUCTION

I originally had the idea to write a book, similar concept to this one, when I was 18. I was keen to find out the behind-the-scenes stories, like the struggle to obtain a licence, dealing with councils and land owners – pretty much anything relating to the raves, the set-up, police, contracts and crazy DJ demands etc. Unfortunately, nobody replied, except for rave giants Helter Skelter, who were very helpful. However, due to the lack of interest, that idea was put to bed.

The acid house and rave scene was my first introduction to nightlife, an underground experience with which I soon fell in love. The people, the music and the sheer excitement of the night ahead was compelling. The house sound was born in Chicago back in the early to mid-80s when the legendary DJ Frankie Knuckles was experimenting with music and where mixing the records together became the new norm for those grooving on the dance floor. Frankie was playing at The Warehouse, in the Windy City, which is where the term and genre house music originated. Sadly, Frankie Knuckles is no longer with us, but what a legacy!

Don't forget, also, that the music was also being produced at home, in a *house*, before the music studios took over.

By the end of the 80s the acid house and warehouse scene was growing and taking over and, eventually, led to the birth of the rave scene, especially in the UK.

Acid house was not about taking drugs, as the mainstream UK media and government machinations, at the time, would have you believe. But instead it was a term for the sampling of music, a process which was simply known as acid-burning, and the musical genre of acid house was born. Meanwhile over in Chicago DJ Pierre discovered what a second-hand Roland TB-303 could do. In doing so, the term acid and the genre also became associated with him and his discovery.

Top of the Pops, a very popular BBC television music show, refused to play any music which featured the word acid. D Mob's We Call It Acieed made it to number three in 1989 but would never feature on TOTP because of its title. Incidentally, D Mob had about 20 gigs cancelled because of their involvement with acid house and the negative press that came with it, as did international legend Carl Cox, who was labelled an outcast in his hometown due to his involvement in the scene. His story is included here.

The UK soon became a go-to destination in Europe for the new underground sound revolution that was beginning to boom from town to town, city to city and even from field to field in some obscure locations. The original motivation came from Ibiza, from the mid to late 80s, and its inspirational summer of love. DJ Trevor Fung, who also features in this book, was dropping musical bombs upon the white island, together with DJs Paul Oakenfold, Nicky Holloway and Danny Rampling. From 1987 clubs and weekly nights began to appear regularly in the UK, especially London, on the back of the inspiration of the Balearic music revolution. Paul Oakenfold organised Spectrum and Future at Heaven, while Nicky Holloway devised Trip nights at the Astoria and Danny Rampling kicked it all off with his Shoom nights. The Shoom flyer was the first to feature a new design – yellow smiley faces. A symbol that was to become synonymous with the scene, and now recognised worldwide in all walks of life.

12

Manchester had the Hacienda, which featured local artists Dave Haslam, 808 State and A Guy Called Gerald, all of whom feature in this book. Incidentally, the Hacienda survived financially on the back of the success of New Order and, in particular, their huge 1983 hit Blue Monday.

Each town and city eventually had its own scene, with some locations more influential than others. Ethical hedonism took over. At the time, 1993, I was going to the local clubs in Suffolk and Essex, in the south-east of England, which dominated the rave scene locally. In particular, Tooto's and Oscars in Essex, as well as the Raven and Mindwarp raves at the University of Essex in Colchester, alongside heavyweights Fantazia, Dreamscape and Universe, which always required a road trip. Still, to this day, the Mindwarp parties are the best I ever attended.

Amsterdam's acid house soundtrack was provided by Black Love Cabaret, Mayhem, Soho Connection and Multigroove, whose choice of music was certainly harder than that of its competition. DJs Dimitri, Monde, Jaydee and Gino were all major players in the beginning in Amsterdam and their personal stories are included in this book.

Two years later, in 1995, I moved to that beautiful, stunning city, after relocating for six months to do work experience as part of my two-year hotel management course. I was sacked after just three months following an altercation with the hotel's food and beverage director. I complained when I was refused my tips from each shift, which on some days amounted to 100 guilders a shift, and I made it clear I wasn't happy. I was told that because I was only a trainee I was not entitled to tips. "What a load of bullshit!" was the phrase that sealed my fate. I don't write this with a smile – okay, maybe a cheeky grin – and I most definitely would never
13

recommend using such fruity language with work superiors.

Looking back, I have no regrets. If I hadn't been sacked I would have had to work the following Sunday, July 23rd, 1995, which just happened to be the day of the first Dance Valley festival. I remember going with my mates from our student accommodation – Sam, Nick, Lisa, Hannah, Cathy, Terry, Clodagh, Kaisa and Nicola – and it was the first time any of us had ever been to an outdoor dance festival at 10am!

Best outdoor party ever, in my opinion. That party, all those years ago, shaped the way Amsterdam and the rest of Europe partied, with various all-day extravaganzas popping up all over Holland, and now worldwide on a regular basis, after the initial success and popularity of the original Dance Valley.

Amsterdam is now the European capital for weekend summer dance festivals, featuring the finest international artists.

But back to 95. I wasn't due to return to England until the end of October but since I had recently been sacked I needed an income of sorts to see me through. Together with a few friends, especially those who'd made it to Dance Valley, we decided to sell beer and soft drinks in Vondel Park, Amsterdam, to finance the remainder of our time in the city. I returned to England in October 1995 but within a few weeks I was back on the ferry from Harwich, not just sailing back to Holland but to stay forever. Amsterdam certainly made an impression on me. Everything I had been told about this amazing city was certainly true. It was a real eye-opener, especially my first walk through the Red Light District.

I had been going out to the raves back home, but the Amsterdam nightlife was a lot deeper, with a more hypnotic style of
14

underground music. Especially at Mazzo – I absolutely loved that place! The Dutch rave scene was going strong, filling sports centres every week. Events such as Thunderdome, Hellraiser and Multigroove were ruling the Dutch scene and anniversary parties are still being organised today, due to the popular demand and the new generation of hardcore lovers.

The rave scene in Holland was very hard and fast; the gabba sound was immense. It is still an amazing sight to witness a few thousand bald Dutchmen and pony-tailed girls strutting the hakka, the infamous Dutch dance to hard and fast hardcore music. You dance on the tip of your toes almost, kicking and twisting to the beat. Check it out online – it looks bloody awesome!

Mazzo became my new regular haunt. DJs Cellie and Carlijn rocked the Saturdays with DJ Angelo on Thursday, DJ Paul Jay on Friday and DJ Lucas on Sunday. We were completely spoilt for choice. Cellie's tales are featured in this book.

I fell in love with this new sound and Mazzo was rocking. Gaining legendary status within the Dutch, and specifically Amsterdam, nightlife, it really was something else. I was fortunate to DJ there myself a few times alongside resident DJs Cellie and Estroe.

Over the years my DJ career began to prosper but I always took gigs for granted, something I wouldn't recommend to aspiring artists today.

I used to work at The Greenhouse Effect Bar and Hotel in Amsterdam, and one evening a guy from New York checked in. He was really friendly and was a big tipper, much to my delight.

The next day he was sat at the bar and he was telling me about life in New York, where he lived, and about his early life. He said he was a record producer and managed rock bands, one of whom was punk outfit Television. He said he discovered them and managed their early career and also mentioned sharing an apartment with Iggy Pop in the 70s, where Iggy would always walk around naked.

His name was Terry Ork, but he is sadly no longer with us. He passed in 2004. Incidentally, and rightly so, he features a lot in the 2013 movie CBGB, the story of the infamous live rock and blues club in New York. I highly recommend it.

I told him that I was a DJ, and that I was playing in Utrecht on Friday. He came with me and a few others, and we had a great night. He said he really enjoyed the music and that he was organising a reunion/anniversary party for his Ork Records label in New York later that year, 2001, at CBGB in Manhattan's East Village.

He asked if I wanted to play. Wow, first some big tips behind the bar and now an offer to go to New York to DJ. Of course I said yes. Soon after that he flew back to New York but promised to arrange everything once he returned.

Two weeks later a letter addressed to me arrived at the bar. Inside were travellers cheques worth 1500 dollars. I exchanged the full amount for euros and bought myself a return flight. My mate Paul Freestone came along for the ride. We went in May 2001, just four months prior to the devastating attacks on the World Trade Towers. We spent some time in the cocktail lounge situated on the top floor of one of the towers, while the other housed an open roof garden.

Unfortunately the night at CBGB, which had Talking Heads and Debbie Harry on the bill, was sadly cancelled due to the fact it couldn't be recorded with a video camera. Fortunately, we found two new gigs elsewhere in the city and still had both the hotel and gig fee paid, so that was a result. We met Terry a few times while we there and much to my amazement he gave me another 500 dollars. "To enjoy New York and to apologise for the cancellation of the gig," he said.

We did manage to have a tour of a closed graffiti-covered CBGB one day and shared a drink with owner Hilly Kristal. I even used the famous toilet where Janis Joplin is said to have been caught giving Iggy Pop a blowjob.

Another night, we were hanging out with Rob Rives, aka Floppy Sounds, Matthias Heilbronn and Francois Kevorkian, an absolute legend of the scene, after meeting them at a bar called Idlewild, where Floppy Sounds was having an album launch. Rob even gave me a signed CD. Cheers Rob! We all shared a taxi and they took us to the Plant Bar after closing.

We also saw Laurent Garnier and Tony Humphries play at Centro-Fly on a Wednesday night and the following day we had a guided tour of the Wave Records office, just off Times Square. We were also kindly given several records from the label. I even spotted Francois Kevorkian working in his recording studio, which was built within the label's office.

We were among New York DJ royalty for a week. If only I'd shown more respect for those moments, instead of taking it all for granted, then the career of DJ Kreed may have turned out differently.

Fast forward to 2013 and I was about to become a father for the

17

first time, together with my fiancée Stacey.

It was around this time that I noticed several social media posts from a few artists in which they briefly described incidents, both good and bad, from the weekend's gigs. I wanted to explore those moments in more detail and had the idea that it would be good to combine their anecdotes for a book.

Remember, I had originally tried to write a book in 1993, but I felt the time was now right to re-visit the idea and do everything possible to bring it to life.

Originally, I concentrated on acid house and rave artists, mostly from the UK. But they're a lazy bunch, in the most positive of ways, and only a handful of artists replied to my original email.

One English rave originator I was keen to interview was Billy 'Daniel' Bunter. He originally replied to my request for an interview with interest and even agreed to put one hour aside. Great, I thought, but then I never heard from him again.

A few weeks later Billy was advertising his own book and I had not even been aware he was writing one. He certainly never mentioned it to me. I have to say, I'm pretty sure my original email outlining my own book's concept might have provided him with his own light bulb moment, and the books that featured other rave DJs, also published by Billy, did nothing to change my theory. Not a problem, though; I'm happy to inspire others!

I was very grateful to those who took the time, not only to reply but grant me an interview. My original DJ hero, DJ Slipmatt, one half of rave pioneers SL2, even offered to publish the book if it was solely about the rave scene.

But there still weren't enough rave-related artists or topics to fill a book. So I reached out to my favourite artists, from the acid house days right up to the present day and regardless of musical genre. I waited for the replies to fill my inbox – and they did. Everyone was very positive and very keen to share stories, so this baby grew some legs and started to run.

The following January, 2014, my other baby was born. Louis Jack Henderson had entered the world and this first-time father had to get his arse in gear.

The response to the book exceeded all expectations and I was now having regular email, texts, etc. with many of my heroes. I was arranging interviews online and even managed to organise a lot of them during Amsterdam's wonderful summer festival season, a convenient fix for all parties.

Wooferland – in my view the best old-school festival in Europe, perhaps even the world – were particularly helpful. Many thanks to Manon, Lars and Bas for their wonderful hospitality. Awakenings, Cheeky Monday, Loveland, Dockyard, Paradiso and Dance Valley were also very hospitable, so a big thank-you to you all. I tried every ADE, Amsterdam Dance Event, for press accreditation, but they always refused my application. Perhaps I could have managed another 10 to 15 interviews with other heroes if I had been granted access.

Sadly, I broke up with Stacey, Louis' mum, when he was 10 months old. Stacey moved to Leiden and we became single parents, sharing joint custody of our gorgeous boy. That was when the book project had to be put on hold as Louis became my main focus, which took up a lot of my time and concentration.

However, it was always my intention to complete the book. My

19

enthusiasm never wilted but the time I had to devote to it became very limited.

Further delays became inevitable when, in November 2015, I was diagnosed with testicular cancer. My operation was a success and I was told no further treatment was necessary.

It took about three weeks before I could walk straight and properly, but in that time I had an interview with Leftfield scheduled at the Paradiso. There was no way I was going to cancel. I'd been looking forward to this moment for ages. I absolutely love the Leftfield sound, and Leftism is an absolutely timeless production, so to be sat next to those responsible was a very big deal for me.

I watched the soundcheck then sat down with Neil and Adam to conduct the interview. They were hungover following the gig and after-party the night before, while I was also under the influence of a few heavy painkillers and too many coffees, while sporting a fresh and tender tight wound in a sensitive area proved a further distraction.

It really was the worst-possible preparation for an interview. I didn't know where to start and everything I thought I was going to talk about didn't even enter my mind. I had a total brain freeze. I've since spoken to Neil, offered my apologies and tried to arrange a second interview, but to no avail. I was keen to redeem myself since I was convinced Neil and Adam were unimpressed with me, despite the mitigating circumstances.

They were not rude but we didn't seem to connect in any way. They put me on the guest list for that evening's performance, gave me a tour shirt and I had a photo with the entire band, so it wasn't a complete waste of time. I actually had to leave the
20

concert early because I couldn't cope with the crowds and the constant knocking of elbows into my stomach.

I can honestly say that was the only time an interview didn't go to plan. It was a learning curve for me, despite my health, and pushed me to be more professional next time when sitting in the presence of such stars.

My recovery was good, although only six months later I was diagnosed with lung cancer. My oncologist scheduled me in for three weeks of chemotherapy over a nine-week period. But just two days before it was due to start I was informed that the chemo was being put on hold. Instead, they would monitor the nodule for four weeks, ending with a scan.

By this time, I had become aware of cannabis oil and how well it could apparently treat cancer. I immediately bought some, used it many times a day, and after four weeks, following a scan, the nodule had shrunk by half. Two months later I was told that I was in complete remission and, to this day, the cancer has not returned.

It was certainly a massive help that I had this project on the side. It proved a great distraction at a very difficult time. I continued to work on the book and, despite a few delays along the way, I finally completed what you are holding in your hands right now.

I hope you enjoy the many pages that follow.

THE INTERVIEWS

In England and pretty much all over Britain and Ireland, the rave scene was massive. From illegal events being ambushed weekly by police, and, in some cases, raided by gangs, to superstar events in amazing locations, I wanted to explore the artists' personal experiences, with the hilarious, mad and downright crazy tales at the very top of my list.

All artists were hand-picked, with my original heroes from the acid house and rave scene, through to the national and international, deeper-slower house and techno artists I was introduced to after relocating to Amsterdam in 1995.

The Mazzo in Amsterdam soon became my new nightlife home and Billy Nasty was a regular favourite of mine. One night in particular, at the Mazzo's temporary home on the Oudezijds Voorburgwal, since a fire on Queensnight in 1995 had gutted the place, Billy was playing alongside The Advent and went all the way through to 11am Sunday morning.

The upstairs had a wooden dance floor and that floor was pushed to its limits that evening and morning. Everyone bounced all night, even those who didn't want to. Happy days.

The interviews vary from artist to artist. Some were completed online via Skype, video calls, some over the phone and the majority took place face-to-face backstage, or in their dressing rooms at festivals and events.

There are particular moments in each artist's career that I had either found interesting, unbelievable, wild, particular tracks, certain gigs or particular incidents that I was especially keen for them to elaborate upon. Anything that had captured my attention, I was keen for them to explore in more detail.

In some cases they went very deep and personal. This was very much an eye-opener for me, with certain heroes showing their passion for life outside of being an international, non-stop touring artist.

I reached out to well over 100 artists but, for one reason or another, the contact dwindled with many.

Rave legends Slipmatt, Micky Finn, Mark Archer, and Phantasy are included. House pioneers Paul Johnson, Tyree Cooper and Gene Farris gave up their time to be interviewed, as did Love Parade head honcho Dr Motte. Dutch legends Dimitri and Miss Djax, together with fellow countryman and Plastic Dreams mastermind, Jaydee, also kindly offered their support, as did Slovenian techno chiefs Valentino Kanzyani and Veztax. Amsterdam stars such as Mazzo's very own DJ Cellie, San Proper, Diablo, Juriaan, Melon, MC P-Pholl, JP, Oliver Kucera and Aron Friedman also feature. UK artists 808 State, Leftfield, Mr C, Bushwacka!, Vince Watson, Darren Emerson, Dave Seaman and many others share their fondest memories, while the one and only Carl Cox opens up about his involvement in the acid house scene, acting, Amsterdam and much more.

The early days of their careers, why a DJ?, tours, albums, the creation of seminal anthems including Voodoo Ray and Plastic Dreams, the wild weekends, particular gigs, and many, many more revealing, and, most importantly, humorous stories about the life of a DJ.

Much to my amazement – and huge disappointment – one rave

legend asked me how much I was going to cough up for the privilege of interviewing him. After telling him I had purchased every record he released back in the day, and how I looked up to him as an exceptionally skilled DJ, I crossed him off the list and deleted him. Cheeky bugger!

You may be reading this and thinking to yourself 'What about such and such?' but that would be your experiences, and only you may know that, so it's pretty much from a personal angle that numerous interviews were conducted.

This book includes many mad and humorous moments, from the believable to the downright unbelievable. A naked DJ locked outside of his hotel, police searching for a missing DJ, dynamite, the legendary Hacienda and the stolen amp, war zones, Diego Maradona, kidnappings, police raids, tear gas, airport adventures, illegal warehouse raves, hotel fires, gun-wielding mafia maniacs, raving behind the iron curtain, driving through the Berlin wall to get to a gig, the camel jockey trainers, the birth of the Love Parade and the time an international legend was chucked into the cells after a police sting!

There are drug and alcohol references, but what did you expect? It's only rock and roll - but with a kick drum.

That's just a brief outline of what you can expect and I really hope you enjoy the interviews.

Put the needle on the record...

DJ PHANTASY

We kick-off with DJ Phantasy, who was actually the first DJ to confirm an interview right back at the beginning of this project.

After selling rave tickets in the late 80s on behalf of organisers Phantasy, from which his DJ name originates, to performing for 20,000 people on a regular basis, Steven Hannon, aka DJ Phantasy, has become a household name in the UK and International Rave scene. He was initially a builder with his father in the family business but felt more inspired by music.

Still performing to packed international dance floors, Steve continues to be on top of his game, rocking the finest drum and bass.

"I'm a DJ first, a producer second, a record label boss third and a promoter fourth," he says.

Steve has also written a very entertaining and interesting book called Three Generations Deep which is available to buy.

For this interview, Phantasy spoke about upgrades, being on the road with Carl Cox and delivers a hilarious tale involving the police and a missing DJ.

Back in 1993 I flew overseas to play with Micky Finn and MC Reality, and at the airport I announced, full of confidence, that I was going to get us all upgraded. Micky laughed and said: "Yeah, go on then," with a smile on his face. I walked up and down the check-in area to try and find a camp member of staff. After locating him, we headed to his desk and I asked him, in my finest camp voice: "Can you check us in please?" "Oh yes," he replied. I then leaned in with a smile and asked if he could upgrade my friends and me. He pressed a few keys and, hey presto, we were upgraded. Easy! Micky and Reality were shocked but happy with my efforts.

So there we were, upgraded and feeling great. As the flight was about to take off I couldn't help noticing that the stewardess kept smiling at me. I thought nothing of it but she kept smiling. Every time she walked past she gave me a smile and so I thought I would smile back, being the gentleman I am! She was very attentive to all three of us but it was me she was smiling at. The drinks were flowing and we just thought that this was the treatment you received in Business Class.

So the smiles and the personal attention continued. Micky couldn't believe the interest she was showing in me and eventually said: "Maybe you're going to be the next member of the Mile High Club."

A bit later on she came over to me with another of her colleagues and asked if I was a musician. 'Wow, fuck me,' I thought. 'She knows who I am!' I leaned over to Micky and Reality, and told them that she recognised me. "Yes," I replied, "I'm a musician."

"Are you Simply Red?" she asked, with obvious excitement. We all just fell about laughing then looked at each other and I replied "Yeah, we're Simply Red," much to the disappointment of Micky. And to be honest I was really pissed off that she thought I was Mick bloody Hucknall!

I was playing at the legendary Eclipse club in Coventry with Carl

Cox, right back in the day. The Energy boys, who were the promoters, asked if we were able to do an interview for the TV programme The Hit Man and Her. At the time Carl was managing me and we were also regarded as a team, so we agreed.

So, I was stood there talking to Pete Waterman and I asked him what he was going to ask me, and he just said he would make it up as he went along. Suddenly, the lights went on, the camera was rolling and it completely took me by surprise as Pete stared into the lens and introduced me. Check the video – it's available on YouTube – and you can see me looking very worried as the microphone is suddenly shoved in my face without any warning.

I must say, though, that Pete Waterman was an absolute gentleman. He didn't know me from Adam. And after the interview he handed me his business card and asked me to give him a call. I did, we met, and he took me to the Stock Aiken Waterman studios, followed by dinner. He didn't have to do that; I was just little old me in those days but he treated me with the utmost respect. I then agreed to remix one of his tunes, Papa's Got a Brand New Pig Bag by Pig Bag. In my quest to keep it real I made the remix rave orientated because that's what the vibe was at the time.

After completing the remix, Coxy asked why I didn't use any of the original sounds and I hadn't a clue how to answer him. For me, I just made the remix relevant to my sound at the time, one for the ravers! It was well received by the underground massive. One regret, though, is that I don't feel I gave that remix enough justice, which could have taken my career down a different path. I wasn't business orientated in those days. At the time I was just too interested in the scene. I was playing regularly to 40,000 people and I wanted the world to know, not just about me but the entire UK rave scene.

Carl and I were great mates, we did lots of gigs together and I spent a lot of time in the studio with him making records.

Carl was a massive influence on me in the early days and influenced the way I played too. I used to go raving and see Carl play so for him to then take me under his wing was amazing. Alongside Top Buzz and DJ Seduction, he signed me to his agency. There I was, raving to Carl Cox one minute and the next suddenly working alongside him. Very surreal. We had a wicked laugh and became good mates. Our friendship grew and we spent a lot of time together, sometimes on the road for two to three weeks at a time, travelling all over the place, staying in hotels. It was pointless to come home after a gig. I remember we had bookings in Derby, next night Middlesbrough and then, say, Leicester 24 hours later and then on to Wales. We just jumped in the car and drove all over the place, up and down the country; it was mad. He also arranged gigs for me in Italy, Japan and Australia back in the day.

CDJs were not about in those days – it was 100 per cent vinyl.

One thing I remember about Carl is that not only was a massive influence on my career and development, but he was also a hindrance on my pocket. When Carl Cox goes, or went, record shopping he didn't just buy one or two records, he'd buy the entire shop! It was really hard to keep up with him. If we were playing in a town that had an underground record shop we would always visit it because we were always surprised by the amount of gems we could find.

However, the records did vary from place to place. For example, in Manchester they would have a load of records only available there and in the surrounding area. The same would be the case in, say, London. People in those days were selling records out of the boots of their cars. Each town or city had its own crews, DJs etc. and this was represented by the vinyl available up and down the country.

I remember one weekend driving to Portsmouth with Carl. I had never been there before as a DJ, only as a Chelsea fan on away days, driving two to three hours just to buy records. I remember the huge stacks of records on the counter. I had to move them to the side just to be able to speak with the guys behind. And, of course, whenever they saw Carl walking in they would rub their hands together, knowing they could take their girls out for a meal that evening after Coxy bought the lot! The beautiful thing about it is they always gave us a discount.

We were supporting the scene and the industry. We were active artists, playing almost every night, and we felt we had to give something back and support the labels.

Carl would always buy the most, sometimes 200 to 300 records, then it was me with 100 to 200 and finally Gemini, who usually bought about 12. Gemini was really selective about the tunes he bought.

The funny thing is that some of the records I bought I never even played, because my collection was so huge. I then sold a lot that had never even been out of their sleeves.

No matter what, it was always a costly day out record shopping with Carl Cox. Good times though!

Some artists can let their status go to their heads, whereas Carl was always just a very normal guy. He would often chat with my mum, a proper down-to-earth bloke and a really lovely guy. I

29

wouldn't have anyone say a bad word against him. He was a massive influence on my career and it was a shame that our musical paths crossed. I loved the jungle and breakbeat sound that was emerging and Carl went down the techno route. The rest is history.

I was producing more and more with my mate Gemini and we would sell our records from the back of our car. We sold enough so we didn't need a real job. Job done!

In 1991or 1992 – can't remember exactly – Gemini and I were playing at the Energy weekender and we were accompanied by our girlfriends and mates etc. After our sets Gemini, our driver Mick and I headed for Skegness to play at another gig. One thing I do remember is the really long road that leads into Skegness, probably about seven to ten miles long. So we made it to the party, played a blinding set and then the three of us jumped back in the motor. Mick was driving, Gemini was wasted on the back seat and I was falling asleep in the front – despite the tunes on full volume!

So we're heading out of Skegness, that long road again, and we got perhaps 20 minutes into our journey when Mick woke me up and, with a hint of panic in his voice, asked: "Where's Gemini?" 'Don't be so stupid,' I thought. 'He's in the back seat, you nuttier. Where else could he be?' But when I turned round to see for myself he was nowhere to be seen. What the fuck was going on? By this time we'd covered perhaps 10 to15 miles, or maybe even more, and had absolutely no idea where Gemini was!

I was looking around the car trying to make sense of it all and I noticed the car door in the back was ajar and all I could see was a coat on the back seat. Where the fuck was Gemini, how can this be, what the hell was going on? He was there, now he wasn't – I couldn't work it out. To be honest, we were going round the roundabouts like Nigel Mansell and I thought to myself 'Fuck me, he's fallen out!' Panic started to set in. What were we going to do? How was I going to tell his missus?

By this time it was around 3-4am, it was pitch black and we couldn't see a thing. We had no idea what the hell had happened or if we'd ever see Gemini again. I told Mick that we would have to go back, so he turned the car round and we headed back for probably a total of 20 miles – but driving really slowly. Mick was looking out the right side and I was on the left, praying we were going to catch sight of him at any moment and put an end to the nightmare. Every time we approached a roundabout we would creep round it really slowly so as to get a good look and try to spot him, but he was nowhere to be seen. Bloody hell, how was I going to explain this? By this time I was panicking, really panicking, thinking I'm never going to see my mate again!

Each roundabout had sandbags round it and from a distance they could easily be mistaken for something else – Gemini perhaps – but no, they were all sandbags. Time was passing rapidly and I decided I had to do something. In those days mobile phones were very rare but I had one. So I called his girlfriend, woke her up, and tried to explain what had happened. I told her that one minute he was in the car and the next he had vanished. Poor girl; God knows what she must have thought. I had just told her that I had lost her boyfriend from a moving car, which isn't really the type of incident you want to explain to a loved one, even the police for that matter. They were next. I told them: "My mate was in the back seat when we left Skegness, I fell asleep and when I woke up my mate had vanished, and I don't know where he is." The police were like 'Huh, what are you on about?' So I replied: "The car door was open so we think he's fallen out somewhere. Can you send a car to try and find him please?" They agreed,

31

noted our location and said they would try to find Gemini.

There we were, driving at a snail's pace looking for him, with his missus shitting herself thinking something awful had happened and a police car was speeding to our location to look for a wasted DJ lying in the road. Just a normal night out!

We were driving back down the winding country roads in complete darkness, Mick looking out his side and me frantically doing the same on my side. By now the tears were starting to roll down my face. What a fucking mess. What have we done?

Suddenly, in the distance, I spot something.

As we got closer the image got bigger and after a minute or so I worked out it was a moving object. Not any old moving object but one that was staggering right towards us. It was a small country road, no footpaths and suddenly I could see what it was. It was Gemini. He was alive!

We pulled up next to him, he jumped in the car and he only said one thing: "Turn the fucking music up!!!!"

We asked him what on earth had happened, thinking we were going to hear one hell of an explanation. He said to me: "Don't you remember?" Mick and I looked at each other and had no idea what he was on about. He continued: "When we stopped at the traffic lights I told you I was going for a piss!" Now you have to remember I had fallen asleep and had not heard any of this. So the fuzzy picture started to come sharply into focus and we realised that poor old Gemini was standing at the side of the road, we were at the lights and when they hit green we went, completely oblivious to the fact that Gemini had got out of the car.

He saw us driving off and was probably thinking 'Yeah, yeah, funny one boys, now stop the car.' But we had actually carried on for nearly 20 miles before we realised he wasn't in the car. All he could see was the back of our car getting smaller and smaller, thinking it would stop at any time, but instead it completely disappeared from sight. While we kept driving in the dark, if you see what I mean, Gemini, poor bugger, had no option but to start walking!

Now, just after we left him, perhaps three or four miles, there was a left turn, a right turn and we also had the option to continue straight on. We turned left but Gemini had no way of knowing this. Yet when he approached he, amazingly, also chose to go left, luckily for him, and continued walking. It must have been a total of 15 miles before we eventually spotted him. He said he had tried to find a house so he could knock on the door and ask if he could call me to come and pick him up from some stranger's house.

I called the police and told them we had found him and that they could call off their search. I also called his missus and she was one happy lady.

At the time it was anything but funny, but nowadays I admit I can't stop laughing hysterically whenever we speak about it!

One of my very good friends, DJ Hype, was having a meal for his birthday and invited a few select friends along to a restaurant in east London where we had the entire top floor to ourselves.

Our agent, Caroline, managed to spill a bit of her drink on me accidentally and so, jokingly, I flicked some water on her. It was nothing serious, just a bit of fun, until she decided to throw her

33

entire drink over me. 'Right then, game on,' I thought, so I responded by emptying my drink all over her. Then, suddenly, the top floor erupted into a massive food fight.

There we were, leading members of the rave scene, covered in cakes, rice, noodles, ice cream and topped off with a selection of different drinks! Even the bloody ash trays got in on the act.

Cheers Hype, I've still got the scar!

Anything that wasn't nailed down was flying across the room, all in the name of fun. Nothing negative, just a group of grown adults having a good old food-ash tray-liquid fight.

In my attempt to escape the carnage I ran downstairs and the entire restaurant staff were heading upstairs in a state of sheer shock and panic. In the middle of the top floor there was a huge feature statue taking pride of place and it was obviously of some value, even if it was only sentimental rather than monetary. We, however, didn't pay much attention to it and the look on the staff's faces was one of sheer shock. This statue-type thing was dripping with ice cream, rice, noodles, alcohol, pretty much everything. Thank God it wasn't my local.

I don't go to restaurants with Hype any more.

TREVOR FUNG

Back in the day Trevor was one of the original DJs to emerge from the UK and spread the underground house sound worldwide, long before the scene became the dominant force we know today.

Trevor was hanging out in Ibiza in the early 80s and in 1987 he started to DJ on the island with fellow superstar DJ Paul Oakenfold, who, at the time, was unknown in the world of DJs. The rest is history.

Without his passion, perhaps the scene that is often referred to as the Balearic sound may never have come to light and go on to grace the world's dance floors for decades.

It was Trevor's early involvement and leadership that inspired many hungry youngsters to buy a set of decks and start a studio in their bedroom etc. The UK scene grew and grew, with Trevor inspiring many to not only turn to acid house but go on to become artists in their own right.

From Trevor's early German DJing experiences, it's clear to see that East and West were already being unified on dance floors. As one, in dark, smoke and strobe-filled underground techno clubs – and long before the wall came down.

For the interview, he touched upon flights, Ibiza, Las Vegas and more.

I used to co-promote and play Rage at Heaven and was also responsible for the programming. I used to book a lot of international DJs like Carl Craig, Derrick May etc. But not just Americans; there were also a great many others from around the world. Westbam was actually the first German DJ I booked and the first German DJ to play in England. He's a great DJ and a great bloke, and it was through him that I met all the other DJs from the Dutch and German scene, like Jaydee, who produced Plastic Dreams, DJ Hell and the Love Parade crew. I actually played at the very first Love Parade party back in 1989.

In the late 80s I used to play a lot in Amsterdam and Rotterdam, and played in East and West Germany a number of times – especially Tresor and Planet in Berlin, which was next to the river.

This was just around the time the wall was being pulled down because I remember being picked up and we used to drive through a hole in the wall to reach East Berlin. This was probably 1988-89 and I'd often be playing with the big American DJs plus the Underground Resistance boys.

I remember playing in this really mad place that was like a dungeon. I would play for two hours then get driven back through the wall to West Berlin. It was mad.

Hamburg and Munich started to grow on the back of Berlin's success and Germany now, especially Berlin, really has some of the best clubs and parties around.

I was booked to play somewhere in Wales, right back in the day, and when I turned up there was no bloody party. This particular evening started with a gig in Chelmsford, in Essex, before driving to the non-gig in Wales and then back to London for the last gig of the night.

In those days it was nothing like today. We had to find a dirt road and back then we didn't have sat nav to show us the way. Then we had to find a gate, then another gate and keep going until we could see the party. And all of this while carrying a box of records!

On one particular occasion the police had beaten us to it and shut the party down. Unfortunately, there was a lot of this stuff going on in those days and we didn't have mobile phones so we never really knew what was going to happen. In a way this saw the birth of agencies and management for DJs. We were all missing out on work and with an agency things were more concrete and official. Well, most of the time.

Don't get me wrong, it was fun in these weird places in the middle of nowhere but as I became more professional I decided things had to change.

I first played in Ibiza back in 1982, then 1983, and then I started going out there to have a holiday towards the late 80s. It was then that I really fell in love with the island and I've been back every year since. I love it.

Back in 1987 I rented a bar for the summer and took Paul Oakenfold and Danny Rampling out there to play. We kind of started this whole crazy Summer of Love vibe and it was amazing. It was the first time Paul and Danny had played in Ibiza. They couldn't believe it and they were hooked.

I remember playing in Portugal with Paul many years later and afterwards we flew back to Ibiza for a gig at Pacha, before I flew

37

on to Tenerife for another gig later that evening. Anyway, we were at Pacha and my flight time was fast approaching when I decided to change my flight to the evening and stay at Pacha with Paul to keep the party going – like you do.

Later that evening I made it to the airport on time and almost immediately I noticed these two guys with shades on. I boarded the evening flight to Tenerife, via Barcelona, and again I noticed the same two guys with the dark shades. I changed at Barcelona and yet again these two guys were on the plane.

I landed and by this time I only had about 30 minutes before I had to be on stage – and it's about a 45-minute drive!

Already a little stressed, I approached the customs gate and once more these two guys I had first seen in Ibiza were there. They were only undercover police officers! I was taken to a room where I was questioned and then strip-searched. Charming. I didn't have anything on me, of course, but they still kept me behind. Eventually they let me go and I arrived at the gig almost two hours late but still managed to play. My good friend and fellow DJ, Alvredo, had filled in until I finally arrived.

I guess, looking back, these guys must have been tailing me since Pacha. What a wasted journey – in more ways than one.

I remember playing in Los Angeles back in 1991 with Frankie Bones, Lenny Dee, Joey Beltram, Blake Baxter etc. at this massive outdoor party called, if I remember correctly, City of Angels.

I was picked up from the airport and taken to my hotel but something didn't feel right. The promoter didn't have any credit cards, or even cash, and he made his girlfriend pay for my room, which I thought was really strange.

I had been there for a couple of days, played the gig and gone back to the hotel, and being the only English DJ booked I was kind of on my own. I tried to get hold of the promoter because he still hadn't paid me and after I found him he told me he had no money. I didn't have any gigs planned for a little while so I had nothing to go home for. I decided to stay for another five days – in the room for which his girlfriend had originally paid.

Eventually, I received a call from reception telling me that the money on the room had run out and it was time to go. I still hadn't been paid, and wasn't likely to either, so to get my money's worth I started running up a huge drink bill on the room. Ha-ha.

I left LA and when I was back in London the broke promoter started ringing me and calling me all sorts of names. He was telling me I was out of order etc. when, in fact, it was him who was out of order by not paying me in the first place. In fact, he basically pretty much screwed over every DJ there. Promoters!

Back in 1990 or perhaps it was '89 – I can't quite remember – we had been playing Love at The Wag in London. At closing time, around 6am, we all headed for Heathrow Airport. The Wag boys had arranged a Spanish tour for us and that particular morning we were heading out to Valencia to play at a place called Big Ben. They had actually sold 10,000 tickets in advance – a complete sell-out.

There was Dave Dorrell, CJ Macintosh, me and a few others, and we were waiting for our early-morning flight. Suddenly, we discovered our flight had been delayed…and delayed…and delayed.

By this time it was about 2pm and we had all been there since 6am without any sleep. The boys were getting restless and everybody had pretty much had enough, and just wanted to go home to bed.

I decided enough was enough and called Rob, our manager at the time. I told him that we were not waiting any longer and that we were all heading home. "No, no. Wait, wait. I'm coming down there...now," he replied, sounding half asleep. So Rob arrived, still in his bloody pyjamas, passport in hand and convinced us all to stay put and wait for the re-arranged flight. Too tired to argue, we agreed.

So there we were – complete with Rob, who decided he would join us – on the very much delayed flight to Valencia. Tired but happy, we were all going to make it to our gig so everybody started to relax and enjoy the flight.

About halfway through the journey, the pilot made an announcement that due to the bad weather the plane would be landing in Madrid and there would be no connecting flights anywhere due to the awful weather conditions.

We all looked at each other in disbelief and started laughing as we were that tired. What next? Madrid? How are we going to get to Valencia? What about the gig? We were the only DJs booked and we were all stuck in Madrid, with 10,000 people expecting us in Valencia. It was a proper nightmare and with Valencia more than 200 miles and four hours away we ended up enjoying Madrid's nightlife.

I played in Gothenburg with Danny Rampling in 2010 and our gig was on a Friday. But we both had gigs in England on the

Saturday so we couldn't hang around and headed straight for the airport after playing. But unfortunately it was snowing really hard and the airport was covered, and no planes were flying in or out – except for one flight to Brussels. I'd never seen anything like it, there was so much snow. We didn't really know what to do, so we just thought we would take the flight to Brussels and make it to England that way.

By now we'd been at the airport all night. It was 8.30am and we were heading for Brussels. We had the idea that if there were no flights to England we would just catch the train. But little did we know, no trains were running. So there we were, stuck in Brussels and it was probably late morning by then, and there are no trains and no planes. Eventually, at 10.30pm, we boarded a flight to London and after landing we headed off in different directions to do our gigs.

It wasn't really funny at the time but looking back I can laugh at it now.

What a night…and day…and night!

DJ SLIPMATT

Matt Nelson, aka Slipmatt, is my absolute hero. It was an absolute pleasure, not only to be in his company but to also interview him.

I was fortunate enough to see SL2 live on several occasions around the south-east and beyond in the early 90s, as well as the numerous stomping DJ sets from the man himself.

Mindwarp at the University of Essex, in particular, was always a memorable night when Slipmatt was in town.

Known fondly as The Godfather of Rave, Slipmatt still continues to fly the flag and represent the scene worldwide, of which he has been on top for decades.

Matt spoke about wild weekends abroad, road trips, awards and a Kylie Minogue kiss.

We had a gig in Mexico back in 1992 as SL2. There were five of us – our MC, two dancers, Lime and me. It was booked through a big agent at the time but somehow it all felt a bit flaky. I don't know; it just wasn't right. We flew to Los Angeles and then we jumped in a tour bus for a 10-hour drive to Mexico.

Halfway down there the bus ran out of fuel and the driver didn't have any money on him. He had to leave his watch at the petrol station and told them he would be back. He was going to drop us off at the party, pick up some money and pay on his way back.

Anyway, that was one thing. He dropped us off at the rave and there were only 20 people there. It had taken us 12 hours to Los Angeles, another 10 hours on the tour bus and there were only 20 people. We only stayed for two hours before we had to drive back to America and then immediately fly straight home.

It was actually the same driver on the return trip who had initially driven us down there. God knows how he stayed awake. He actually had loads of ready- rolled joints stashed in the back of the bus.

At the border we got caught. We all had our hands up against a wall and the driver hadn't arranged any money so was still broke. He couldn't pay the 500 dollar on-the-spot fine, so Lime had to withdraw the money from his own account. Fortunately, we only had to pay the fine and then we were allowed to be on our way. We were dropped at the airport and flew straight back to London. But that wasn't the end of it. Upon landing at Heathrow we went straight from the airport to do Raindance at Jenkins Lane, where we had another show.

That was one complete journey. We were at the party in Mexico for two hours, on a coach for 20 and flew to and from Los Angeles – plus we got nicked at the Mexican border along the way.

Just around the time On a Ragga Tip came out in 1992 we were again in Los Angeles, where we had a gig for someone. The promoter had booked us in at The Holiday Inn in Hollywood, which was really nice, right on the edge of the ghetto. Just so happened that KRS-One was staying there too and we managed to say hello. If you walked out of the hotel and did a left, which we did once, you were right bang in the middle of the ghetto. We

43

were all warned not to go down there. Do a right and you're safe.

We arrived back in the UK to find out our hotel had just been burnt down the day after we left. The LA riots had just started, Rodney King and all that.

We were there for one day; any longer and we would have been seriously caught up among it all.

Here's a bit of a funny story and a bit of a claim to fame story at the same time. I remember meeting Kylie Minogue at Top of the Pops. She was absolutely lovely. She came into our dressing room after we had requested earlier to meet her and she gave us all a little kiss on the cheek.

I know Carl Cox quite well. We were quite close back in the early 90s and I'd been to his house a couple of times. One night in 1991 I was playing at the Forum in Kentish Town at my mate's party. Carl came in and he was complaining that he had the wrong records, as he'd been doing a techno gig or something. He asked me if he could borrow my records. "Yeah, no problem, fill your boots," I said.

We, SL2, collected a silver disc at an awards night at the Royal Albert Hall at what I believe was a DMC (Disco Mix Club) competition. We'd sold, like, 200,000 copies of Ragga Tip. We had to go on stage and I was really shy at the time. It was bad enough that we had to go on the stage but I was the last one to leave because the guy who presented us with our award wanted me to stay on stage and hand over the next one. And at the fucking Royal Albert Hall of all places. I was absolutely shitting myself but I managed to pull it off.

I played in Toronto, Canada, at the end of the 90s. I can't

remember what the party was called but it was something to do with United Dance from the UK. The promoter's mate was running around with a record bag but it wasn't full of records, it was overflowing with drugs and he kept dishing them out. We were all absolutely smashed for days and at one point I even threw a television set out of our hotel room from the tenth floor. It was carnage, proper mad!

There were quite a few of us there, including Ellis Dee, Chris Brown and Terry Turbo.

When we had to leave the hotel the organisers were waiting for us and tried charging us for all the drugs. It wasn't really us that were the problem; it was more to do with the promoter's mate who was running around dishing them out freely. We heard that people with guns were coming to sort it out so we headed to the shop across the street. Some of them loaded up with tools but I don't think anyone would have used them. They were purchased more in a state of panic than with any real intention of using them. One of the promoters did have some trouble, which we found out later on.

That all got really naughty. We were in fucking Canada with guns floating about and people demanding money for drugs – SHIT!

One year, I was playing together with another DJ, Eddie Lock, and we had to fly via Athens to Cyprus. We had missed our original flight to Cyprus. After we got back to Athens they told us we had been removed from the flight because we missed the original flight and so the airport automatically cancelled our return flights. We were flying back to Ibiza, maybe Majorca, not sure, but we had to wait 10 bloody hours. We were so tired because we had been on the piss and all sorts all night long. We fell asleep on the floor and I actually woke up at the time our flight was supposed to leave. I ran to the gate, was told we had missed it and then we had a massive row. After arguing we were taken outside, told to quickly jump into a little van and they drove us frantically on to the runway where we boarded the plane.

There have been many occasions I've played at a party where I was absolutely loving it and ended up cancelling my other gigs because I didn't want to leave. Ibiza is the place for that! I've missed loads of flights in Ibiza. Missed a flight, booked another and missed that one, booked another, missed it and so on.

There was one year that I often ended up in a villa somewhere absolutely spangled!

I flew all the way to Sydney, Australia, once for a gig. The flight took all day and I was actually only there for the night. I went back to my hotel after the gig but I passed out and woke up so late I missed my flight home.

MARK ARCHER / ALTERN-8

'Top one, nice one, get sorted' was a phrase synonymous with the rave scene, and can be heard in Altern-8's 1992 rave anthem Activ-8 (Come With Me). Check the Altern-8 videos on YouTube; they're actually pretty funny and capture the crazy rave scene and its many characters.

Altern-8 were a major part of the UK's rave scene right back in the beginning. Performing in their trademark yellow A masks and their large khaki hooded jackets, they soon built a solid reputation for themselves as consistently entertaining and live performers.

Mark is also a founding member of old school rave outfit Bizarre Inc., and I was a fan of them too.

These days Mark is still an internationally recognised artist, and remains on top of his game decades after starting out.

Altern-8 are still performing live, and Mark has built an excellent reputation as one of the finest old-school DJs anywhere. His sets are mixed to perfection and I wish he would play in Amsterdam more often!

Mark spoke about his early career, certain gigs in London and recalls the day he met his hero.

I was a painter and decorator until one day when I was laid off. That same day I was walking back through Stafford and met my old mate, Dean, who I had known since the breakdancing days.

He asked me to pop round one day to his house, because he had recently bought turntables. He invited me to hang out and have a mix, and that was the day that everything started to change for me, in a musical sense.

Thank God I was laid off that day, otherwise I met never have bumped into Dean.

In 1988 I bought a sampling keyboard, so I could sample sounds and noises from other records. I didn't have any know-how or knowledge and absolutely no production skills at the time. My mate had a set of turntables, and while he mixed tunes I would play basslines over the top from my keyboard.

That same year, a recording studio opened in Stafford. They placed an advert in the local paper and I wanted to get involved.

There were a lot of small clubs around Stoke and back in 1988, on a Tuesday night, I used to go out partying to Frenzy, a night organised at a club called Freetown.

In those days it was the norm to go out in shoes, trousers, shirt and tie. The music would be a bit of this, then a bit of that. I would normally wait for the dance music to come on, while watching fights at the bar, and eventually stumble home with a kebab.

That was a normal Saturday night out.

In 1987-1988 house music came over from the States and it didn't just head for London. It came over in a wave and hit the entire country. It didn't matter where you were from, or lived, each town had its own little club that was playing house music, or the next big town, at least, was playing house music.

All of a sudden we were wearing smiley shirts, jeans and trainers, and partying on a Tuesday!

With just the one genre of music, a pitch black club with a strobe and a smoke machine, we had acid house all night long!

E-Vapor-8 and Activ-8, both recorded back in 1992, began as little demos I made at home. We used to create songs to play out and if the crowd went off to them we would turn them into proper tunes. All the Altern-8 stuff was made as a demo at home in our studio, and road tested at events. The crowd's reaction at these events was what determined the final edit of that particular song.

I was a big fan of Tyree Cooper in those days, and still am. I loved his tunes and had a star-struck moment when I met him at a festival in Amsterdam called Promised Land, in June 2014.

I'm really bad in those situations; I get all nervous meeting a star.

We were both performing on The Founders stage. After being inspired by such a legend, it was really great to be on the same stage as him!

Back to Stoke, and it's 1988. It's like the place has just turned completely on its head. It was a different world, absolutely.

By 1988, the Hacienda in Manchester had already been playing and promoting house and acid nights for a couple of years, thanks to Dave Haslam and Mike Pickering, among others.

It wasn't like Paul Oakenfold and Nicky Holloway went over to Ibiza and brought the music back with them. That was what they, and Danny Rampling too, had experienced personally. For London, maybe this was the case, but not for the rest of the country.

Those DJs weren't going up to Manchester to see how the scene was developing. They had witnessed it first-hand in Ibiza and concentrated on creating their own vibe in their home town, which for Paul, Danny and Nicky was London.

The music was coming from the States, spreading up and down the country, and at the same time the Ibiza and Balearic scene was growing in London, so everybody was involved with something.

Being from up north, we had only played a couple of times previously in London, one of them being at The Brain, in Soho.

The Brain had a lot of live acts back in the day, like Orbital, Adamski etc. and released two albums featuring live recordings from acts that had performed there.

We were performing pretty much in the middle of the dance floor and The Brain boys were recording our set. We finished our PA, turned all the volumes down, turned all the equipment off and the crowd were demanding an encore.

We turned everything back on but the levels were all different, completely ramshackle. But we still managed an encore of this one track. The Brain boys told us they were going to release this track on their forthcoming album. "What's it called?" they asked.

At the time, we didn't have names for any of our songs; they were just things we would play out. But when I was asked I was holding a Pot Noodle. On the pot I spotted the words 'Fill container to this level' so the track ended up being called Container, although it wasn't the best recording of that song.

I remember a couple of gigs we did with 808 State, one of them taking place at Brixton Academy in London back in 1991. When we did actually perform down south, especially London, we were always told to "Fuck off back up north." And not in a friendly manner, either!

The gig was pretty much done and dusted in terms of preparation and promotion, with the 808 State guys organising and releasing all the promotional material, including the flyers, posters and lanyards.

They were being supported by N-JOI, and somehow we got booked too. We weren't on any posters or anything, and we weren't added to the promotion unfortunately.

Anyway, being 808 State and the headliners, they had a very theatrical stage set-up – lots of keyboard rises, big drummer at the back, dancers and all the rest that filled the entire stage.

Being an added support act, we had two 2 little X-stands in the middle of the massive stage.

We were performing as Nexus 21 and we had Richard Benson, from Astrix & Space, as our MC, and we had John, our mate from Stafford, dancing for us.

So there we were, playing this huge venue and we just felt so small on stage. Everything coming out of the keyboards and drum machines was 100 per cent live and, fortunately for us,

51

there was no hostile reception. It properly went off in there! It was just one of those gigs, you know. Right time, right place.

Unfortunately, we did a number of gigs where the promotion was a complete shambles.

For example, lights at the front of the stage, which resulted in the crowd only seeing flashing lights and no actual live performance. There's no point in anybody performing on the stage, if that's how they think it should be set up. Also, anyone and their dog would just walk across the stage when we were trying to play live and they would have a bloody loud chat in front of our keyboards. I'd often think that there was no point in me even being there!

I had a similar feeling during an Altern-8 gig at Club Roxy in Amsterdam back in 1991. The gig was being broadcast live on BBC Radio 1 back in the UK – no internet radio in those days – and Bizarre Inc. were also on the line-up. There were a few old-school DJs playing too.

Because it was live on the radio, it was time friendly for the UK audience, but way too early to attract the Amsterdammers. They like to start late in the Dam. We did manage to get a handful of people on to the dance floor but one crazy woman was running around with her tits out, screaming: "Woooooohoooooo," at the top of her voice.

As well as being a live broadcast, the gig was being recorded and all we could hear on the playback was that crazy woman screaming wooooo bloody hoooooo!

There was a lot of unprofessionalism back in the day but never anything where, say, in an emergency, we had to stop playing and leave. Except, that is, for one occasion down south in London.

There was still a north-south divide back then and it was pretty dominant. We are from the Midlands but anywhere above Watford and you were considered a northerner. We got lumped in with the whole northern techno thing, which we didn't mind at all, because in 1989 that was the sound we were going for.

I remember an Altern-8 PA in 1992, again at Brixton Academy, as part of an all-night rave with other live acts and DJs.

During our performance our MC decided to say: "The north has risen," and that seemed to upset the southerners. We had to leave by the back door because there was a lynch mob waiting outside for us. Fortunately, we all made it home safe and well.

Whenever we played south of, or around London, it was okay, but central London always seemed to have a problem with us. It was a bit of a strange one, as the rave scene was all about uniting people, regardless of where they were from.

Nowadays, everything is cool.

It's funny, it's 30 years that I've been in this game and I still get the same buzz playing our songs that I had when we started, which is why I'm still going today. If I had got jaded or bored with it, I wouldn't have been able to keep doing it, you know. I'd have got really fed up. The reason I got involved in the first place was purely for the love, and especially the love I had for the wax!

Then somewhere down the line money comes into it. Everybody has to pay bills – even though several years ago I couldn't and unfortunately lost my house. But that's another story.

People would say we were milking the scene but that's absolute bollocks. Everybody has a right to earn a living but one thing I would say is that if you're doing it only for the money, one day soon you'll end up having enough of it, get bored, lose interest and quickly move on to something else.

You've got to have the love.

MICKY FINN

Michael Hearn, aka Micky Finn, is a UK drum & bass and jungle legend, hailing from south east London, England.

Since the illegal warehouse days in the late 80s and beyond, playing cat and mouse with the police each week, to touring the world and flying the flag for the UK drum & bass scene, Micky is truly a part of the foundations. He is an icon to many, an ambassador, and it was an absolute pleasure to be sat in his company and hear his experiences.

Without a doubt, he's a British music institution. Dating back 30 years and more, Micky is still very much an in-demand DJ, playing around the world. He is also responsible for drum & bass holiday experience Sunbeatz.

He runs record labels Urban Takeover and Finn People, and was responsible for one of the most influential tracks from the early-90s UK rave scene. Some Justice features a sample from Marshal Jefferson's Someday track, originally released back in 1988, and went on to be an absolute classic, which still hits the spot today. There's more on that in the interview.

Before moving to Amsterdam in 1995, I grew up in a village called Capel St Mary, near Ipswich. Raydon is a much smaller village that we would drive through twice a week for training sessions at nearby Hadleigh Swimming Club. We would drive along the road through Raydon, which was actually an old runway, next to this huge warehouse. Much to my surprise, Micky spoke about a particular illegal rave near Hadleigh. It was actually at Raydon airfield, in the same vast black warehouse we passed twice a week.

I was only 14 at the time, but at school on the Monday morning there were a few older kids who attended and they were talking about it. There was also a lad in my class who lived in Raydon and he said cars were just pulling up on people's front lawns to park, with hordes of baggy-dressed ravers running over to the warehouse.

There's a great quality video of that rave on YouTube, with Evil Eddie Richards playing...and no mobile phones! Oh, happy days.

Micky touches upon the early days, warehouse raves, touring, festivals, the making of Ruff Justice, riots, and the chance meeting with a Lord etc.

Enjoy...

I was always having a tear-up as a kid and I was chucked out of school when I was 15, but my criminal life actually began when I was only 10. I kind of grew out of it eventually, although I do come from a criminal background. Both my mum and dad were in prison, my brother too. My two sisters are the only members of my family who haven't been to prison, ha-ha.

I was in prison a few times myself as a kid, which resulted in me never minding my own company. Do I wish that I had never been sent to prison? Of course I do, because I wasted three years of my life. My life turned around when I started to DJ and that was when I thought that I could earn a living. I was just about earning a pound note legally and I no longer wanted the shit that came with it. I have managed to turn my life around and have done something good with it.

I loved raving and I loved playing music, but it took me ages to give myself a DJ name.

I originally knew nothing about the drink Micky Finn – I really hadn't a clue what it was – and it was my sister who first called me that. She used to be a promoter and I worked for her back in the day, in 1987. At the time, I didn't have a DJ name, but I was a skinny bastard so my sister said: "Why don't we call you Micky Thin?" So it was my sister that eventually gave me my DJ name. But cockneys don't pronounce their T's or H's, so my DJ name was pronounced as Finn.

I started raving back in 1987 and those days were a brilliant time in my life. My first club was Future, in Heaven's backroom, and I was at Paul Oakenfold's Spectrum every Monday, which then became Land of Oz.

Coming from the acid house scene, Someday was a big tune for me. That's the original tune from which I took the sample for Some Justice. I always considered Marshall Jefferson a legend in the game. For me, CeCe Rogers' vocal on there was just to die for. A lot of people thought it was a woman singing, probably from how we pitched the vocal up a little bit. CeCe is an incredible vocalist and Marshall – well you don't need to say anything about Marshall. What more can you say? He's a house legend but, sadly, I've never met him.

Someday was 1988, Some Justice was 1991, so we had to clear the samples. We literally took the samples from the acapella from the 12-inch record. We were never supplied with anything, but we got by and we cleaned the samples up.

Some Justice was dedicated to my brother Ronnie, who at the time had just been sent to prison for 12 years. It was either going to be called Ruff Justice or Some Justice, but because I had nicked the sample from Someday, I went with Some Justice.

I backed all of Some Justice myself; I paid for everything. Gavin didn't have enough money. Once it had sold so many volumes, and everybody was playing it, the majors came knocking on the door.

These days I think studios can make everything perfect, but for me everything is just *too* right and tunes can often lose their true character. I used to like tunes where the kick was a bit off, but nowadays there's an app to make it perfect. Somebody who can't sing can now sing. I liked it when somebody was a bit out of tune and it showed a bit of rawness. I kind of miss that. Nowadays it's all a bit too polished for my liking.

I have some great memories of the cat and mouse with the police, like them sending out helicopters looking for tents going up, parties starting at six in the morning, warehouses getting crashed etc. The art of it was to get it started and if there was a DJ on you were usually left alone because of the amount of people already there. The police tended to think it would be too dangerous to stop it.

There were a couple of promoters from Brixton, Paul and Dave, who used to be ticket outlets. This is going back to the Sunrise days, right back to the beginning of the scene. They were heavily involved with the early rave scene and organised a party called Beyond Therapy in east London, back in 1989.

There were hundreds of police stood at the gate trying to stop the party, resulting in a lot of commotion and we couldn't get in. My childhood mate, Mark Epstein, and I decided to walk along a little ledge under a bridge in a canal, with me carrying my record box. The ledge was probably only 18 inches wide and at any moment we could have fallen in the canal. We sneaked along the ledge, then under the road, before climbing into the warehouse. I was inside and I was the DJ, so the party got under way.

Once it had started it seemed as if the police had basically given up – or so we thought. They actually went on to smash one of the generators to pieces. We had won the first battle, though, to start the party and after I finished playing it was Grooverider who was on after me. We left and drove back through the Blackwall Tunnel, which runs under the Thames. At the top of the tunnel there were lot of gypsies and travellers, who had all sorts of fairground rides that were clearly visible.

Travellers and showmen are well known for having generators.

We pulled up onto the travellers' site at 3am and we rented a generator off them. You should have seen it – it was just like a scene out of the movie Snatch. Ha-ha.

In my opinion the travellers are really good people to deal with…you just don't want to play about with them!

That was all part of the parcel back then, and what we had to do to get, and keep, the party going. This shows you the lengths to which we would go, regardless of what time it was in the morning.

We drove back to the party with the generator and it was so funny when the sun came up. Obviously, the night before everybody wanted to party in the dark, dance and have the time of their lives. Most of these warehouses were disused, nobody

59

knew what was on the floor and you always kicked up the dust –
thick black dust! In the morning, everybody had black rings
around their eyes. It was hilarious. People had layer upon layer of
dust in their hair and on their faces. It almost looked like they
had just emerged from a coal mine.

My mate Mark Epstein, who was at the party with me, did go
down a mad road in his life before eventually going on to
become an MMA fighter – Mark 'The Beast' Epstein.

Mark and I were telling stories backstage in the green room at a
party once and some people sitting near us asked us which film
we were talking about. Mark said: "We are not talking about a
movie, we are talking about our lives." I'm sure he certainly has a
great book inside him!

He did walk a dark road for a while, but he successfully turned
his life around. He fought in Cage Rage, the UK-based mixed
martial arts championship. It's actually a shame he got into the
cage when he did – a few years too late in my opinion. He had to
learn his ground game and had to adapt, but after a long training
session he wanted to smoke weed. I said: "Mark, you can't do
that!" The discipline, or rather the lack of it, was the problem.
Mark was a street fighter and he had to learn new techniques. If
he had been perhaps 10 years younger, it would have been
different because he had the biggest heart in the world, but
recovering from injuries was also a problem.

Ever since we were kids, Mark has never been bothered by how
big someone else happens to be. He was a fearless fucker and
actually went on to fight fellow British MMA fighter Michael
Bisping twice. Mark clipped him a couple of times at Cage Rage
#7, and once more would have been enough, but Bisping caught
him and knocked him out. Bisping then went over to the UFC –

Ultimate Fighting Championship – of which I've always been a fan.

Mark's best mate was former UFC fighter Lee Murray, who was the mastermind behind the Securitas depot robbery in Kent, England, back in 2006. They got away with 53 million pounds!

Lee is now serving 25 years in a Moroccan prison. At the same time as he was flying all over the place for MMA showcases, his face was all over the news for the robbery. It's sad, because he was a really tasty fighter, but the street life never left him. Another mate of mine was involved with it, and he's just served an 18-year sentence for his role in the job. He was more Lee's enforcer, though.

During his career and before the robbery, Lee fought the former UFC Middleweight Champion, Anderson Silva, at Cage Rage #8 back in 2004.

My other mate, Julius Francis, went down the boxing route and even fought Mike Tyson. Mark, Julius and I used to lead different lives but we all turned it around and did something positive with our lives. Julius did get a hiding from Tyson – but, you know what, he climbed in the ring with him. The moment Julius was offered that fight, for that reason alone he was the winner as far as I was concerned.

Julius was born big. Mark was always the chunky muscle type but Julius was huge, even at 16! We are all still good friends from the days we grew up in Woolwich, south east London. I love that I stay in touch with my old mates. I believe it keeps me grounded, although I'm quite a grounded person anyway.

Mark is a stunt man nowadays in the movie industry. He was in

Bulletproof along with Ashley Walters and rapper and actor, Kano, both of them playing police officers. In season two, Mark is a cage-fighter, plus he also had a role in Guy Ritchie's King Arthur, too. That's his world right now. He keeps himself in shape, and has always had an eight-pack.

Back in the day, mostly every party was illegal and they often went under the guise of people shooting a music video, and everyone inside were extras. The film studios in Battersea, in south-west London, were used a lot for illegal raves. The Gasworks and the Blackwall Tunnel, also in London, were also used a lot, often making out it was a film-set and, again, everyone was an extra. Some great parties! I have some great memories of those days but the government kind of put a stop to it. I do miss those days, but the safety aspect has improved since it was forced to become a legitimate business.

I played at an illegal warehouse rave near Ipswich in 1989. It was actually in a warehouse near Hadleigh, close to Ipswich. If I remember correctly that party didn't even start until 6.30am, because that was actually the second site. The first site had been crashed by the police. I can remember people not having the patience to queue in the car park and somebody actually drove straight onto a farmer's field. Others followed and before long there were cars driving in all directions, not in a civilised line either. The fields were getting badly cut-up and there was dust everywhere, making it resemble a scene out of Mad Max.

The organisers brought in two 40-feet lorries, pulled the curtains back and loaded them with the sound systems. They had been driven down the motorway fully loaded and ready to go. They just literally pulled the curtains back and had one lorry either side of the DJ. That was it....go!

It wasn't about the DJ, either, in those days. It was all about the music. "Where's the DJ?" someone asked. "It doesn't matter, it's about the music," I told them.

There have been many, many memorable gigs! Finishing the Dance tent at Glastonbury in 2001 – that was a great gig. I like Glastonbury and it has a special place in my heart. It's just an amazing festival. There are a lot of tents now at Glastonbury and they resemble film sets. A few years back, at Boomtown, I played on a stage built like a ghetto blaster. The DJ was playing where you would put the tape in. A year later I played at a Hillbilly shack. They are building and creating some amazing stages. I think it's really cool, especially in England. I can't speak for everyone, but dance music has been a part of life in the UK for such a long time. It goes beyond just music now, which is great, because I like an art installation. There's nothing wrong in wanting to entertain people and not just with the music. In the old days, a strobe machine was enough!

Boomtown is such a great festival, 10 out of 10 for me! Those boys do a great job, for a lot of good reasons. It's nice to see that people are working from their heart. There are a lot of festivals out there, whose organisers are just jumping on it and only for the business element.

There are a lot of festivals around the world, but the UK have been doing it for a while, so they should be getting it right.

I did a gig in New Zealand, exactly where Lord of The Rings was filmed. The party was on the film set, the whole of which was just left there. There was a castle in Germany, too, that was a pretty special place to play.

For me and a lot of people AWOL at the Ministry of Sound, plus

63

AWOL at the Paradise Club, London, was something that will be etched into the scene forever. It was a great underground club with a ridiculous sound system, you know, and great people too. Security kept you safe in there as well. It was a great club and I used to love it every week. Everyone looked forward to going there.

I played in Birmingham, at the Institute on Digbeth Street, when all these shenanigans went on. It was right at the height of the jungle scene, which would have been mid-90s. It was crazy in there. People had guns, machetes and all I could think was 'Fuck that, I'm off.' The security staff were nowhere to be seen. I mean, they were proper firm-handed that lot. They were going to town. "Fuck the records, fuck everything. I'm not staying here, I'm off to the roof," I said. It was going off in there but I knew that club like the back of my hand and so I headed upstairs. In the end, they all managed to get out and no one was caught, but MC Moose was chopped with a machete and he had a head injury I think.

A security guy was also hit with a sword, it just went crazy in there. All I wanted to do was play records!

Another time, I was convinced that from the DJ booth I saw a couple having sex over a barrier. I really was convinced, and I was telling people that they were having sex, but nobody believed me. I was sure that I had seen that – well it looked very much like that anyway. I once saw a crazy geezer in Germany who looked like he was tripping, and he picked up one of the turntables and threw it while the DJ was playing. I think it was Ellis Dee who was playing, can't quite remember. Another time a geezer flipped out in Australia and security took him away.

The music industry is very fickle. In fact, it's a nasty industry. I decided years ago that I would not allow it to consume my life. To me, it's just a job, but people get it twisted and think it's a life. I do my work, and come back and try to lead a normal life. People that think it's a life, they're the ones who come crashing down.

I've been on tour with a few people, but I really don't mind travelling alone. I don't mind being a lone ranger. I rely on me and I have to get myself going. Some people can go a bit loopy being alone but, wherever I am, I always go and see something of that country. The first time I played in Canada, in 1997 I think, there were a few artists there and I asked what they were all doing. They were just going to their hotel room to watch movies, but I wanted to visit Niagara Falls. I even learned the artists had played there before, but it seemed none of them were interested enough to visit one of the biggest must-see tourist attractions in the world. So guess what I did. I got them all up and we all went to see the Niagara Falls. I appreciate I'm there to do a job, but I'm also totally up for looking around and discovering the country.

I've had some strange situations on planes before. We spend a lot of time flying and I always try to blag an upgrade, if I'm not already flying business class that is. Once you get to gold card or even platinum card status, chances are you'll most probably get upgraded anyway. In 1988, Aphrodite and I were on a British Airways flight to Tokyo. We were playing in Tokyo and Osaka, and I had a tear-up with a real Lord. Sadly, I can't remember the twot's name!

It was a long flight and I had claimed four adjacent seats because the flight wasn't full and there were enough seats vacant. There were also some spare seats the other side of me, so I sat there and opened the window and did some writing. Suddenly this guy came marching down and stood staring at my four seats. "Is that your stuff?" he asked. "Yes," I replied. "Oh, my mate has a bad back," he continued. "Is there any chance he can lie down there for a couple of hours?" "Sure," I said, but the couple of hours became five, then six hours.

I thought 'Nah, this ain't happening.' I wanted my seats back, but he wouldn't move. He then said that he was going to go to the front and get some staff, but by now everybody on the plane was awake. "I'm coming with you," I replied.

We both marched down different aisles, and when I think back it was so fucking funny. He stormed into business class and all I could think was that this guy has seats in business class but he wants to lie in *my* seats? He was yelling at the staff and demanding that I give up my seats. "Who does he think he's talking to?" I said to the cabin supervisor. By now, the supervisor was really trying to bite his lip, and he told me that this guy and his mate did have business class seats.

"Get the fuck out of my economy seats," I told them both.

At the end of the flight, the cabin supervisor came up to me and said: "Thank you for standing up to that guy. He always talks to the staff like they are a load of shit. He flies all the time with us, always talking down to us, so it's refreshing to see him being talked down to for a change."

It's a brilliant career, don't get me wrong. I've toured the world, but it's still just a job. I'm not being horrible to the industry, I've loved the chances I've been given in life but I keep it grounded as it's only a job.

Some people find it really hard. Some people get catapulted to a luxury hotel room with the big high life and find it difficult to deal with. I can just walk into a hotel room and think 'That job is done, next...'

My son, Danny, does the same job. He is DJ Logan D and he has his own record label – Low Down Deep. He kind of rules the jump-up scene. It ain't really my bag, I'm 53, but the youngsters go mad for it! It's not like the jungle stuff of old for me, but times have changed. He's a DJ, has a label, and literally lives out of a bag because he's here, there and everywhere. He's touring a lot, especially in America.

He did actually fill in for me once, over in Amsterdam at Cheeky Monday. I couldn't make the gig because I have three crumbling vertebrae in my back and they were playing up so there was no way I could travel. Danny was in Amsterdam at the time, so he ended up filling in for me.

It is a different world these days, compared to when I started DJing. You have to set up the parameters, otherwise this job will have you working at whatever time. You have to try and map it out, a bit like a school timetable, when you knew which lessons you had and in which classrooms. You have to live your life like that because at some point you have to switch off and have a bit of a life. Arrange your timetable and know what you have to do to achieve your goals for that particular day. Sometimes you have to be brutal if you have too many things on the go.

Nowadays, I like to get up early, attack the day and get going. At my age I feel there is a bit more to life. The social media side, for example. I get it, we need it, but I'm not going to be a slave to it. I see some people online and they've just become like whores. Their life is all about likes! I'm way too old to play that game. I just post what I like – often a picture of me enjoying a beautiful sunset.

I sometimes put stuff up just to rebel a bit, but I do get it. I do use it as a promo tool, to help promote a campaign. It is something we can use, but only with a proper thought process behind it.

If Rage asked me to do a promo video then I would dig deep, pull out a banger and talk about it. Get the Rage nostalgia across, provide a bit of entertainment and that's it. You won't find me saying 'Hi, this is Micky Finn, and you can catch me this Friday playing at.......' Fuck off! I just find it a bit biased. I used to have the mini toy Volkswagen camper van, which had a record needle on it. So my videos would be me asking who remembered the dub-plate as I kept the camera on the little camper as it raced around the vinyl. I had it for the best part of 20 years and I was always using it. Sadly, it gave up on me last year.

I do my agency stuff almost every day, starting off speaking to my colleague John every morning to see what we have to do that day. I then move on to something else, whatever project I'm working on. I find life is happier that way, rather than being on the go 24/7.

I enjoy reading books. I'm a bit of an SAS and ex-MI6 agents freak. I've come across a lot of good writers that can transport you to the actual moment and you're captivated. You are living and experiencing the scene.

When I'm reading Andy McNab and his SAS stories, it's like I'm dressed in camouflage with canned grease all over my face!

I have started to write my own book, although I'm not a writer. I just started writing down different points in my life. It kind of has humour in it and is very much like the movie Snatch, because some of that shit really went on with my mates and me. There's a lot crime in there – that was my background – but I turned my life around and I don't get involved with that any more. There's a lot of criminality, but it also includes many very funny stories.

I want the book to end just as my DJ career begins to take off. That way, hopefully, everybody will be looking forward to book two!

808 STATE

The Rolling Stones of the underground dance scene! Not because of their age, but the fact that they've been around since day one. They helped build the scene and inspire the next generation of electronic producers, and they continue to perform with a smile on their faces to a forever growing fan base. And rocking it!

Celebrating more than 30 years in the game, 808 State are still sought-after around the globe, continuing to perform worldwide at sold-out venues and produce new music.

In September 1988 Newbuild, their first offering, was the album that made people sit up and listen, especially as this new sound was taking over the UK. After emerging from Manchester, the city soon became the place to be in the late 80s as the Hacienda and acid house takeover was in full swing. After some initial line-up changes, 808 State went on to release many influential albums over the years.

Aphex Twin liked Newbuild so much that he re-released it on his label Rephlex Records back in 2005.

From David Bowie to Soundgarden to the Stone Roses, 808 State have remixed some of the world's biggest artists.

MC Tunes joined along the way, with the album The North at its Heights providing a platform for Tunes to do his thing. That album reached number 26 in the UK charts and the tracks Tunes Splits the Atom and The Only Rhyme that Bites still sound timeless today. At the time, I could even rap along with Tunes because I knew all the words. If 808 State song lyrics were an exam I would have passed swimmingly, something that I didn't manage at school, sadly.

I remember listening to a concert on my 3D super-woofer ghetto blaster, as you did in those days, broadcast live on BBC Radio One on Friday January 18th 1991, live from Wembley Arena.

The line-up was Happy Mondays, The Farm, James, Beats International, Northside and 808 State. I was really into that music and scene, still am, and the fact that all those bands were performing live on the radio made it the perfect moment to record a tape. I must have listened to that concert every day for years.

I was in my bedroom, pushing my homework to one side, and when they played Cubik, an absolute stomper, that was the cue for my dad to tell me to: "Turn that rubbish down." I don't think I complied, well not until that track finished anyway.

Together with a friend, Amsterdam DJ Diablo, we made a tribute remix of Cubik. When I interviewed Andy Barker, I gave him a copy. Not long after, I was speaking again with Andy and he told me that he liked the remix we made, so much so that after editing it a bit he was going to use it in his DJ sets.

What a compliment! After listening to that track for the first time when I was 15, here we are decades later and the man responsible for it is telling me he'll play our remix when he's out DJing.

For the interview, Andy spoke about 808 State's early days, his involvement in Manchester's illegal warehouse rave scene and the legendary Hacienda etc.

Back in the late 80s there were a few of us who would often hang out in Eastern Bloc Records on a Saturday, checking for new vinyl imports coming in from the States and Europe etc.

Between us, we all had various pieces of equipment and when we got together and set everything up it was just like a studio. Unfortunately, though, some people became frustrated with the scene. It wasn't moving fast enough for some – but it was for others.

Some went down a different path but those of us that were still interested became 808 State.

One of the guys involved was doing a sound engineering course and, being a trusted sort, he had a spare set of keys to a local recording studio. Some nights, after the Hacienda closed, we would head for the studio, set everything up and start making music. By 7am we had to have the place cleaned up to make it look like nobody had been there and then we were out the door. Our first two albums didn't actually cost us anything in studio time.

I spent my youth in the Hacienda, just as the house music revolution began.

You used to have to walk through these big plastic flap type things into the club, just like an old warehouse. Once inside you noticed it had many little compartments and corners. We used to congregate in one corner with the Happy Mondays, Stone Roses etc. All the bands would gather in that corner, we knew everyone around us. It was a crazy time, to say the least.

At the time Manchester wasn't the best city in which to live. For us, we all felt a lot safer in our corner with a group of trusted mates.

This was around the time that clubs in Manchester were closing at about 2am and nobody wanted to go home. There were regular cries of 'One more tune, one more tune.' It was usually Mike Pickering or Jon Da Silva who would have been closing and they had to tell the crowd the sound system had actually been turned off because nobody would leave.

This was when the rave culture started to come in. It was in those days, around 1988, that my brother and I, along with a couple of others, would drive around Manchester looking for warehouses with a To-Let sign visible. When we found one we would break the locks off and put on new ones, which we had brought with us, and sneak inside for a peek. We would go back the following week to see if anybody had changed the locks, therefore knowing if anybody was looking after that particular building. More often than not, they hadn't.

So, on Saturday morning we would enter the chosen building, clean it up, put a sound system in and away we went! This would go on for many months, purely through word of mouth. Incidentally, our first-ever party, back in 1988, was across the road from the Hacienda on City Road, by the arches.

We went about it the usual way, changed the locks, waited and then pounced. This particular place had no electricity so we put a generator in but we had to wrap it with mattresses just to keep the noise down! Looking back, it was a pretty dangerous thing to do, seeing as the generator ran on petrol!

Outside, we had a security team on the door to keep the

undesirables out and one particular guy, who had been refused entry, decided to call the police. They then turned up in what we called tag vans, like riot vans and full of shields. Fortunately, my brother went out and spoke with the police chief. He told him we were throwing a leaving party for 'Barbara.' He showed them the car park which was full of nice cars, proving that a good, decent bunch of people had been invited and no scallies. The police were happy to let us continue, with the fact that there was no alcohol on sale counting hugely in our favour.

At the time there were no rules in place regarding that type of party so nobody had the power to shut them down. But that soon changed!

In 1990 we played at the GMEX in Manchester, supporting the Happy Mondays, and the place was rammed. A few months later we, as a band, decided to put on our own party at the same venue.

We built the stage in the middle of the crowd and we had Tony Ross playing, alongside Sasha and Nipper, a great local DJ who you don't hear so much of these days. We were also doing a live-set.

At the time KLF were massive and we approached them to be on the line-up. Jimmy Cauty said they would but only if they could catapult live sheep across the stage during their set, a novel way of saying 'No thanks.'

The party itself was massive, a complete sell-out, the hottest ticket in town. All our money went into production and we had the biggest sound system the venue had ever seen. Unfortunately, due to the massive production costs that were down to us to cover, we ended up with a profit of precisely 1 pound and 25 pence!

We were playing Glastonbury for the first time back in 1991 and we were actually headlining the Other Stage.

At the time, we were taking laser systems with us on the road and they were big – the size of a coffin with water coolers. Nowadays, with modern technology, it's comparable in size to a laptop.

Anyway, prior to our gig, everything was being checked and, unfortunately, our laser wasn't working. The company that we used at the time – Laser Dynamics – said they would have another laser driven from Shropshire to Glastonbury in time for our set.

Our set was fast approaching but still no laser in sight.

So, the sun was setting and our set started, minus the laser. We had some fibre-optic tubes placed at the front of the stage which read 808 when lit and they were supposed to work in sequence with our laser system. We later found out that our new laser system was stuck at the entrance and wasn't allowed in because no one had issued a backstage pass for the driver. We had been in touch with the production crew in order to get our new laser past the gates but to no avail.

It was still a great set, though. I remember looking out to the massive field full of people dancing and all the concession vans at the top of the field were rocking with people dancing on top of them. A great experience, just not the complete experience.

Nowadays at Glastonbury, Tony Ross and I are the resident DJs at Bez's Acid House.

808 State were booked for a DJ set at a festival in Tel Aviv, Israel, back in the 90s. The plane touched down and as we made our way down the stairs to the tarmac we all noticed a van with blacked-out windows and a driver with a sign reading 808 State.

We headed for the sign and were told to get in the van. We jumped in and the driver set off, asking us for our passports and demanding to know what our luggage looked like. We all thought this was a little strange, no customs etc. Suddenly our passports were stamped and our bags had been found but we had not seen anyone apart from the driver. No queues, no checks, no standing in line, nothing, and we all felt like royalty. Anyway, off we went and we were driven to the festival site. We played, everything went well and we left on the Sunday to return to the airport.

Leaving Israel was a whole different experience to entering.

There I was at passport control and after having my passport checked I was suddenly surrounded by huge armed Israeli military and they asked me to go with them. I hesitated at first and asked: "What's wrong?" They just told me I had to go with them immediately to the police station within the airport. The others had all managed to get through without any problems.

Just me, then!

I was placed in a cell for two long, silent hours and I was still trying to understand what was going on. I just couldn't work it out. What could I have done, I kept asking myself, even though I knew I'd done nothing wrong.

Eventually someone came to me and told me they were expecting Andy Bakker, not Barker, and I told them to contact the British Consulate and they would confirm my identity. Now, time was ticking and my flight had long gone, with the rest of the band on it.

Confusion sorted, the officers explained it was a simple case of mistaken identity. They simply gave me back my passport and told me to be on my way. I headed straight for the ticket desk, explained my situation and, fortunately for me, they put me on the next flight to Manchester at no extra cost.

JAYDEE

Like many others in this book, Jaydee was responsible for another acid house anthem, which still graces any sound system today with great effect.

Plastic Dreams was, is and will always be a stunning production. Robin Albers, aka Jaydee, has played all over the world due to the popularity of Plastic Dreams. It reached number one on the US Billboard Hot Dance Music charts back in 1992.

A regular on the Dutch DJ circuit and an old-school ambassador, Jaydee is still doing the business.

Robin spoke about the early days, the story behind Plastic Dreams, prison riots, the mafia and boxes of dynamite etc.

Enjoy...

I used to work for the biggest national radio station, AVRO Radio, back at the beginning of the 90s and the usual music I played was disco, funk, R&B etc. I was inspired by artists who, at the time, were not in the mainstream, like Prince for example.

I approached my boss and asked if I could do a new show in the evenings playing this new genre called house music. He replied: "What's that?" I told him it was the new sound that everybody wanted to hear and that I had discovered it in a club called Boccaccio in Destelbergen, near Ghent in Belgium.

People kept telling me to stop with the disco, funk sets and switch over to this new sound called house music. I went along to Boccaccio to see what everyone was talking about and when I arrived I was told that, before we go in, I had to take this little pill. I asked why and I was told it would be good to feel the music and the vibe. So I said 'Give me one' and, for the first time ever, I took one. After half an hour everybody in the car park wasn't walking any more – they appeared to be floating – and that's when it was time to go in.

'Wow,' I thought, I felt like I had just discovered something new, like a new tribe in Africa, and I was hooked. I looked around and white women were dancing like black women. Everybody was dancing for themselves, not with each other, because the music was so powerful. From that moment on, I fell in love with the music and the scene.

When I approached my boss from the radio station I told him this music was the revolution, rising up all around the world. My boss said it was just a phase and the music would die. I told him it was the music people wanted to hear, I was amazed and I said 'No way!'

I was so passionate that I wanted people to experience what I had experienced. I managed to get it up and running for about a year. It was called For Those Who Like to Groove, and was the first-ever show on Dutch radio to play house music.

There was a convict in the prison who would write letters to me every week. I didn't know what the convict did to be in prison and I didn't want to know, but he was really crazy about the show.

One day all the convicts had their ghetto blasters, about 72 in total, and they were all on at full volume at the same time listening to my show. The entire prison turned into one big club.

The partners and the children from the convicts had earlier smuggled in lots of weed. The guards from the jail were walking into what appeared to be a club, one that smelt suspiciously like a coffeeshop in Amsterdam!

The prisoner who initiated this event was put into a solitary confinement cell for four days. He later wrote me a letter telling me this and he said that even if they had locked him away for 20 days he would still have done it because, he insisted, it was worth it!

After this the prison made new rules and ghetto blasters were not allowed after 4pm.

This was before Pete Tong began his Essential Selection show on BBC Radio One. I think everybody, including Pete, was so inspired by the music that they wanted to do their own show. That's how I started and I think it was the same for Pete. I played with him recently and maybe I should have asked him if my show on Dutch radio inspired him to start his show on English radio.

It turned out to be a very intense time for me because my boss wasn't feeling it. We had our problems and he was trying to lay down all these rules. He wanted me to make a playlist for weekends and he didn't want my guests to smoke in the studio.

I couldn't do what he wanted. I was inviting these house artists to perform on my show and, of course, when they asked if they could smoke a joint I didn't say no as it became a part of the vibe, a part of my show. The listeners could connect with me, the show, the music and my guests. I had a really strong connection with my listeners. But my boss said that if I didn't play by the rules I had to stop it, so I said: "Okay, stop it, because I will not change my decision to do a house music program."

At the time I wasn't producing music but I was DJing and thought it was time I started to produce my own house music. I always felt it would be great to be out at a club with friends and see everybody dancing to my tune.

So I started piano lessons and my teacher told me my timing was perfect and after about six months I made Plastic Dreams.

Once I'd produced it I began to promote it myself to other producers, radio DJs etc. but nobody believed in it – only I believed in it. I tried to sell it to record companies in Holland but nobody wanted it or shared the passion I had. I didn't give up because I knew I had something new.

"Take it or leave it," I would tell them.

I originally took Plastic Dreams out of Holland, but my good friend DJ Marcello would still be playing it every week in Holland, plus it was used in the gay scene. "This track is something special," Marcello told me.

Plastic Dreams started to be played in gay clubs around Belgium, Germany and Holland, and then all over the world at every party!

The gay scene is great. They really love their music and I think they're more progressive in the music they like, let's say, than a hetro guy.

Plastic Dreams changed my life, but it's a story with a lot of angles. If you begin to produce music but know nothing about the business, then you immediately become a target for many record companies. There are a lot of bosses that would try and take advantage of you because you don't know shit about contracts, lifetime guarantees, options, exclusivity etc. There are a lot of sharks out there on the road.

You know, Plastic Dreams is like my business card. Sometimes people change their business cards, the design or colour etc., but I've changed nothing since 1992. The kick was so heavy for that time and it can compete with songs made today because of the specific kick I used.

At the time record labels, DJs and producers were telling me the kick was too heavy and that there was no break. I was told it didn't work and that every time someone played it in a club the sound systems would break down because they couldn't handle the kick.

I know that's 100 per cent true because I have also blown several systems around the world playing my track!

Nowadays the systems are made to handle the heavy kicks and basslines with sub woofers. Every club which started playing house back in the early 90s had to change their sound systems to incorporate subwoofers in order to feel the music properly. The mainstream disco sound was on the way out and instead came the heavy kicks and basslines, and new speakers. Acid house was born.

After I made it, I couldn't recreate it any more. It was made on an Atari and I used 14 floppy discs. I think I still have them somewhere in my basement, but I did throw my Atari away. If it was to be re-released I could maybe recreate it nowadays if I had the chords and grooves again, and if I could find the old keyboard online that I used, a Juno 106, because it has the bell, another thing I don't have any more. It was actually a twinkle bell but I recorded it as a low bell.

The organ was only played by me, and I even used my elbows, whilst the grooves were sampled. I had two grooves and one was cut with the snare and the kick – because I'm a funky man, ha-ha-ha.

There were a lot of mistakes when producing the song but these mistakes turned out to be great. When you are producing you have to follow your heart, plus people were talking a lot of bullshit to me. They would tell me I didn't do this or I should have done that, but if I had listened to them the funk would be out. I was told it should have a break in it, so that it could be mixed. I didn't want my track to be mixed. It was ten minutes long and I can go to the toilet, and after ten minutes you mix it out. What I learned was that you shouldn't listen to other people, even if they might mean well.

If you hear a mistake in the studio, don't try and make it correct, because a mistake can be that certain twist in a song that makes your song special.

It was a long struggle but I'm actually the owner of the track after having to go to court. I have lost a lot of money but have gained a lot of contacts and experiences in life. It's not all about the money but you have to be very clever. If you're not clever you are going down because all the youngsters just want to make music but know nothing. Be careful what you're signing, that's my advice.

I've played all over the world and everywhere in Europe, but I've never played in the UK. I always took my own bookings and never asked an agency if they wanted to represent me.

I know friends who didn't make a track like mine but still played in Birmingham, Manchester and at Cream, for example. I'm surprised that no one in the United Kingdom heard my track and then thought they would like to have this guy come and play. That type of guy existed all over Europe but sadly not in Britain.

In Italy there was one guy from an agency that absolutely loved it. He loved it so much that the rest of Italy fell in love with it. From east to west, north to south, everywhere. But for that to happen there has to be at least one person who wants to book you.

I met Lil Louie Vega at an Amsterdam Dance Event – ADE – and he said to me: "There is always a mystery around you – who are you? What do you do? What music do you play? Do you still play music?"

"I like to be a mystery," I replied.

Back in the mid-90s I was playing in Russia. I don't remember where exactly but this particular party was in an old factory. I remember, after my set, being outside with the promoters, a bunch of massive Russians you don't want to mess with.

We were chilling, sitting on boxes smoking joints. I asked the guys where we were and, to my surprise, they told me we were at an old explosives and weapons factory. But they said there was no need for concern because they didn't envisage the police venturing out that far as they would never believe people would take over a factory full of explosives and weapons, for the purpose of throwing a party.

But they did – and when we were outside, enjoying a smoke, somebody had a torch and shone it on the boxes we were sitting on. They were only full of TNT and other highly explosive stuff – and there we were smoking away!

Looking back, it was very special to be there and do that with these guys, despite the added danger.

In those days, if you were caught by the police you would be sent to Siberia, never to be seen again. A lot of stuff from the western world is forbidden there. You may believe that Russia is now a democracy, but that's just not true. If you do something wrong you end up in a place you don't want to be. I've played there about four or five times and you always have to be careful.

I felt lucky that night!

I remember a gig in Porto, Portugal, in 1992 when I was playing together with Danny Tenaglia at a big castle. I was with Danny and Rob from Twisted Records, and we were being picked up and driven in a touring car. On these journeys you always put your life in the hands of the driver. I kept watching him and he was driving recklessly. As I was talking with the guys I had to keep shouting at the driver to watch out.

I had soon had enough and told him I would drive. The driver said that only he knew the roads but I insisted, although I told him he would have to tell me where to go. The driver climbed in the back of the car, with Danny and me in the front. I put on a track that Danny and I were working on together – Karnak's White Rain & Black Moon. It hadn't been signed yet but Danny and I made a deal, while I was at the wheel, to have Twisted sign the track. I was being told where to drive and also making a
85

record deal at the same time!

Another time, in Italy, I was booked to play near Naples somewhere, in the southern part of Italy, but I really don't remember the city any more. I was booked by the club's promoter.

After arriving there I got a phone call but I didn't know who was on the other end of the line. He asked if I was Jaydee, the DJ playing at the Phoenix in the evening. I said I was and he told me that I would be playing that night, but not at the club, at his private party.

I said I was booked for Phoenix but he said I wasn't listening before adding: "You play for me tonight and I give you 5,000 dollars." I had to call Phoenix and tell them I couldn't play and cancelled. They didn't react badly because they knew that if the mafia had made the call they had no choice but to back down.

I was picked up and driven to this huge villa, which was the home of a mafia boss. There were a lot of people and I couldn't see a DJ booth or anything remotely resembling one. I was told to wait and go to a room they had for me. They would come and get me when everything was ready. There must have been 500 people there, most of them either beautiful women in big dresses or good-looking Italian mafia guys.

They came to get me and I asked where the party was going to take place. Suddenly, these walls lifted up and at the same time some huge doors opened up, leading to a huge swimming pool. Above the swimming pool they had built a bridge, which was where the DJ booth was. I was escorted to the booth and told in no uncertain terms that I must start with Plastic Dreams.

I did and the place just erupted. Boooom!

Another mafia story took place in Minsk, the capital of Belarus, when my girlfriend and I were picked up at the airport and driven to our hotel. There were three cars, one at the front with bodyguards, a second car in which we were travelling and a third behind us with more bodyguards. There were also two bodyguards who stood outside our hotel room all night. They were obviously there to prevent any issues relating to the gig but also for our own safety.

I have to say, it felt good. We liked that.

DAVE HASLAM

Everybody knows how influential Manchester is around the world with its music scene and, of course, the mighty Manchester City – best team in the land and all the world!

But there are certain individuals who helped to shape that musical soundscape and one of them is Dave Haslam. Originally from Moseley, Birmingham, Dave was a student at the University of Manchester before going on to join the Manchester, and ultimately the United Kingdom, list of DJ royalty.

Dave was a prominent part of the Hacienda's rise to fame alongside the likes of fellow residents Mike Pickering, a City diehard, and Scottish DJ Graeme Park.

When Dave and I met in Amsterdam for our interview I had to admit to him that being in his presence was initially a nervous experience. Dave is a DJ, like me albeit on a different level, plus he works as a freelance journalist, like yours truly wants to do. He also writes brilliant books – the likeness is uncanny! He made me feel at ease immediately and before we had even started he was assuring me it would be a great interview.

Dave spoke about his early days, pre-Hacienda, the late Eric Morillo, starring in the movie 24 Hour Party People, touring with the Stone Roses and much more.

Enjoy...

In the early days, 1984-ish, I was a concert promoter at a club called Man Alive in Manchester. That title makes it sounds really grand but basically I put on bands with friends of mine in a very ad-hoc, endearingly amateurish kind of way.

One of my roles was to play music when the bands had finished but I didn't think of it as DJing, I just thought of myself as the guy playing music when the bands had finished. I had a DJ set-up with two Garrard turntables but no vary speed. I remember playing Trouble Funk, that kind of stuff, and old James Brown records, but also post-punk, A Certain Ratio etc.

One night, back in March 1985, we decided that instead of booking a band I would DJ the whole night and that was basically the first night that had ever happened. I had to get my head round the fact I was on for three hours and I had to prepare a playlist as I had a dance floor to fill.

I was really evangelical about music and I wanted people to enjoy what I enjoyed. I really enjoyed the DJing and I knew I could do a good job, so I started playing at a few other little clubs and it went from there.

I used to work with pretty good bands before any of them kind of made it and they were always really grateful that they had a gig in Manchester. It was the same with the DJs. I booked Eric Morillo twice back in 1992 for the Boardwalk and I paid him about 200 quid. This was around the time Reel 2 Real was about and on one occasion Eric came with The Mad Stuntman and did I Like to Move It, as a special live PA and again for 200 quid. When you're dealing with people on that level it's not about egos, it's about connecting and feeling their enthusiasm. I've tended to opt out of that side of things once it's become about the contract, the cash, splitting the door etc.

In terms of A&Ring the night I would always look to do things others weren't doing. I always thought if you're going to intervene in culture, you should intervene when nobody else is doing it and be original. You don't want to get involved just so you can imitate someone else and you should always believe in yourself and be original.

I remember one of the Friday nights I did at the Boardwalk; it was called Yellow and I started it in February 1992. The DJs were me, Elliot Eastwick and Jason Boardman. It took us about four months before we broke even but the night went on to last seven years! We knew it was a great night and we knew it would work. It was different to what everyone else was doing and we really believed in it.

This was between the time of punk and rave, and there was a lot of stuff happening. John Peel was my biggest influence; he was very eclectic and would always look outside the box. I didn't know any other DJs from the scene; I was just doing what I wanted to do.

I started a Friday night at The Venue in Manchester, just near to the Hacienda, and it became a very popular night. So popular, in fact, the Hacienda poached me from The Venue.

At the time I had a fanzine called Debris and that had given me a reputation for knowing music and, in terms of getting a job at the Hacienda in 1986, knowing music was probably the most important thing. It wasn't necessarily a technical thing, it was just that the club was run by New Order and Factory Records and their ethos was always quality music and to do something different. I was doing something different, I knew the music and

I could carve out a little something for a Thursday night – I was the man for the job.

Remember this was May 1986. It didn't start with a bang and I certainly wasn't carried into a mega successful Hacienda.

It was just about pre-acid house and there were a few tracks about like Farley Jackmaster Funk's Love Can't Turn Around and Steve Silk Hurley's Jack Your Body. At that point I was playing Shannon's Let the Music Play and I would play go-go, a sub-genre associated with funk, and bits of hip-hop etc.

There was already a culture of new and different things at the Hacienda, like the new sounds from New York, and then the Chicago and Detroit sounds were next to come over and, to us, with some great new imports to choose from, it was a music revolution.

Mike Pickering and I used to programme the music we would play and we would consider ourselves as eclectic DJs because, if you imagine in 1987, I was doing two nights a week at the Hacienda, Mike was doing every Friday and we would play from 9pm to 2am. There wasn't five hours of acid house to play in those days, so instead we had to create and define a sound as we went along and, to us, we were just basically playing music.

It wasn't until the middle of 1998 that things became defined and people could recognise that this was acid house and this was techno. It was a revolution. In the two years leading up to it we were sowing the seeds and doing things in an undefined way, which was actually very exciting.

Mike Pickering, Graham Park and Jon Da Silva were heavily into the music and they were great at what they were doing, and their audiences often went with them on their musical trip.

People would travel from all over to be at the Hacienda and by 1990 we had a very clued-up audience. Very few would come from London because Londoners thought they already had everything. I've met people since who have told me that they used to come to the Hacienda and see me play around the end of the 80s and early 90s, and it was fantastic. I used to say "I didn't realise you were from Manchester," and they always replied no, I lived in Glasgow, or I lived in Leeds, or I lived in St Helens etc. A lot came from Wolverhampton, too, and it was fantastic.

They would come because in 1989 we were playing music that you couldn't hear much on the radio, plus a lot of other clubs weren't playing this music and, of course, there was no internet.

If you wanted to hear what we were playing then you had to come to the club. There was something brilliant about that.

Nowadays everything is a little diluted in terms of clubs and venues because if you want to hear a certain type of music then you can find it without going to a club. You can find it on YouTube, it's very easy to track it down so you don't really get that same excitement any more. Nowadays, people go to a club and they want to hear the music they've already heard, not the new stuff or music that isn't played on the radio, so it kind of changes the demographic a bit.

I would play on Saturdays together with Jon and we were very much on the acid house tip but my Thursday nights, I believed, were much more eclectic.

I've always felt as a DJ that I never wanted to be in a position if I heard a great record, from whatever genre, I couldn't play it as I

92

felt my audience wouldn't understand it or it wouldn't fit with everything else. I felt I would be doing something wrong. I always wanted my music to be flexible enough and the selection eclectic enough. If a record was to suddenly appear on the horizon, it could be the next big thing, and if I was stuck in my own self-defined pigeonhole I would be washed out as a DJ, so the eclectic tag has always stayed with me longer than most artists from that generation.

I always used to enjoy my time in the Hacienda; it was an adventure. The best years for me were around the end of 1987, November time, to the summer of 1989, because we were undiscovered and didn't have to think about it too much and, you know, being unselfconscious about what you do is a good thing.

Having said that on Saturday June 28th, 1997, I went into work and at that point Elliot Eastwick was DJing in the main room, playing what we would probably call deep house today, and I was playing in the basement which could hold about 500 people. I was playing right across the board, anything from psychedelic soul, perhaps, to more modern soul and Mo' Wax music, with a few classics thrown in. I remember the club was absolutely packed and it was a fantastic Saturday. On Monday morning, I woke up to a phone call saying that the police had closed the Hacienda, so even the last night was a great night.

I played with the Stone Roses and because they were such a maverick band they didn't like support acts. When they played at Blackpool Winter Gardens and Alexandra Palace, for example, they didn't want another band on stage as they didn't think anyone was good enough to share a stage with them. They had such high beliefs and flash arrogance, so they would employ DJs to play before the band.

At Spike Island they did have some guest bands but they didn't really want them and they booked them right at the end. They always preferred a DJ and to be honest they didn't play that many gigs.

They had various big gigs between 1989 and 1990, the landmark gigs, and they were like stepping stones in their career. As the gigs got bigger, they would book extra DJs and I was booked.

I had a couple of conversations with them about what music I would play and the order the DJs were in. They knew what we'd play would be exactly right for them, with a Hacienda-inspired playlist, and they also knew we would warm up the crowd in such a way so that when the Stone Roses came on it was just the perfect environment.

Just before they came on at Blackpool Winter Gardens I played Sympathy for the Devil and just before they came on at Alexandra Palace I played Good Life by Inner City. In 2000 I did a few gigs with Ian Brown and we had no conversation about what to play but I was just on the right wavelength.

One night, just before Ian and his band were about to come on, the tour manager said to play one more, so I played Fight the Power by Public Enemy and Ian came over to the side of the stage and smiled because for him it was just the perfect record. I really liked having that role and would often play before and after bands at a number of my Hacienda gigs.

As a DJ I loved the understanding of how you could create a vibe and how you could hold stuff back and bring it in at the right time. We learnt all these things as DJs because we were playing five-hour sets twice a week. You learnt how to rise and fall during a set, with programming being absolutely key to what we wanted to do.

The television and radio work that I do, I don't really control. Sometimes when I wake up there's an email or a phone call for a programme regarding such and such. I don't always say yes to them because I find it's too nostalgic, you know 'I Love the 80s' etc. I tend to find out who else is doing them and if Mike Pickering is doing it then I tend to get involved. Or another friend, Richard Boon, who managed The Buzzcocks, because he can usually sniff out what's good and what's bad. If the researcher says we have Richard Boon then I'll do it.

I have various little rules. Because you're a Hacienda DJ people assume you're an expert in certain things, some of which is true. With programmes covering gang warfare or ecstasy, they think because I was a DJ at the Hacienda I'll then know about the other stuff because it's connected to the Hacienda. I tend to say no to these programmes.

I talked earlier about the bands I put on and DJ gigs, and with the current on-stage interviews I do, it's the latest manifestation of the same thing. For me it's a form of live entertainment that nobody else is really doing, or not bothered enough or not clued-up enough to do. It's something I like to do.

There are a whole load of people who have come on this journey with me who really understand where I'm coming from and at each gig I get a different audience. I A&R it the same way; I sit down and I have a list in my head of people that, I think, are interesting, intriguing and imaginative. And maybe people who aren't heard much from, like Nile Rodgers for example.

This was before the explosion of Chic and Nile Rodgers back into the scene. He was absolutely brilliant and did a two-hour interview, and for the second half he bought his guitar on stage and ran through the writing processes of Let's Dance by David Bowie, among others.

I really do believe in the magic of those events. I believe being in a room with all those people and making something happen is a great thing to do – but they can be very exhausting.

There were 700 people at the Jon Lydon event, paying 15 quid each. Jon Lydon is a very interesting character, a bit uncontrollable and a bit prone to be a bit mischievous. I hadn't met him before but I managed a 30-second conversation with him before we went on, which was okay but it didn't really make much difference. He really enjoyed the interview.

The other thing that I try to keep doing is to keep doing things well. I'm at that point now where younger people are asking me for advice for making it in journalism, or as a DJ, and the music business generally. One of my pieces of advice is for everything you do, just do it really well, and do it properly. Always give 100 per cent because you only get one chance, whether it's a little DJ gig that you think is beneath you. I've done these gigs and there's someone there who has danced all night or stood listening to you all night, and they come over to you and ask if you would play at an event they're organising. This would not happen if I didn't take the gig seriously.

It's the same with the on-stage interviews. The interviewees respond really well if they know that it matters to you and you care about it. Jon Lydon responded really well and actually said during the interview that he enjoyed the effort I went to in making it a great night.

The odd thing about the movie 24 Hour Party People was that it was filmed one year after the Hacienda was demolished. They had found this huge warehouse in Ancoats, Manchester, and recreated the Hacienda inside the warehouse. They used the original architect drawings by Ben Kelly and spent something like 125,000 pounds recreating it for just one night of filming.

It was my job to arrange all the extras for the party scenes. They didn't want all the old people who had been there back in the day, they wanted it to look like a cool and happening night, except for myself and the other DJs up on the decks!

There were people there who had been to the original Hacienda and couldn't believe just how close it was to the original design. If you go on Google Images you can see stills from the movie and original Hacienda pictures where they all intermingle, which is a weird little quirk of history.

The filmmakers wanted 20-minute mixes from the DJs so they could feel the vibe and the audience could acclaim them. The original idea was that every so often they'd stop the music to run scenes with Steve Coogan etc. but the minute we started playing the music and the crowd responded we forgot that we were actually part of the film and even the filmmakers forgot they were part of the film. They came up to us and said it was brilliant and to just keep going.

The mad thing was that there were more drugs on set than there were ever in the real Hacienda. To add to the realism you had Bernie from New Order, Bez from the Mondays, and Mike Pickering etc. on set and they were meeting the actors playing them in the movie. It was a memorable experience.

One evening back in 1989, I noticed on the Hacienda line-up a DJ called Laurent Garnier, who was playing from 9-10pm

97

warming up for Jon and I, which would probably have been one of his first gigs, not just at the Hacienda.

He was originally employed by the French Embassy in London and came up to Manchester chasing a woman and went to the Hacienda. He thought it was the best club ever and soon moved to Manchester, managing to get a job at the Dry Bar as a chef. He managed to arrange   some gigs at the Hacienda but had to return to France not long after. While back in France he learnt to DJ properly and moved back to Manchester and was a part of the early rave scene. In 1991 he was doing a lot of nights in the north of England and then moved back to Paris and created the scene there.

Laurent walked into the Hacienda in early 1989 and that was the day his life changed. He took what he learnt back to France and changed Paris. He was involved with the opening of the Rex Club and in 1994-95 he was doing a regular Sunday afternoon in Paris, where his warm-up DJ was David Guetta.

For me this is why I love touring, why I love writing, describing and discovering those links and networks, and realising what happened next.

With the Hacienda, it's not just about what went on within the four walls but what happened subsequently. If Laurent had never walked into the Hacienda all those things he's been responsible for would never have happened, and as a historian it makes you realise you can change culture quite easily.

That original moment with Laurent in the Hacienda wasn't marketed or promoted. Mike was playing what he wanted and Laurent just got it. It's a lesson to not hold back, if you want to do something you do it. You never know who, 12 years later, will look back and say that was culturally significant – even if you never knew it at the time.

I played together with Laurent in 2014 and I think the crowd were expecting a techno set, but we kind of got carried away and within half an hour he was playing Donna Summer's I Feel Love and ended up with Nirvana's Smells Like Teen Spirit.

Sometimes I think DJs should just throw off all the chains and preconceptions and just play a load of party tunes once in a while. It really invigorates you and you can really open up. I saw Seth Troxler play once and he played Love Tempo by Quango Quango, a band which was signed to Factory Records and featured Mike Pickering. I've not heard anyone play that record since 1980 and the way he played it he made it sound like a great record rather than an old record.

GINO LIGHTNER

Since day one Gino has been one of Amsterdam's more influential DJ figures and there's more about that in his interview.

Back in the late 90s, Gino used to organise a club night on a Tuesday at Trance Buddah, the ex-home of Mazzo.

I had been playing in the Vaaghuyzen one Tuesday and after closing we all went to Trance Buddah. DJ Ram was playing upstairs and I asked him if I could play. In those days, if you had your records and could talk the talk, you could often talk your way on to the decks, but not at those big parties with international DJs.

Ram said okay and I did my thing. A bit later on Gino walked over and asked who I was. He said I could play next Tuesday too but as a booked DJ. I was blown away, couldn't believe it to be honest. I was just a youngster, no name and hardly any experience.

Next Tuesday came and I was really nervous. I had new records, a new haircut and even bought a new outfit for that evening's gig. I was very excited and, if I remember correctly, I even bought a record box just to appear more professional.

My then girlfriend, Roberta, and I had told all our friends and we were really looking forward to the party. We headed for the club but as we were walking down the street we couldn't see anybody. Usually, there was a buzz outside on the street, people in the queue etc., but there wasn't a soul to be seen.

We made it to the front door, which was closed. I was not happy. I rang the bell, and after about five long minutes, the cleaner opened the door. He seemed really bemused, and asked what we wanted. "I'm here to DJ tonight," I told him. "Er, no, not tonight. We are closed. Sorry," was the response.

What the fuck? My original excitement soon turned to frustration and anger, but we didn't have mobile phones or social media back then and, annoyingly, I never saw Gino again for months. Eventually, he did apologise, and just said he got his dates wrong, but all is forgiven. Gino and I are good mates these days, but back then it was an unfortunate experience for a wannabe DJ.

Gino spoke about his early career, road trips, Ibiza and the beginning of Amsterdam's acid house and rave scene.

Enjoy...

I was originally organising underground parties in Los Angeles, where I was at college.

I left that college in May 1986 and went to Amherst, Massachusetts, for a holiday, before moving to London in June 1986. This was going to be my first experience with European nightlife and, I hoped, the emergence of something big.

There wasn't any house music back then, especially where I lived in the States. You had to either be in New York, or in Chicago, or in that network of people from New York to Chicago, like Frankie Knuckles for example, who was key to linking the whole sound from Chicago and New York simultaneously.

Another key, I think, in linking Chicago and New York, was to get the likes of Derrick May, Richie Hawtin and Juan Atkins playing between those cities. Philadelphia was close to New York, easy for the DJs to drive there from New York to play, and they were also making house music, with local boys Josh Wink and Foremost Poet Johnny Dangerous setting the standard.

They were the two key players responsible for the Philadelphia sound, among others, but those two were very influential.

My first experience of what London had to offer was at a club called Heaven, and its many drag queens. They played a lot of high-energy music and eventually opened a second room, which played more hip-hop. That room went on to be known as The Soundshaft, a club independent from Heaven, but both clubs were still accessible via a back door.

I loved it. It was the beginning and the music was new.

Outside Heaven, at the end of the party, we were always handed flyers advertising after-parties, and also what London had to offer during the week. Jungle at Busby's, on Tottenham Court Road, for example, was open on a Tuesday and I was there every week.

It was actually in London where I had my first introduction to Chicago house, despite being American, plus the new sounds emerging from Detroit and New York. I never DJ'd in London and had never played a club in England. I was just there to party and to work.

The scene was new, but I was a part of it and didn't actually pay to get in anywhere. Much like Amsterdam; I moved there in 1987.

I had only originally planned a two-week holiday in July, but I liked it so much, and had met some really great people, that I decided to move away from London. I had a few things to arrange before I could make the move, so it wasn't until September that same year that I made Amsterdam my home.

I was in Amsterdam for a whole year before the first house party came along, courtesy of Soho Connection. The party was called London comes to Amsterdam and this, for me, was the big-bang of the underground party scene in Amsterdam, the birth if you like, just like I had experienced in London in 1986. I went to all the parties they did in the first year and wanted to be involved myself.

Black Love Cabaret began as an illegal warehouse, underground party concept in Amsterdam in 1988. Our musical concept was to bring Chicago, New York, Philadelphia and Detroit DJs to Amsterdam, so we could introduce the music first-hand by the artists. The Soho Connection, featuring Paul Jay, Maz, Graham B and Groovemaster Johnson were more responsible for the Manchester and UK sound, during the late 80s and early 90s.

They were bringing the English sound, and we were bringing the American sound, and the Dutch people just ate it all up.

With Black Love Cabaret, we wanted to create a new vibe, something like the Paradise Garage in New York, even though some of us had never been to the Paradise Garage. DJs Abraxas and Crazy Shaun, who was originally DJing with Soho Connection and moonlighting, were the resident DJs. I eventually started to DJ more and more, after managing to practice regularly
103

when a friend asked me to stay at his home while he went on vacation. He had decks, so I used them and he had all the latest records.

I usually opened, or an early set, warming up for the other DJs. We were blending Dutch DJs like Dimitri, Per and Marcello with our American guests, who we booked every month. Josh Wink, Juan Atkins, Keoki, Eddie Flashin' Fowlkes, Frankie Bones, and Stacey Pullen etc. were the American DJs we booked form 1988 to the early 90s. Back then people didn't know who they were, unlike today.

Byron was also involved. He is American but we didn't know each other until we were introduced in Amsterdam, where we had both moved to be part of the same scene. I kept hearing his name mentioned and was told many times that I should meet this guy from DC, America, because he liked the same sounds and artists as I did. DJ Abraxas actually introduced us and we just hit it off. He used to organise parties back in Washington DC, on the college circuit, and I used to do parties in California, also on the college circuit.

Byron was responsible for bringing Derrick May and Frankie Knuckles to Amsterdam for the first time.

Every party was at a different location, but usually always a squat. We did a party at B-Bop, which later became Club It, and we had flown Frankie Knuckles over to play. We had stencilled a paper flyer together, which looked more like a ransom note with lettering cut out from a newspaper.

There had been no reason to book foreign, especially American, artists, before then. But the scene was growing and he was at the top. I think it was Frankie's first gig in Holland.

Rocco Veenboer was at our first party in Amsterdam, and he went on to start the Awakenings concept, after falling in love, and being inspired, with the Black Love Cabaret parties.

Back in 1989, 1990 maybe, towards the end of the Black Love Cabaret series, I think some of the competition were at our party – because tear gas was used. We had managed to find this amazing location near Weesperplein, in the centre of Amsterdam, and some people were jealous and unhappy that we had come across it first.

That same night, another group of people were doing a party, and at that time there wasn't enough of a crowd to go around. There was a big crowd at our place and they basically wanted them at their place.

In return they decided to throw smoke bombs, combined with some form of tear gas, at our party. We were already using a strobe and a smoke machine, the basics, but now it was full of tear gas too. People's eyes were itching and it felt like bleach had been poured into them. I was on the decks when it happened and it took me a little bit of time to work out what was going on. All I could see were people frantically rubbing their eyes and running out of the room, and then it started to affect me. People were really suffering and the whole place emptied out. We had to douse the whole place with water. Nobody wanted to stay in that room because it was such an awful mess. The event was also a financial disaster and we didn't recover after that. But we didn't stop the party; we eventually resumed and kept going!

It was at the time when there were a lot of people trying to get things off the ground, but there were not enough people to fill all the parties. We still don't know the names of those who attacked us. There are a few theories but nobody knows exactly who was responsible.

In 1988, George Clinton was hired by 5th World, a record label, for six months to make some new tracks. I was already working with the label, as house music was the next big thing, and I was there to teach them house and help the label produce some new music. It was four kicks on the floor, wrapped with a sample, and then you were on your way to the bank – but the label never did that. It was rubbish.

I did some vocals on a track for George. I remember being pushed into a recording booth, and being told to write, just write. They wanted me to write something on the spot for a track they were going to release, featuring me doing the vocals. It was called No More War and we even went to England to record a video at 2Unlimited's company, plus many live PAs to promote it. But the track was never actually released publicly, although it was available as a promo.

It was actually a really annoying process making the track, and then the video wasn't regarded as good enough, which meant we had to re-shoot the lot. The track had a few different versions with different singers and took three years for a remix to be produced. I can't even listen to it any more. It's really bad and the vocals are so annoying!

I remember playing in Prague, in the Czech Republic. To get there, we decided to go on a road trip. I hated flying and would always prefer a road trip. But if someone insisted, or there wasn't enough time to get there by car, I would consider flying.

My mates were really into their gabba, the fast and heavy hardcore sound. They were looking for a party so we all went to

106

Prague. The car was loaded with people, and loaded with other stuff too. They were sniffing all the way and when we arrived at the Czech border, everybody was searched. If you were caught in possession it meant you would be denied entrance to the country.

Everybody was held at the border for hours. Actually, we were basically hanging on the side of the road and we were all searched. Together with my mate Rienzi, from the Party Animals, I decided that we were going to stay and make it to Prague. After all, I was there to work and I was getting paid. My mates had to drive back to Holland, not surprisingly, but Renzi and I were picked up at the border by the organisers.

The location was a squat, situated high in the mountains, and if I remember correctly it was an old orphanage. There was an old basketball court and at the end of the party we all played a game, while one of the organisers made off with all the money! It was quite the adventure after we had made it all the way down there and barely got into the country, only to see our cash disappear. We hung around for another two days, until the other organisers worked out what to do regarding our wages and the missing money. We did our job, we came, we played, we partied – we did our thing. Not surprisingly, the guy who stole all the money proved elusive, so the other organisers couldn't get in touch with him. They did the decent thing, though, and scraped enough money together for us before we made our way back home.

It was quite a strange experience, especially as we were having trouble at the border. All the signs were telling us to head back to Amsterdam, but I wanted to export my sound to other countries and that is what I did.

In 1995 I played in Ibiza and again we went by car. I first flew home to the USA for my sister Renee's wedding. I actually have
107

seven sisters and three brothers, and I hadn't been home in a while. My two younger brothers, Sundown and Timothy, who I also hadn't seen in a while, were going through a difficult time. They didn't know what to do with themselves. They had no motivation, so I asked them if they wanted to fly back to Amsterdam with me – and then do a road trip to Ibiza!

Sundown, the youngest, decided to come and I paid for his ticket but Timothy didn't want to come. My father drove us to the airport and we flew back to Amsterdam. I had a lot of upcoming gigs, including the trip to Ibiza.

We arrived back in Amsterdam on the Wednesday afternoon around 4pm, by 6pm we were in the car heading for Ibiza, so Sundown had to wait a further two weeks before he could discover the pleasures of Amsterdam.

I had played previously in Ibiza, back in 1989 and 1990. In those days I was a fan of Sven Vath, who I actually met on a beach one day and he signed my cigarette packet for me. I was playing with some Italian DJs in those days, such as Francesco Farfa, and DJ Dak from Germany.

Back to 1995-96 and I was playing in Space, which opened only from six in the morning until the afternoon. They had a patio outside with slow, clubby lounge music, and inside was techno – the harder stuff. Inside, it was dark with air conditioning and a strobe. It was great and we had the best of both worlds. I played at Amnesia and Pacha in the two weeks we were there, also.

I was playing together with another DJ from England, Fat Max, and we played under the name Funky Fakirs as a DJ duo. It was cool; Ibiza still had its hippy vibe then. Together with Max, we also did some remixes for R&W Records for an artist named
108

Tabitha, and her track was called Amsterdamcing.

Mysteryland had their first festival in 1994 and it was one of the first big festivals in Holland. It was originally called Mystery Island, but they changed the name at the last minute because they lost the license to use the island. I said: "Why don't you just call it Mysteryland?" So they did and I had my own area as well. It was the only area open for the entire 72 hours from start to finish. We had only three DJs per day, and I was one of them. When everything else stopped we kept going. DJs were playing 10-hour sets and my set on the first day, with Spider Willem, was 15 hours long. The next day was Jeroen Flamman, Abraxas and me.

It was the first real dance music festival to happen in Holland, running through the night, outside and in multiple areas with different styles of music.

In 1995, one year after leaving, Ricardo came back to Amsterdam. I had gigs in Paris, Switzerland, Germany etc. and would always go by car. Ricardo wanted to come along and he joined me, along with his girlfriend Krissy, when I played in Switzerland at Planet-E, so he could see for himself how the scene was going.

Planet-E was a similar concept to the festivals, where they would start on the Friday and finish Monday morning. A non-stop, three day party. It was in Basel, right on the border with France and Germany, and very well organised, with a great flyer too. Train times from various locations were provided, showing the fares in different currencies, depending on where you bought your ticket, like the French franc and the German deutschmark, for example.

There were several massive rooms with the best DJs from all over Europe – no, make that the world. There were different styles, like the acid room, the techno room and so on.

Enrico could see what they were doing, from the flyer to the various rooms and sounds – and he was inspired!

On the way to and from Switzerland, we had been discussing the possibility of doing a festival in Amsterdam. I said we shouldn't do one like Mysteryland, but instead get everyone involved. The Mazzo, Roxy, Time Machine, Maz from the Soho Connection, later the Paradiso – just get everyone on board. We should do a big outdoor party, with at least five to 10 outdoor areas, and that's exactly what we did.

The first one was in 1995 but, unfortunately, it wasn't really gated well and lots of people sneaked in.

I was playing and I took the shuttle bus from Sloterdijk station. I arrived quite early, before it had officially started, and they were still trying to figure out how to get everyone in safely and quickly through the turnstiles.

Tents were still being set up and sound systems installed. Our area was the only one ready to go, so when everybody came charging in they headed straight to our area as it was the only one with music!

I actually played the very first record at the very first Dance Valley festival. For me, it was another beautiful event at a new beautiful location – another door had been kicked open.

I actually thought it was a pretty good effort, their first festival, and everybody pretty much knew what they were doing. I don't know how they found the location but I'm glad they did. It was at a time when lots of people were offering their land to promoters, as they knew there was a growing market for that type of festival. Back then, a lot of people were renting any type of location to organise a party.

That location in Spaarnwoude is now the go-to place for lots of events.

I was asked to play again in 2009, but in the old-school area. I wasn't too keen to play the same records I had played at the first party back in 1995, so I changed it and played elsewhere. I really wish I hadn't because, annoyingly, it was really quiet where I played and the old school area was booming and packed all day!

LOUIS OSBOURNE

Louis is the owner of All Night Artists, a management company for electronic music artists. He has hung up the headphones and puts all his efforts into helping others within the scene. What a kind soul.

Louis is the son of international megastar and Black Sabbath vocalist, Ozzy, and has gone on to forge a successful career in the music world for himself. Stepping away from the eye-liner and bats, which is just a myth apparently, Louis entered the industry as an artist in his own right with a successful career within the electronic music sector.

Louis spoke about life as a DJ, early days as a raver, artist management and recalled some lovely tales of him and his father sharing some quality moments during Louis' DJ career.

Enjoy...

I remember a time when I was still at college and along with a few mates I had started to get involved in the rave scene. We bought tickets to Fantazia in West Point, Exeter. The plan was to take the train but my mate's mum found out and grounded him. But my mum didn't seem to mind as she drove me to the station, bought me a return ticket and sent me off to Fantazia – all on my own.

From Exeter I hitch-hiked out to the rave at West Point. I was only 16 at the time and I can still remember the date – February

20th 1992. I had been to some smaller events locally but that was my first big rave.

I loved the music, especially the drum & bass and early hardcore. I started buying records and I must have bought everything from Reinforced and Moving Shadow. I needed a DJ name, too, so I chose DJ Hardcore-Rush. We all have a skeleton in the closet, don't we?

After some time the scene, for me, turned a bit moody. The music was getting darker and, just around that time, another mate of mine introduced me to New York house. Strictly Rhythm, early Armand Van Helden stuff etc. From that came my love of Chicago house, then Detroit, and that was it for me. I'd found my new sound.

My first gig, under the pseudonym DJ Hardcore-Rush, was in the student union at Birmingham University back in 1994, and then my first proper club gig as Louis Osbourne, playing house music, was at Crunch, in Birmingham, not long after. DJ Hardcore-Rush wasn't a very good house DJ name after all!

Also in 1995, I started work at a record shop in Birmingham called Hard to Find Records. People had a love-hate relationship with the shop. It was still the early days of mail-order and records were going missing all the time. We had customers screaming at us down the phone but, I have to say, for the bunch of stoners that worked in the shop we didn't do too badly. Ha-ha-ha-ha!

During this time I had a residency at House of God, the techno club in Birmingham. The owner was a huge Sabbath fan and when he knew Ozzy's son was working in the record shop, and loved techno, he had to come and speak to me and offered me the chance to play at his club. This was a massive learning curve for

113

me. I learned how to build it up and play a warm-up slot all the way up to the main slot. In the end I'd proved my mettle and I was getting headlining slots.

In 1998 I left the record shop and decided to go to Ibiza and join two other Brummie DJs, Steve Lawler and Pete Gooding.

I remember being done by Thomson at the airport before leaving. I had six record-boxes with me and they stung me for 600 quid's worth of excess baggage. After a two-week trial I became a resident DJ at Cafe Mambo together with Pete. I also managed to become a resident for Cream at Amnesia, on the infamous terrace, in my first season.

I was playing seven days a week, six hours a day, for the entire season and every Thursday evening I was playing for Cream at Amnesia - everything from deep house to down-tempo, jazzy sets, all sorts really. Working in the record shop helped a lot because we stocked so many different styles and I was lucky enough to have access to it all. I was really into the French trip-hop sound and played a lot of that, before Air came along and killed it. Except for their first album, I liked that.

I managed two seasons in Ibiza and the second saw me reside at Bugged-Out, also at Amnesia. I was mainly playing on the terrace but was fortunate enough to play in the main room occasionally and opened for Carl Cox, Basement Jaxx, and Josh Wink etc. My greatest DJ experience was probably when I played the main room at Amnesia. The DJ booth was amazing, as was the sound.

I did actually get into trouble with Mambo's owner, Javier, one day. I was playing different styles, from jazz to down-tempo to disco classics etc. and some of these tracks lasted forever. It was boring just standing there. So, because we were next to the sea, I decided to put on a 22-minute mix of MFSB - Love is the Message - and set the timer on my watch. I went snorkelling for 15 minutes then walked back and changed the record...ha-ha!

In late 1999, for the first time, I was signed to a booking agency in the USA and they looked after me from there on.

Another time back in '98 or '99 I was sat outside Space with an old mate, Adam, who used to be Paul Daley's PA, and he started telling me about his trip with Paul to San Francisco for a gig a few weeks previously.

They were sat on a flight from London to San Francisco, and sitting just in from of them was this old washed-up hippy-type guy and he was sat there drinking something from his own flask, which later turned out to be mushroom-brew.

They were approaching San Francisco and the guy in front started to lose it. He began shouting at everyone, going on about psychotic conspiracies etc. and, just as they flew over San Francisco Bay, the guy leapt from his chair, while the other passengers and crew were all seated waiting to land. He only ran to the back of the plane and tried to open the doors. Adam and Paul both jumped out of their seats and started to wrestle the guy to the ground, with a few punches here and there, and they sat on him until the plane had landed. Waiting for them were the police and the FBI.

Because Adam and Paul were involved they were escorted from the plane and taken away for questioning but, obviously, they were released as they were actual heroes.

Now, remember, this was back in '98 or '99 and in 2002 I met my wife, Louise, in Los Angeles. Shortly after we started dating I went to pick her up one night in one of my dad's SUVs. I put a CD on and she asked who it was. "It's Leftfield," I told her, and she just said: "Oh my god, I was on a plane with Leftfield's Paul Daley a few years ago, and this weird guy sat next to me was drinking mushroom-brew. He went mad and the guys wrestled him to the ground."

Wow!

Adam had also told me that Paul had taken a liking to an Irish girl during the flight, and there was me, a few years later, hearing the same girl tell me the same story. I called Adam and told him that I was dating that very girl.

The funny thing is, the boys were chatting to Louise during the flight and Paul told her he was from Leftfield, which prompted Louise to ask if it was "Near London?"

Not long after we had launched our O&A project, Jamie Anderson and I played together in London. At the time I was in Birmingham and Jamie was in South Wales. We weren't being paid a huge amount – around 300 pounds between us – and afterwards I was going back with Jamie to his place for a Sunday studio session.

We decided against a hotel and thought we'd go to an after-party at someone's house and catch the first train back to South Wales.

Our problems started when the electricity meter ran out. I was in the toilet at this house party and I couldn't see a thing, so I turned on the light from my phone and, in doing so, managed to drop it down the toilet – while I was in full flow. I managed to catch it as it hit the water, completely covered in pee, and looked round for something to dry it.

This was just the start, and don't forget my phone was on the blink. Sometime later Jamie and I left the house and headed for the train station. We thought we would sleep on the train and be fresh for the studio.

We needed a taxi, but there were absolutely none available, and we couldn't find our way back to the house to ring for one. We decided to stand on opposite sides of the road to try to spot a taxi from both sides. We had to be at Marylebone for 7.45am and we had booked these really cheap tickets in advance, so if we missed that specific train we would have to pay a lot more.

It was getting late, we were still trying to locate a taxi and I was bursting for the toilet. I needed to go so I shouted over to Jamie and headed round the corner, out the way of the road to avoid getting arrested. As I'm busy, I spot a taxi and raise my hand and he stops. Excellent, I thought. I jumped in and we drove round the corner to pick Jamie up. But he had disappeared and my phone was covered in urine so I couldn't call him. I just thought he had found a taxi and headed for the same station, and he had my record bag, train tickets and my wife's expensive video camera.

Anyway, I'm running through the station with only minutes to spare and Jamie's nowhere to be seen. I have my reservation confirmation for the train – but no tickets as I didn't have time to stop at the ticket machine to collect them.

I'm on the train, in my reserved seat, and the conductor walks into the carriage and asks for my ticket. I explained what had happened, he didn't listen and told me that I had to pay the full fare of 120 quid. Now, I had been up all night, and I was pretty

117

pissed and I started to have a massive ding-dong with this guy, and he just said: "Right, that's it, you're off at the next stop!"

As we pulled in at Reading station, the British Transport Police were waiting on the platform and immediately boarded the train to remove me, and threw me out of the station. Other passengers were trying to stick up for me because they knew I had my reservation but the jobsworth didn't want to know, and off I went. I managed to call my wife, Louise, and she went mad. I asked her to call Jamie's girlfriend and tell her he's lost in London somewhere.

It turned out that Jamie, after seeing I had gone, had spotted a train station and just got on the first train he saw, fell asleep, and woke up in Essex somewhere.

Eventually, after being evicted from the train station, I sneaked back in and caught the next train to Swansea. With my original confirmation in hand I explained what had happened to the conductor and he just laughed. He said that some people are like that and told me to sit back and enjoy the ride to Swansea.

Upon arrival, my phone was starting to come back to life and I spoke to Jamie's girlfriend, who was furious. She came to pick me up from the station, dropped me at their home, and then she had to leave immediately with the kids. Jamie didn't show up until 10.30 that evening. He still had all the bags, including mine and my wife's video camera. We both got so much heat off our respective partners. They even suggested O&A was a bad idea!

I started to produce my own music and after a few business issues with a certain label I decided to form my own label. I had to think of a brand name and decided to call it Mija Recordings, an amalgamation of my two children's names – Mia and Elijah. A made-up word, I thought, but it actually means dick in Brazilian slang and girlfriend in Mexican slang. At the time I didn't know this and it certainly wasn't coming up when I researched the name through Google!

I devoted a lot of time and invested a lot of money in the label but it wasn't really the heyday for the music business. Sales suffered, artists were upset they weren't making any money and I was losing money too, and rapidly. I was fed up releasing other people's music and if I decide to do it again I think I'll just release my own music.

However, I did set up another label with Jamie called All Night Records, which is still actually running but without any new releases. To be honest, it's a lot of work to run a label, plus I was beginning to become more interested in artist management.

I had a gig in Turkey in early 2000, I don't remember where exactly. The day before leaving, I was chilling on the beach, listening to Blue Lines by Massive Attack. Out of nowhere a pack of stray dogs decided to massively attack me. I had to escape by running into the sea and in the process ruined my CD Walkman!

The gig itself was a bit disappointing and it ended up that I was the only DJ that actually got paid.

The next day I had to fly to a gig in Munich, with a changeover in Ankara. The problem was that I was left all alone at a domestic terminal instead of the international terminal for my connecting flight to Munich. To make matters worse, across the tarmac I could see passengers boarding my connecting flight but it was too far away for me to make it on time. I was banging frantically on the glass hoping someone would hear or see me

119

when, suddenly, a baggage handler led me down a flight of stairs and told me to jump on his baggage trolley. He quickly drove me across the tarmac to my flight, undoubtedly one of the most bizarre things that has ever happened to me.

I've only ever managed to miss two flights, once when I was in Los Angeles just after I had met my wife, and I didn't even bother going to the airport as I was having so much fun. The second time was after a gig at No-UFOs in Berlin, when I woke up in the hotel five hours after my flight had left. The annoying thing was I had to pay for a new ticket which took up most of my wage from the night before. My wife wasn't very happy!

When I was living in Dublin, I had two weekends on the bounce where I had to change at Heathrow Terminal 3. I was playing in Germany and when I flew back my records hadn't made it to Dublin. I had to fill in all these missing bag forms, describing every little detail, contents, colour, and all that kind of stuff. After a few days my records still hadn't turned up and I thought 'That's it, they're gone.'

The following weekend I was back at Terminal 3 and I had a bit of time to kill before flying home to Dublin. I decided to go to the lost baggage counter and ask if anything had happened, seeing as I had already filled in the papers a week earlier. They said 'No' but offered me the chance to go into the back room and check the lost and found luggage. As I walked in the first bag in front of me was MY record box. The airline had lost my records and I had actually found them myself a week later.

In the late 90s my dad and I did an article for a Japanese magazine. I had to choose 10 house/techno tracks to play to my Dad and then we had to each give our opinion. I can't remember every track but I do remember one being Armand Van Helden's

120

You Don't Even Know Me and he really liked it. He liked the chorus, verse, melody and from a traditional songwriter's point of view, which of course he is, it worked for him. Then I played him Jeff Mills' The Bells and he said it was really quite hypnotic and it would sound great if you were loaded.

I toured with my dad many times across the USA and I asked my American agent to arrange gigs for me in the same cities where Sabbath were performing. I was trying to break America at the time and because I was already in those cities it meant that promoters didn't have to pay travel costs, which was a massive help to them. I spent an entire summer DJing across America when I was on tour with my dad.

He actually came to see me play in Atlanta, Georgia, back in the early 2000s. It was in an old theatre, a really great club and it was packed. My dad came up a via a fire exit, to avoid the crowd recognising him, and he stood in the DJ booth behind me. You wouldn't have known he was there unless you were up in the booth. His timing isn't the best but he's there tapping his foot, getting into it and enjoying the night but soon after he tapped me on the shoulder and said goodbye.

We were sharing an adjoining suite at our hotel and there was a door from my room into his, and the following morning I was sitting with him when he started talking about the previous night and how he thought the music was tribal and hypnotic. I actually thought that was very perceptive of him because at the time I was playing a lot of tribal and hypnotic stuff from the likes of Danny Tenaglia, Stereo, Steve Lawler, and Boy's Own etc.

Playing in America did, eventually, have its problems. Because of the success of the TV reality show, The Osbournes, promoters wanted to tap into that market. It was starting to get ridiculous. I

121

was playing at Spundae in Chicago, together with The Scumfrog, and they even had a picture of my dad on the flyer.

When I toured the US, promoting my mix album, I must have played at every single town that didn't have an underground music scene and on one occasion someone came up to the decks and said: "You're not fucking Jack Osbourne!"

That was it for me and I had to write everything into a new contract that nothing from the show had any bearings on my own career. I could have gone down that route, a reality star DJ, and made loads of money. Perhaps I could have been the founding-father of EDM! But despite annoying my wife, I was adamant there could be no link between my professional career and my dad's career. Of course, I couldn't prevent people talking about him in promoting events for which I was booked, but there can be no artwork, names, or anything on the billing for my shows and I had to give my approval for all my gigs. This eventually started to affect my bookings and how much money I was earning.

I have had some amazing international gigs in the past and one that really stands out was when I played on top of Sugarloaf Mountain in Rio de Janeiro, Brazil. We had to take a cable car to this exhibition area with a theatre, which is where the party was taking place.

I was playing inside and Derrick Carter was playing outside. In the morning, when the sun came up, I was stood staring down at Copacabana beach and it was beautiful, a very special moment. Unfortunately, and this is something that many DJs share, these amazing moments are always without your family and your loved ones. I've travelled the world but only shared my moments with the people I've met along the way, if that, and eaten alone in the best restaurants. It is such a shame that all the amazing things I've managed to do, I've experienced them all flying solo!

A GUY CALLED GERALD

Responsible for one of the most renowned cuts of vinyl to grace the decks during the days of the acid house takeover, in my opinion Gerald Simpson has grown to legendary status.

Always at the forefront of trying something new, he never fails to move a room, a tent or an entire field. Growing up in Hulme, south Manchester, Gerald was always looking for something different. By the late 80s he had realised there was definitely something else going on, not just the pop rubbish he was hearing on the radio.

Already busy DJing and originally with 808 State, Gerald was never happier unless he was locked inside a studio recording one tune after another. He originally found it hard not having his own proper studio, but then things began to change.

Recorded back in 1988, Voodoo Ray was and perhaps still is the musical background to a scene that produced some of the finest artists we still have today and for that we must all be truly grateful. It began as a bit of an experiment when alone in the studio and the sample was originally called Voodoo Rage, but Gerald ran out of sample-memory during recording and Voodoo Ray was born.

No chart success was expected and it was very much an underground track but it reached number 12 in the UK singles chart. The revolution had begun.

I can remember a really great night with Gerald in Amsterdam. It was December 13th, 2008 and Gerald was booked for the

Redevice Invites night at Studio 80. The music was so deep, positively intense and very soulful, but it was played at the perfect pitch. It wasn't fast or techno-like, but an extremely groovy pitch that kept everybody interested. The resident DJs who were on after Gerald were in place ready to take over, but Gerald didn't stop. I don't think the other boys were too bothered because the dance floor was packed and it was going off!

Gerald is still in demand and so he should be. If you haven't already done so, make sure you get your fix of A Guy Called Gerald because it's never too late.

Gerald spoke about his early days, a chance meeting with Finley Quaye, life in Berlin and how he tried to gatecrash a potential gig.

As a youngster in Manchester I used to walk from Rusholme to the city centre with all my studio equipment every day because I couldn't afford the bus fare and I always had a lot of energy to produce music, despite the long walks.

A few of us would get together and create some music and, eventually, we became 808 State. I worked on Newbuild, 808 State's first album, then a Peel Session mix and also Pacific, plus maybe another three or four tracks as well.

Around this time, I really had the idea that I wanted to go on and create my own music. It wasn't really working for me so I decided to go it alone and the A Guy Called Gerald project was born. I had the idea for a house track, which I later called Voodoo Ray, and I just decided to focus on that and not go into a negative one.

I was really broke, completely on my arse. I couldn't even claim any benefits so my mum kept helping me out and I just made music every day. Sometimes I'd make 10 to 20 tracks a day and record them at home on a four-track machine. I ended up with so many cassettes full of tracks.

My number one goal was to get my music played on Piccadilly Radio, Manchester's local station. Some friends of mine from the local jazz scene had heard the tracks I was making for the radio and put me in touch with Rham! Records.

At the time they were a versatile label with some industrial sounds. They were really interested in this new house and electronic music that was starting to emerge, and I suppose I was the closest one to them making it. They liked the fact that I was a local boy from the North West involved in the production of this new sound.

Being a local boy certainly seemed to work in my favour and they gave me some studio time at Moonraker Studios in Manchester, to work on some tracks. I decided to take the four tracks I was currently working on, plus a fifth which featured a girl singing and sounded a bit R&B-like. I really wanted to take and record the vocal from it so I decided to put that one in too.

I managed to complete the four tracks in their studio and when it came to the fifth, and that vocal, I decided to do something completely different. Basically, just throw some paint at the canvas. I just wanted it to be different and they had loads of equipment in the studio I'd never used before, like a sampler for instance. I asked the girl, Nicola, to sing just anything into the sampler, total improv, but for some reason I couldn't get the timing to work with the sampler, so I asked her to just sing into a tape. She improvised and filled the whole tape with some sounds and vocals. It was easier for me, too, because once she left the studio I could still work with what she had created.

So I listened to the tape, kept forwarding and rewinding it until I found the vocal I wanted to use. I grabbed it then put it through the sampler and discovered that I could play the ad-lib backwards. So I just kept the ad-lib, which was the vocal, playing and played it backwards too, and it was creating this different sound. I was just experimenting and it was from this that Voodoo Ray was born.

I have my own studio and a lot of crazy things have happened to me while I've been recording in there. I'd often try and get random people into the studio to do things and the most famous was probably Finley Quaye. This was probably back in 1992-1993 when nobody had heard of Finley and he was still a long way from being famous at the time.

I used to have a PlayStation in the studio and I had every single game. You name it, I had it. Finley was working in a studio downstairs from mine and one day he came upstairs and just started playing on the PlayStation, and this went on for months and months. Not surprisingly, he knew all the cheats and tricks.

One day we were having a chat and a smoke, and he said he could sing. I thought 'Yeah, yeah' and I just blew him off. I didn't take him seriously. A little while later I was working on a new track and just as I was putting it together he came in. I asked him if he could do some vocals for me and he agreed. I was really surprised – not only could he actually sing, but I liked it a lot.

The way he was coming across was really original and I'd never heard anything like that before, so he did vocals on a couple of
127

tracks for me. I moved on to another project and at the time I didn't really do anything with the tracks and Finley's vocals.

A little while later, Finley turned up at the studio and offered me an amplifier. It looked great and I bought it from him. A week or so later I got a knock on my studio door and it was Leroy, head bouncer from the Hacienda. He said that word had got out that I had an amplifier of theirs and I just thought 'Oh shit, fucking hell, he's robbed it from the Hacienda.' Funnily enough, Finley was in the next studio and once Leroy had left I went to find him but he had gone – completely disappeared – and I didn't see him for ages after that, ha-ha-ha! Obviously, I gave the amp back for nothing. They knew Finley had taken it, but there was no way I was going to say anything.

I didn't get my money back but I did have this track with Finley's vocals on. I came up with the idea that I should put the track out but not pay him, so that is exactly what I did.

I called it Finley's Rainbow and it started to get played all over the place. Maybe about a month after I released it he called me and told me he thought the track was really cool. At the time he wasn't around Manchester and wouldn't be for a while. I told him about the amp he sold me and that I didn't get my money back, explaining that I'd decided to release the track we made but that I wasn't going to pay him. He wasn't happy but he understood.

Finley's Rainbow was starting to do really well on the underground scene and because I had two gigs in London coming up I offered him the chance to come and sing live. He was already in London and was happy he didn't have to come up to Manchester. He agreed but we didn't actually meet and discuss it until the day of the gig at the sound check.

I was spinning some jungle music at the time and had the idea to start with the strings of Finley's Rainbow, and then Finley would just appear from nowhere on the stage and start singing. People were really amazed and it went down really well. After the gig we were backstage and there were a few record label bosses hanging around. They were really interested in Finley after hearing him sing and they pretty much signed him up there and then – and the rest is history.

I was really happy for him. It was great that someone from Manchester, who was basically on his arse, was going places. I was definitely a bridge in his career and did give him a little push but I do think he's really talented and really original. It's just that he often forgets just how talented he is.

I've been working on a project with some computer programmers, between London and Berlin, to try to develop this new artist system, which is completely 100 per cent artist driven and where 100 per cent of the financial feedback is for the artist. The idea is for the artist to be 100 per cent in control – no manipulation from labels – thus leaving the artist's work 100 per cent pure.

One of the things I've noticed is that artists are often swayed, or pulled, by financial decisions and the amount of people that are lost in this is worrying. They never really get out of that net. They really want to do something but instead do something else to get the money. Some people have to do what they can to pay the bills but it would be nice to hear the music the artist really wants to do. There are a few sites around where you can upload your own music but you need management and connection to a label to really make it.

What we are trying to do is make everything for the artist –
129

incorporate them being their own publisher, label boss etc. They would be in total control of their musical property, intellectual property, the business, their portfolio, everything. This would also help to make their business more creative. They could create their own style without being pressured to sound like this person or that person. The aim would be to make them more aware of what they do, instead of looking at someone else's progress. Most of the time the media can promote music, even bad music, so it's good for people to learn how to promote themselves and be active with their music.

If you're an artist and somebody shows interest in you personally there's nothing more inspiring than that and this really helps create individuality. If someone likes you there's no reason to try to impress by not being yourself. If 10 people wanted to sound like this one person and they make it big it basically becomes a wall of the same music and it becomes very uninteresting.

I think I must have spent 10 years living in Berlin and it taught me a few lessons, one of which was DJ-jacking. You turn up at a club with your records, or your CDs, whatever, and you head to the decks or the DJ booth, and it's there you basically tell the DJ who is playing that you're up next. Basically, you jack them off. You start looking at your watch, gesture towards the DJ and point at your watch, and then you've got to try to put on the next tune while the other DJ is searching through his records or CDs. A slight shoulder nudge often does the trick but you've got to watch out the promoter doesn't see you. I've seen it a few times around Berlin, especially Bar 25, when everyone's wasted and nobody has a clue what's going on.

I tried it myself, purely by accident, at the Panorama Bar in Berlin back in 2006, but I kind of got sussed out. I was standing by the front gates with my record box after a gig elsewhere and one of the bouncers came over to me. He asked if I was the DJ and I just looked at him and said: "Yeah." Ha-ha-ha! He took me round the back of the bar and we went up in a lift. Then he turned and asked which DJ I was. He had a list of all the artists playing but I couldn't see it, so I just came clean and told him I wasn't actually playing tonight, before adding that I was a DJ.

Busted!

I tried to buy him a drink and discovered he was not a bouncer but the big boss. Fortunately, I wasn't in his bad books, but I did decide to be more honest in the future!

MONDE

This gentle giant with a heart of gold is largely responsible for how Amsterdam and its underground party scene have developed since 1991.

Andre van der Monde and his Mayhem brand ruled the underground roost with its harder sounds and its many faithful followers, and soon led to the creation of more party organisations within the Netherlands. Specific party-goers were heavily inspired by what they were witnessing as teenagers, as Andre and Mayhem delivered the goods. More on that in the interview.

The go-to man for all your old school acid house needs, Monde is a regular member of Amsterdam's old school family, and always spins a quality vinyl set, with the original classics from yesteryear gracing the decks.

Andre spoke about his illegal warehouse rave days, the unforgettable drama it brings and much more.

I used to organise illegal underground acid house raves called Mayhem with my mate, Neuv. For that time, they were certainly the heaviest nights, musically, around Amsterdam. The biggest sound systems playing the finest underground music and we made a lot of noise. It was before the gabba sound came in; not as fast but just as heavy.

One weekend, we organised a night in Rotterdam, which was not the usual location in those days for a bunch of Amsterdammers to take over. I had booked Quazar for a live set, alongside Turntable Terror, aka Michel de Hey, and Holy Noise, aka Paul Elstak.

I had hired the most expensive laser system available in those days. It cost 6,500 guilders, the old Dutch currency. Once we had the laser system installed at the venue, I noticed the cable wouldn't reach the power point and we had absolutely no way of fixing it. In the end, I couldn't even use the bloody laser!

I lost a lot of money that night and it kicked off a lengthy depression in my life. All my savings were gone. I had to do something after losing so much. I ended up squatting a dome shaped warehouse in Sloterdijk, Amsterdam. It was 300 metres in length on one level and was constructed and wrapped with corrugated steel. I changed the locks and we organised a party on September 9th, 1991.

Seeing as I was broke, we decided to do a pre-sale of the tickets in advance. We actually managed to sell 1,500 tickets at 15 guilders each. There was no turning back; after taking so much money we had to make sure there was a party.

On the morning of the event I went to the warehouse and opened the locks I had previously installed. Somebody drove over to me and was asking a lot of questions about what I was up to, but I told him nothing. Shortly afterwards Heineken arrived with the beer and the sound system was delivered and installed. This was followed by the arrival of the decor and everything else we had ordered for the party, and both the warehouse and terrain were transformed beautifully into an all-night rave.

It was very busy and I couldn't help but notice that it kept getting busier. Something was clearly up and I wondered where they

133

were coming from. I went outside and could see a lot of people climbing through the side of the building. Somebody had cut a huge hole in the corrugated iron and they were crawling through the hole in their thousands. In total over 6,000 people turned up that night – and the majority without even buying a fucking ticket!

We had a few hundred gatecrashers at another Amsterdam party I organised. It was at De Wielingen, near to the Amsterdam RAI and very close to where the Knijn bowling centre is now situated.

We, Mayhem, were honoured to be asked to put on the last-ever party at that location, but we didn't expect what actually happened. They, the hardcore party beasts who didn't want to pay, broke through two doors, charged over the cloakroom and burst into the party. There were so many people already there that it was impossible to distinguish the gatecrashers from those who had purchased tickets.

Funnily enough, it turned out it *wasn't* the last party to be organised there. Instead, one month later, Multigroove organised what was their first-ever party, which was supposed to be the last party at De Wielingen, and they even played the same music as we did.

Another time, I organised a party called Mayhem Summer Trance Garden Party. Multigroove then organised something similar, plus their flyer was practically the same as ours, but they called it Multigroove Summer Garden Party.

Multigroove progressed further into the gabba and hardcore scene, just when Mayhem stopped, but in my opinion they copied us – Mayhem – as a brand and even used very similarly-designed flyers. Their brand logo was almost a carbon copy too, with the
134

same type of design. Was it just a coincidence? Definitely not, because when I asked Ilja, the Multigroove boss, he said it was better to copy something with quality, than to think of something badly. Ilja and I are good mates, no bad vibes at all, so I don't say anything with any negativity.

My girlfriend grew up in Purmerend, a province in north Holland, and was school friends with ID&T's Duncan Stutterheim and his brother. I remember one of my old parties, back in 1992, that I have video footage from, and you can spot a very young Duncan and his brother backstage in the VIP area. They were sitting in the corner looking impressed with what they were experiencing and soaking up the Mayhem vibes. It wasn't long before ID&T was formed and eventually it became a worldwide brand, including their Sensation parties, but with a more commercial sound.

First Multigroove, then ID&T, but Mayhem really did set the standard. It's good that Mayhem is given a mention and some recognition in their first book, which details the start of the rave scene in Holland and ID&T's history.

There's also a part about a party in Nieuw-Vennep, a town about 20 minutes from Amsterdam. In that story it not only claims that I was the promoter of that particular party, but also that I left the party with all the money, meaning no one was paid. I'd like to assure everyone that is not true. It wasn't my party; it was the Beat Club, not Mayhem.

From my days in the game nobody is able to come to me and say they weren't paid. I was always good to my word and always paid what was owed, which nobody can question.

In 1991 I remember playing at a party in a discotheque in

Limburg, a province in the south-east of Holland. The DJ booth was actually a cage suspended from the ceiling overhanging the dance floor.

It was about 7am and I was playing my set when security came to me and asked me to stop playing because the party was over. I had other ideas and after noticing there was a lock I quickly locked myself in the cage, much to the annoyance of the security people, and continued playing for another hour or so.

Unfortunately, they eventually had the idea to cut the main power, which sent the club into complete silence and darkness. At first I refused to leave the cage, but I soon realised I couldn't argue any more with the security guys.

Earlier that evening, the promoters, who had booked several high profile DJs to play, found one of them busy in the toilet with drugs. They weren't really too impressed with him, so they kicked him out, with a few punches also thrown, and said they didn't want to hear him play any longer as they felt disrespected by his toilet antics.

Mayhem was still going strong and we managed to organise a party in the catacombs of the Olympic Stadium in Amsterdam, which at that time was the home of local football club FC Amsterdam.

There were a few guys who turned up and started to make trouble. They were saying that money had been stolen from their jackets, which were hung up in the cloakroom. I had hired security people but they didn't know what to do and decided it was best to come and get me. I knew that there was no money stolen because that wasn't the Mayhem way. They were just trying to create some trouble. They were big guys and continued to make trouble, not just for me but for everyone trying to have a good time. I had soon had enough of these guys and their bullshit lies, so I grabbed a nearby hammer and threatened them, face-to-face, and fortunately they soon left.

By this time, the security guys were standing **behind** me. What a waste of money!

The Borneokade in Amsterdam was the scene of another memorable night, also back in 1991. We decided to arrange an event but there was already a party organised on the same day nearby. We were right next to each other. What a coincidence – same day, same street. But when we looked at who they had booked to DJ we thought our party would be better so we weren't too bothered about the competition.

The organisers got in contact after hearing of our party and wanted to have a meeting with us. So my mate, Neuv, and I arranged to meet them in a local restaurant to discuss the parties. About nine of them turned up, which we interpreted as a force of intimidation, but they were surprised that there were only two of us and we weren't intimidated in the slightest.

What was really funny was the fact that two of them owed me money for cocaine and this was the first time I'd seen them in a while. I asked them for my money and they immediately paid. I think they were a little surprised by that, seeing as we were outnumbered, but it seemed to work in our favour. Instead of telling us that they were first to arrange the party and that we should cancel ours, they actually asked to join forces with us and hold a joint event. We thought about it and decided to give it a go.

On the day of the party we were there during the day to set up the sound system, bar, cloakroom etc. A few guys turned up and I didn't know who they were. Nobody recognised them but they walked over to me with a bit of a swagger over to me and demanded that I cancel the planned party.

They insisted there was no way they would allow us to hold the party. They said they had a weed crop growing in a large warehouse close to where our party was to take place and didn't want to risk it receiving any unwanted attention. They were worried somebody would spot it because it was almost time to harvest their weed.

They were asking me to cancel but I stood firm and said I had no intention of complying with their request. I walked off and continued to arrange our party, while they also departed but returned quickly with another guy who was flashing a gun at me. When they saw the firearm the other promoters in attendance, who we had joined forces with for that night, decided to walk away, making it clear they no longer wished to be involved and were happy for us to sort it out.

Incidentally, in those days I was a fucking crazy guy and nothing intimidated me. I was using a lot and had lost some good friends, so I wasn't bothered about anything. I simply didn't give a fuck. I told them all, to their faces, that if they wanted to stop the party they would have to shoot me. That was their only chance of stopping the party; otherwise we would party all night.

Unsure how to react, they stepped back and opted to leave. But they didn't leave it at that; they actually drove to where the electricity lines that provided energy to that entire district of Amsterdam were located and set about destroying them in an effort to destroy our party. Their crop was not in danger, however, because they had their own energy supply in their warehouse, so it wasn't affected.

Fortunately for us, though, somebody had a huge generator they wanted to lend us. After a delay of an hour or two we were back in business and it was quite funny to see the entire neighbourhood blacked out while our party shone brightly.

The weed boys were still not happy with us and in the early morning hours they decided to set our warehouse on fire.

But this time, much to my amusement, they really fucked up. The fire began to spread rapidly to the warehouse where they were growing their weed and eventually it destroyed the whole lot.

Ha-bloody-ha, result!

BUSHWACKA!

He may be one half of tech and breaks duo Layo & Bushwacka! but these days Matthew Benjamin is also known as Just Be. But the name Bushwacka! is never far from a flyer or two. With a New York residency recently announced, and more and more gigs with original DJ partner Layo, Matthew continues to perform at the finest locations worldwide.

Growing up through the acid house explosion in London, Matthew progressed to be the artist we know today after first being inspired by the new craze sweeping the nation back in 1988.

Matthew is one of my favourite producers, as were Layo & Bushwacka. Like so many top producers, he always has a signature sound pouring through the speakers, with a lazy breakbeat to keep you grooving. That signature sound can often be heard through his own record labels – Plank Records and Oblong Records.

One track that instantly springs to mind is his remix of Billie Jean, the Michael Jackson stomper released on vinyl back in 2001 and still sounds fresh today. Timeless music.

Matthew's son Oliver is following in his father's footsteps and building a solid reputation as a performer in his own right, but heavily influenced by his father I'm sure. Oliver Moon is the name, check him out.

Matthew spoke about the acid house explosion, Amsterdam and a certain gig in South Africa which involved the gun-wielding

140

mafia etc.

Enjoy...

I left school in May 1988 when I was 16 and managed to get a job at Young's Disco Centre in Kentish Town, London. Through working there I got to know the customers. These guys were coming in each week to hire lights and equipment for warehouse parties – acid house warehouse parties, although at the time I had absolutely no idea what they were.

One Saturday in August 1988, these boys were in the shop again and I was helping them out with the required items for that evening's warehouse party, which was actually being organised by rave legends Rat Pack. They told me and the other staff to come down and check it out.

I decided to go with my sister and three of my best friends. The location was an empty indoor old swimming pool, in Merlin Street, north London.

Up until that day, it had always been the norm to go down the pub on the weekend and drunkenly move on to the local disco, where I would stand around the edge of the dance floor, feeling paranoid, praying people didn't fight and hoping I wasn't going to get beaten up.

These nights usually ended up with me throwing up on the bus on the way home.

So back to Merlin Street. We walked in and immediately got involved and life was never the same again after that night.

We arrived home midday the following day and my mum said: "Where the hell have you been?" I told her she wouldn't understand and that I now knew what I was going to do for the rest of my life!

I wanted to be part of that DJ culture and I immediately felt so at home at the Rat Pack parties. To begin with, I used to pay on the door, be a raver and dance all night high on acid.

I was having the best time of my life.

Eventually, I began to get involved. I started to help out with the smoke machine and the projectors. I helped out with carrying the sound system in and out to the vans, plus I also helped with distributing flyers in the evenings.

There is one particular warehouse party in Rosemary Avenue, north London, that stands out. Everson Allen, from Rat Pack, had to leave the party and talk to the police outside. He asked me to go through *his* record box and put some records on.

My hands were shaking. I was a skinny 16-year-old little kid and that was my first introduction to being a DJ, and playing at an original acid warehouse party!

I was in the right place at the right time and what I believe is very different these days is that I had actually worked really hard to be allowed the privilege of warming-up with someone else's records.

I would be there all day, all night, helping out in any way I could. I was standing on street corners handing out flyers, loading equipment up and down stairs. I really had to earn my place and I did.

Right place, right time, with added desire!

Back then, I was DJing under the name Matthew B, complete with my newly acquired purple tracksuit with Matthew B in white letter patches sown on the back of my hooded top – as you did back then. That was my rave uniform and usually complemented with a pair of Converse trainers.

It wasn't until the mid-90s, when I had left a sound engineering course I was doing at a college on Britannia Road, in West London, that I managed to get a job at Mr C's recording studio, which was called The Watershed, in north London.

Richard, aka Mr C, had built the studio off the back of his success with The Shamen.

I kind of walked into a dream job but I was working 80 hours a week. I was generally making cups of tea, reading manuals, sitting around getting stoned. During this I was constantly learning everything I could. I was producing music; I would just jump on the synths, the mixing desk and the computers, and start doing my own stuff.

One day I was sat with the head of A&R of Plink Plonk records, Mr C's underground label. His name is Paul Rip and he used to put on the Rip parties at Clink Street back in 1988.

We used to work quite close together in the studio, and one night during a studio session I was rolling a spliff, something I did a lot of back then, and Paul just looked at me and said: "You're the bushwacka, man. That should be your DJ name."

Some people think it originated from Millwall Football Club and their hooligans, but it doesn't. It's from the weed, man!

My early DJ experiences were around London and Essex. I used to play monthly in the early 90s at a place called Tooto's in Frating, between Colchester and Clacton-on-Sea in Essex. I used to play alongside Mr C, Eddie Richards and The Prodigy, who were local boys from nearby Braintree.

I'm still friends to this day with those that used to run the club. Great times and I remember it well!

I first came to Amsterdam back in 1998 and went to a party at the Melkweg.

I walked in and noticed Evil Eddie Richards was playing. I knew him from the London scene and thought it was pretty surreal to walk into an Amsterdam club and see a DJ from London playing. I bought a pill on the dance floor and danced all night.

Many years later I was back in Amsterdam but this time I was the DJ. I was playing at Chemistry, a club night in the city, alongside Layo, Mr C and local resident DJ Marcello.

It was back in the day, the 90s, and it was a ridiculously good party. In fact, they were pretty much running things back then in Amsterdam.

I had met this really hot girl there, but it was whilst I was playing. She smiled, I smiled, she winked, I winked, she said hello, I said hello and then we kissed each other on the cheek. Then she kissed me on the lips, so I kissed her on the lips. This was all happening behind the decks, during our back-to-back set. I was like 'Wow, what's going on here?' She had this Pamela Anderson Baywatch look and I just thought 'Oh my God!'

I looked for Marcello, asked him if we could have an after-party at his place and if I could invite this girl I had just met. He agreed, so off we went back to his place on the canal with many more people following from the club.

We were all pretty spangled, and I was sat with Layo and Richard on the sofa. I asked them if they had seen the girl I was talking to at the club and at that very moment she came up the stairs and sat down next to me. She put one hand on my knee, the other on the back of neck and she started to tickle me. "Wooooooh, oh my God, I'm going to have to take you away from here in a minute," I said.

Just then, Marcello came over and asked if he could speak to me. "Yeah, sure, what is it? Be quick, I'm kind of busy," I said.

"You do know that she has a boyfriend? He's sitting over there, but he doesn't mind. Do you want to use my bedroom?" said Marcello.

I had no idea she was taken.

I was kind of like 'Hhmmmmm, okay,' but I really couldn't believe the situation I was in. It was weird but I just thought 'Sure, okay, let's go.'

Marcello's bedroom had two entrances. One was via the double swing doors that led to the living room and the other was a door leading around the back from the bedroom – and neither had locks.

We were lying there and she asked me if I knew she already had a boyfriend, gesturing 'Shhhhhhh' with her finger on her lips.

145

Just at that moment I immediately had this awful image in my head of a load of Dutch guys, with their trousers round their ankles and video cameras, storming the room from both entrances. I had to call it all off, immediately. "I can't do this," I told her. But not before kissing her!

We left the room and continued the after-party.

Man...only in Amsterdam!

Playing in South Africa was always memorable, especially the time I played in Johannesburg with Mr C and Pure Science.

We had played earlier on at a huge rave and afterwards Peter White, the promoter and our go-to man, took us to another party. It was actually almost finished by the time we arrived.

We were sat in a back room with Peter White and then the club's head of security, Pistol Pete, came in. This guy was a gun-wielding maniac who had previously been asked to leave the UK following an allegation of attempted murder. He was actually upset about that, because there wasn't *actually* a murder, just attempted!

It was all starting to get a bit raucous. Peter was exchanging words with Pistol Pete and his security, who all had guns and this was all over somebody skinning-up.

I was actually petrified by what was going on. It was ridiculous. I mean, these people were just casually throwing guns around to each other.

Pistol Pete didn't know who we were, or that we were with Peter, and he had a few words for us. Fortunately Peter was there to sort it out for us.

Pistol Pete seemed embarrassed that he'd got us mixed up. His way of trying to deal with it – apologising if you like – was to demand that we drank shots and sniffed loads of gear with him – for the next three hours.

Once he'd had enough of that he insisted that the three of us – Mr C, Pure Science and I – should go with him and his girlfriend to do some shooting practice at his home. We weren't really in a position to refuse.

We left, but Phil – Pure Science – realised he had forgotten his jumper – so Pete said he'd drive back to get it.

On the way back, Pete decided to stop off to buy more cocaine, this time from a dealer that owed him money.

We pulled up outside this mansion with Richard, Phil and I petrified on the back seat. He gets out of his car, swinging his gun in the air and shouting out to the dealer over the garden fence.

"You'd better come out of your house right now, there's going to be a fucking war if you don't," he screamed.

We thought that at any moment the car was going to be sprayed with a machine gun and so we decided to get out and say we needed to find a toilet. Fortunately, that didn't happen, and we somehow managed to avoid any trouble. Pete drove us safely back to our hotel.

What an experience!

Brazil is a favourite of mine and I've actually been there more than 70 times since my first visit in 1998.

I really love it; I love the people and especially Bahia in the north. I have some wonderful friends in Brazil, ex-girlfriends too, and have had some amazing gigs there over the years.

Layo and I were really on top of it since the noughties. We played for more than two million people at the Rio Carnival, alongside Fatboy Slim and DJ Marky, perched on top of a juggernaut. That was pretty special. Great memories of Rio and Salvador too.

I still go back at least once a year, just to get involved. I absolutely love it.

I'm so lucky. I feel so blessed to have been in a position to play music that I've enjoyed, mix it the way that I want to mix it and play it to a captive audience all around the world who really appreciate it and enjoy what I do.

That has happened so many times and I really am blessed to have been able to do what I do and to have had so many memorable gigs. An unbelievable amount! Despite that, however, there are still some crazy weekends flying around the world. The most recent one was when I was playing in Australia, back in December 2016.

I had to fly from Sydney to Ho Chi Minh City then from there to Phu Quoc, an island in Vietnam, for a gig. I had to fly somewhere else after that plus a five-hour drive. I then flew back to Australia for a one-hour gig at a festival run by the KaZintip guys.

There have been a lot of those weekends.

I think the most memorable gig I've been involved with has to be the closing of The End on January 24th, 2009.

It wasn't just the build-up to it but the fact that at that point in my life Layo and I were so close. We had played there together every month since it opened, right through to the day it closed, plus a few more times on top of that.

It was a feeling of deep pride, euphoria and joy. The build-up of energy in that building was just amazing. I felt immense pride and joy from seeing what we had created in the club and from every person that came to dance to our music over the years. People didn't want to leave the dance floor, even at closing time.

It reminded me of when I played in Canada and at the end, instead of leaving, they would start banging drums for hours as a sign of appreciation for the music.

You couldn't get a better gig; the place felt monumental. The End really was something else!

It was a very personal experience too. My small part in it was playing there every month, where I forged the sound of the breakbeat stuff. I've broken lots of new music in there and had so many adventures in and around the place. I don't think London has seen a party like that since.

Yeah, I am biased, but I have a good reason to be. I've had residencies in London since I was 17 right up until The End closed.

It generally was better than anything else.

Fact.

DR MOTTE

Love Parade is an international brand, spreading positive vibes worldwide through the power of music. Very loud music, with a kick to make you skip – often alongside a truck with a monster sound system. Unfortunately, the annual bash, often held in Berlin, is no more.

Dr Motte is the man behind the rise of such a major force within the music and Europe's festival scene. Originating in Berlin, this day of celebration has become recognised throughout Europe, Australia, Mexico and America.

Many major cities began organising their own street parades after the popularity of Love Parade.

In the beginning he was playing at underground acid house and techno parties in Berlin, often organised in any suitable location they could find. He was a very prominent part of a growing techno community that eventually spread across Germany, more so after the collapse of the wall.

In the early days, along with other legends and pioneers of the Berlin scene, like DJs Westbam and Tanith etc., the Dr would often have to fight over records in the local record shops as there would only be one or two copies available. They always had first pick and any other customers would have to wait a week or two for the next delivery.

Dr Motte continues to spread the love through music and his old school DJ sets are an outstanding trip down memory lane, nothing but positive vibes. Reminiscing at its best.

151

For this interview, the Dr spoke about the rise of Love Parade, and a rather unfortunate train journey.

Once upon a time I had a dream that the turntables were three metres high and I couldn't reach them. I actually woke up from the disappointment so I don't know how the gig went!

It was many years ago, I really can't remember when – late 90s I think – and I was invited to play at the Full Moon and Solar Eclipse Festival in Chile.

My flight was from Frankfurt and I was living in Berlin. We decided to take the night train to Frankfurt and in the morning I would be there, leaving me plenty of time to reach the airport and catch the flight. There were other crews and DJs heading to Chile, so we were not alone.

During the train journey the cables above the train were not able to provide electricity any more. We were stuck on the motionless train while I tried to work out how I could get to Frankfurt Airport? It just wasn't possible and I was thinking to myself 'What can I do now?' I realised my only choice was to catch the next train home, back to Berlin. I had planned to be away for two weeks but there I was heading home before I'd got any distance at all.

I was crying because I really wanted to be there with the people and to be at the festival. I was the only artist who couldn't make it because the others were flying in from other places and had no problems.

That was one of the worst experiences I've had. To be on a train and having to just sit there meant I couldn't make it to beautiful Chile. Happily, however, I did manage to get there another time later on.

When the Berlin Wall was still up today's creators were thinking back then what could be done to create something positive out of this. There were a lot of illegal parties starting in the UK at the time and the police would stop them. But the party-goers would simply move outside and dance in the streets with a ghetto blaster.

I really liked to hear those stories, how everybody kept on going, and I wondered how I could get this to happen in Berlin.

One night, I was playing at a small party in Berlin and a lot of my friends were there. After my set I was standing there and the universe gave me the idea and inspired me to start something. We have a saying in Berlin 'Just do it,' whatever is on your mind.

I decided to declare a demonstration and announce music as a new way of communication. Peace and happiness was our message, we also proposed a ban of all weapons and the music became our new way of communicating and connecting with everyone.

Just do it!

I had to get permission to use the streets because what we really enjoyed was going out on the streets with our own music and just dancing. The first one was in 1989. We decided to keep doing it every year and every year more and more people wanted to dance. Street parades started in other countries and have been going since 1992. Mexico, San Francisco, Israel, Chile etc., all
153

have street parades.

At one point we had 1.5 million people dancing in Berlin. They were all dancing under the umbrella of electronic music. We were a family of humans, united by dancing and music, who wanted to bring peace to everyone.

That was our mission and after 10 years Love Parade became a worldwide brand. It was a culture of electronic dance music.

This was our message:

"In the beginning, there was Jack,
And Jack had a groove,
And from this groove came the grooves of all grooves."

With everything you need a vibe and with the Love Parade we created that vibe. We wanted everybody to join, because to us it didn't matter who they were. As long as you can enjoy the vibe and love the music, you will always be welcome!

People from all over the world tell me that being at the Love Parade was the best day of their lives and they are all part of the message we are spreading. We don't talk about politics; we talk about humanism, friendships, compassion and all these nice things.

DJ ELLIS DEE

I'll be honest and admit I didn't know there were two DJs called Ellis Dee. Coincidentally, both made their names in their respective rave scenes, one in the United Kingdom and the other in the United States.

Say hello to Ellis Dee from Los Angeles.

It took me a while to actually appreciate the difference; it was only when I received his stories that it became clear.

He was very decent – even wrote the stories himself – and for that I am truly grateful.

He talks about the illegal warehouse scene, custom agents and sound systems, plus a spooky gig etc.

I remember going to see Orbital perform at the Shrine Auditorium in Los Angeles back in 1994. The sound system was probably the biggest and loudest system I have ever witnessed. I think there were six separate stacks of speakers, each at least 25 feet high and probably 40 feet wide. The bass bins were so loud and so insane that, for the first time, I was truly afraid that a sound system could hurt me, like cause a heart attack or some kind of internal bleeding and organ damage. I had to go up to the balcony just so I was able to remain in that main room. I felt my bones shake and vibrate so much I thought I was going to break a rib.

Orbital sounded great that night but I have no idea how they were able to physically survive performing on that platform in the centre of the room, let alone concentrate on the music they were making with it being so insanely loud.

I'll never forget the first time I heard EAWs. EAW stands for Eastern Acoustic Works. They make high-end cabinets and large-scale sound systems. There was a little club I was spinning at in Los Angeles for about 400 people and I noticed the sound guy was setting up these jet black, hard wood cabinets which I hadn't seen before. He didn't have very many cabinets compared to other clubs of a similar size I had previously played at. He finished setting up his system, turned it on and the first DJ went on. Wow! This little system sounded awesome!

There was none of the snappy, cracking, high-end issues you get with cheaper two-way cabinets. The bass was super smooth and not boomy like so many cheaper bass bins. I think the secret to EAWs is their seven-inch, mid-range cones and the insane crossover inside. Every sound from 20 Hz to 20 kHz was perfect and transitioned like smooth glass through the frequency ranges. While I was spinning, I could hear far better than ever before, as he also had EAW monitors in the DJ booth.

I was so impressed that I later bought two EAW cabinets for my home and had them for many years.

One of the craziest DJ coffins I ever spun on was hung from the ceiling by thick chains, with one chain attached to each corner of the coffin. The chains were fairly long, maybe 25 feet or so to the ceiling, and the coffin would sway back and forth as you worked the controls. I had to shuffle back and forth during my set about one or two feet which was really disorienting. If anybody ever asks you about having a flying DJ coffin with chains from the

156

ceiling, tell them 'Hell no,' and, please, find another way.

In the 90s, before the airports became crazy with TSA agents, it was relatively pleasant to fly around the country to play gigs on the weekends. When you cross the border into another country, however, it's a different ballgame. The first time I performed in Toronto, the Canadian customs agent started asking me all kinds of questions. Where I came from, where I was going, when was my return flight etc. When they found out I was performing in a local club they seemed upset and said I had to buy a work permit for that weekend, which was a couple of hundred dollars if I remember correctly.

I didn't understand all the rules when performing in another country but I guess I received a crash course that day. The customs agent said I better be back at the airport tomorrow and on my way back to the US or they would issue a warrant for my arrest on the Monday. What the hell? All I was there to do was to play some music for people for a couple of hours.

The next day, I was tired, smelt like smoke mixed with a sweaty nightclub, and I was on my way back through the airport. Suddenly, airport security decided to pick on me again. The security guy picked me out of the line and asked me to come over to a table with my suitcase and record bag. With a really serious voice he asked me: "Son, do you have any drugs in your bag? If you tell me now you will be in less trouble than if you lie to me and I then find drugs in here when I search through this stuff. I can also get my sniffer dog out here and I bet he would bark his head off at you." I said I didn't have anything, I was just on my way home to Los Angeles and he could search though my bags all he wanted. I had nothing to hide except dirty clothes. The security guy didn't seem convinced or happy about my response, so he just searched though all my stuff. To his frustration, he
157

didn't find anything and let me go. Of course I was late boarding my plane and left with the worst seat for the journey home. At least I made it home in one piece and I was paid. I played a great DJ set and had a really good time in Toronto, despite my airport adventure.

Back in March 2000 I played a gig in Memphis, Tennessee. I didn't know what to expect as Memphis wasn't exactly well known for its rave scene. For this night, they had a nice big warehouse location, a huge room that could easily hold 1,000 people or so. I think I went on around 11pm or midnight and played a really good set for about two hours. That room was packed and the vibe in there was amazing. I played one of the best live sets ever.

After I had finished, the next DJ went on. He put his first record down and then two minutes later the cops came charging in, busted the whole party and shut everything down. I felt really bad for the DJ that went on after me because that room was ripe and he probably would have also had a really good set.

It just goes to show that performing at raves is, and always was, extremely unpredictable. You never know if you're going to play the best set of your life, whether the party will be raided and busted, if the sound system will short out or if the generator will run out of gas etc.

Always perform to the best of your ability, and don't have any preconceptions in your head about where you are, the size of the room you're playing in, or how big or small the sound system is. Many times I have been surprised at how well things have gone off in a room that in the beginning didn't appear too promising, but ended up going off with a serious vibe and energy. You need to savour those moments. No city has a monopoly on vibe or

158

music, and amazing raves can happen anywhere at any time.

Back in the 90s, there was a crew in Los Angeles called Zodiac Tribe. I must have played at four or five of their events and every single time that crowd went off. The following Zodiac Tribe had was excellent and they really knew what they were doing. One thing I really liked about the crew was that they never went too big and all of their events were a 300-500 capacity. I think a big part of their success was that they kept their events at a reasonable size, never went over 500 people. A lot of the same people would show up to each of their events, which enabled them to build a loyal following.

I began to love playing for smaller crowds of 300-500 people, in much more intimate settings. Big raves with over 2,000 people were like a three-ring circus and were nowhere near as much fun as a smaller crowd of a few hundred who were really into what I was doing on the turntables.

Believe me, bigger is not always better when you are looking for a good vibe packed with energy on the dance floor.

I played several times in Toronto and I remember the first time I went there I played at a club in downtown. It was a good gig and the crowd were great, but out of the corner of my left eye I kept seeing this human shape standing in the DJ booth. Every time I glanced over there would be nobody standing there. I would turn back to my DJ coffin and, again, the human shape would appear. It was only visible in my peripheral vision. The human shape would sometimes be crouching down and other times it would be standing. When it was standing only the top three quarters would be visible and it faded away at the feet.

The club promoter brought me a drink half-way through my set and I told him: "Hey, there is a ghost over there watching and listening to the music." His eyes grew really wide and he swiftly turned around before walking away without saying anything. Strange, I thought, and after my set was done the same promoter came back to tell me that someone had died in the club and other people had also reported seeing strange things.

So, whatever was going on in that haunted club, I guess the resident ghost just liked the music and enjoyed hanging out in the DJ booth every night, chilling with the DJ!

JOE SMOOTH

Probably best known for his 1987 classic, Promised Land, Joe Smooth is an originator and has played a major role in spreading the house vibes since the very beginning. Joe continues performing to this day at some of the world's finest locations.

Promised Land is a track that just keeps on giving. Never grows old, constantly in DJs' playlists and forever reaching a new audience with a remix or two every few years by various artists.

His international acclaim has come to the attention of many a record label and Joe has helped create tracks for some of the world's biggest pop stars, including Cisqo, the late Whitney Houston, Destiny's Child and many more.

For the interview, Joe reflects on early influences, the story behind Promised Land, working with bands and more.

Strangely enough, as a child, I used to watch a lot of old movies starring Fred Astaire and Ginger Rogers. I liked the show tunes.

To get to the point where I was able to play music, I would just hear some music and think 'Wow, I wish I could do that.'

Music like that would be Stevie Wonder and Michael Jackson. I guess they were my main influences, plus Marvin Gaye, Motown, that kind of vibe. I would figure out how those songs were made, and so I would play around on the keyboard or a piano. You know, I would sit for hours in the house each day. Like eight hours a day, trying to figure it out until I finally got it. They were my influences and that is, kind of, how it all started.

I was on the second Jack my House tour and we were travelling to a lot of countries. People couldn't understand what we were saying but, you know, there was a kindred spirit through the music so you could see and feel the crowd's appreciation of it.

For me, that just kind of confirmed that no matter what's going on in the world, no matter what differences we all have, you know, it was as if the prejudices and all the problems just seem to disappear when you come together through music.

So seeing that, it just made me feel like wow, we can all get along, you know, like brothers and sisters. When I got back to Chicago, I was trying to figure out how to translate the idea musically.

I wanted something classic and, for me, Motown is *the* classic sound. It seemed like I listened to a million Motown records, just to see the structure and how they did it. I then thought about how to translate that to what was going around today, but at that time.

That's where the composition comes from, and you could say it was an inspired piece. Once I got my head around it, the whole thing just came to me and it worked itself out.

Originally, I sang the vocals but I'm a kind of background kind of guy, so it's a mixture of Anthony Thomas, me and another singer called Dohn Conley.

Anthony sings more like The Temptations. You know, more of a rough kind of sound but, like I said, at the time I wanted to stand in the background. So I had him sing like I sing and we just doubled vocals up, and then I had Dohn put a part on top of that vocal. Like the 'Oh, yeah' and the verses are just layered.

You have a vision and you see something, but this particular vocal didn't sound complete, so I was hearing something else. For me, it's just the production of the song, you know, and all the elements seemed to work.

Unfortunately, I had to go to court to own the rights to Promised Land.

The original contract I did with DJ International included a clause that stated any music I had done before signing a contract, I still owned. Promised Land and all the other songs I wrote for the album were actually written before I had signed the contract.

So I decided to level with the company, as long as I felt the label was being honest and transparent.

But there came a point, when I saw the record label wasn't being transparent, that we did end up in court. The case definitely went in my favour and I managed to retain all the rights to the song. Result.

Promised Land probably makes more money for me today than it did back then.

At the beginning of the year, 2019, I did a catalogue deal with Armada to handle my back catalogue. So there are new fresh remixes, marketing strategies, you know, to bring it to the new generation.

The Style Council's remix was a tricky situation. Promised Land was out for a while, a few months already, at the end of 1987 in the States. So it was an import for Europe.

They wanted to do a cover of the record but couldn't before it was domestically released in the UK. So, what they did was release it in the UK on the same day the original came out.

They both ended up in the charts, and it may have hurt the original record – my record. You had two conflicts of interest and styles going on with the same song. But it stood the test of time! It even reached a different demographic of people who would probably never have heard it.

I never did the TV show Top of the Pops in the UK with Promised Land, but I was there with Tyree Cooper when he did Turn up the Bass, and also with Darryl Pandy, who featured on Farley Jackmaster Funk's Love Can't Turn Around. I would travel with everybody, all the time.

Jellybean Benitez was handling the music for the game Grand Theft Auto: San Andreas and he approached me about using Promised Land in the game. If you're a fan of the game you'll know it was included when the game was launched in 2004.

Most of the time when I'm working on music, it just kind of comes to me and I can hear the whole song. Since I can play piano, do the drum programming and all, when I hear it I can just lay it down. So, you know, it's a blessed gift. Even when I was working on remix projects for people. Beyonce, for example, can send you some vocals and I can send them back to her within the same day. I have already heard what I want to do.

I had been releasing songs for a while when I took the decision to hold back because I want to set up a joint venture. I've been talking with a few companies, like Radical Records, Sony and Universal.

We actually have a position with Universal with one of their subsidiaries. I'm just trying to weigh up my options right now, like where I want the label to go.

I more or less held off from making releases in 2019 but this year, 2020, I will probably release some new material.

Working with the likes of Bros, New Order and A Guy Called Gerald, they were all cool guys. I worked with Peter Hook, too. We got together, made some music and worked on some projects together.

I also remixed a record for Bros back then. House was in its infancy, and a lot of labels would approach me with different projects. Back then, I was working at the Spy Bar in Chicago, which is actually still open today, and is one of the oldest clubs in North America.

All those opportunities, and working at Spy Bar, I ended up being managed by a guy named Mark Bevans. Mark used to manage me, Steve Thomson and Michael Bobbierie. They were doing mixes and productions for Guns & Roses and Metallica, and I was doing the dance and house stuff, like Art of Noise, for example, and a whole variety of people.

A lot came from the success of Promised Land, but I was also helping produce Frankie Knuckles' first record, and just about everybody from DJ International. I was the only person who could play keyboards at the time, until Peter Black came into DJing.

165

I worked on everything from Tyree Cooper, Fast Eddie etc., a little bit of everybody's material.

Amsterdam is always interesting. I always enjoy the Amsterdam Dance Event and all the festivals in the Dam.

I enjoy Italy, the UK, Spain, Ibiza and Majorca. Places like that always stand out. I would very much like to get out and do some stuff in Africa. I've never done anything out there before and I think it would be interesting.

ENVOY

I was often buying the latest Envoy 12" in Amsterdam, before I was unknowingly chatting with the sister of one of its members! I used to work at The Greenhouse Effect bar in Amsterdam and one regular, named Annie, mentioned that her brother, Simon, was involved with techno music. Annie was a regular, I was the barman and it turned out we were both from the same English town – Ipswich. After chatting, the name Envoy popped up. I couldn't believe it. What a small world.

Annie and I became – and still are – good mates and I was generously invited to join her and Envoy when they performed in Holland. One such gig was in Rotterdam in an old warehouse. They had flight problems and were stuck all day at a London airport, but managed to arrive in time for their gig. There was no time for a soundcheck but they still sounded immense.

Hope Grant also toured with Scottish techno outfit Slam, from Soma Records. I went to Lowlands with Annie and Amsterdam's ex-pat family in the late 90s and saw Hope live on stage, but this time as lead singer. He looked and sounded great; the guy really is a talented soul!

Hope opened up about the early days, his health struggles, memorable gigs and a certain airport panic etc.

Everyone's truth is a kind of fiction and this is mine.

I used to enjoy acting as a youngster, and that was kind of my thing before I got into making music. I had an electronic upbringing musically and I was really into that synthesiser sound, like Jean-Michel Jarre or Pink Floyd, for example. But also rock, pop, soul, funk, you name it – I wanted to do it all, but somehow do it a bit different, even though back then I didn't know how. I was a singer who still needed to learn how to perform, but I always knew I definitely wanted to be the singer in a band.

I initially wanted the traditional major-label singer's life. Write songs, sing them and record the albums. Let other people take them from there, plus I would need a manager to take care of business.

I don't have much patience and if I had an idea for a song then I'd just want to sit down and do a 12-hour studio session, just to get the song out of my head, rather than in shifts.

Always thinking about being a performer, I really didn't understand anything about the acid house and rave scene in the early days when it first hit London. I just didn't get it. What was all the fuss about? If you had told me then how it was going to shape my whole life for decades, I would have laughed in your face.

When I was 18 I sent some of my early stuff to several major record companies, including EMI. I thought they would probably end up in the bin but, to my surprise, I actually received some positive responses. No record deals, unfortunately, but some useful advice for an impatient 18-year-old who just wanted it all in an instant.

I then completely ignored their advice. 'I'm not making any more tracks for them. If they don't like them then fuck them,' I thought.

Then one night I was at a party and a fella called Adamski was performing live. I noticed he had the same keyboards as me, but he was doing things with those keyboards that I didn't even realise was possible. It just blew me away. I never knew those keys could make noises like that.

That was it. I finally understood what all the fuss was about.

I had an old friend named Carl, who had helped me in the past with sound engineering when I first started to buy studio equipment. I was also fortunate to meet Simon in that 'all back to mine after the party and end up staying for days' kind of way that just seemed to happen back then.

We were all on the buzz and set about trying our hands at creating the kinds of sounds we had been hearing as we'd embraced the incoming techno madness. I bought all the Detroit, Chicago and British records I could lay my hands on, plus a few other things that were emerging back then.

They were crazy days and I wanted to make my own soundtrack to them. With their help and assistance I laid down my first tunes. The three of us put those early demos together, literally in a bedroom, and we actually went on to work together for a number of years, well into the 2000s.

The very first person I sent that first tape to was Richie Hawtin at Plus 8 records. I would call Canada once a week and speak to Richie. "Did you get them? Have you listened to them yet?", I would plead. He would always reply "No, it hasn't arrived," with a hint of 'you again!' in his voice.

This went on for several weeks, until one day he said he had received them and was about to listen to them. I began to bombard him with calls, eager to see what he thought, but instead he asked me never to call this number again, and that he would call me if he liked the tracks. I was mortified. I was a Class A nut job! Years later I met Richie and I told him he very nearly destroyed my dreams, but he totally denies ever having that conversation with me. Good job I never gave up chasing those dreams.

We would hang out in Fat Cat Records on a Saturday morning and in such a small space it was always buzzing with people after the latest tracks. One morning, I handed them a demo – it was cassettes in those days – hoping they would play it in the shop, or at least call me.

They didn't and I didn't hear anything either.

Soon after, I met Dave Angel, a fellow South Londoner. Together we produced a track called Hi-Tech Jazz, which featured a saxophone with a bit of solo. Everyone seemed to think I had played the sax, but I hadn't – I'd just played it live on the keyboard.

But this myth actually propelled me and my career. Even Pete from Peacefrog Records thought I had played the sax. "You're the sax man on Dave Angel's track," he said to me one night when we bumped into each other in club. I was a little perplexed, and he asked if I had any more tracks available. I did, I gave them to him and he put some out. It all helped me to start getting regular gigs and, eventually, to meet the Soma crew and forming Envoy.

I'd kind of grown to think of myself as part of the instrumental underground by then and left behind all the mainstream stuff. But then, in 1997, still being known in some circles as a singer, I was asked to sing for rave combo Bizarre Inc., after they told me they

170

wanted a more techno-jazz-funk influenced style with proper songs. For six months we recorded a load of demos in full major-label country house style – so at least I got that dream out of the system.

The results were actually alright, in my opinion, but the record label wasn't into this change of direction. The whole project was shelved and I vowed to keep control of my own production in the future.

Luckily I had already made the connection with Soma in Glasgow, after falling in love with the city and its people. In Glasgow they work hard but play even harder. Their knowledge and passion for the music is amazing. I had no hesitation signing up with them as Envoy. We started work immediately on our first EP and Soma released the track before it was added to our album, which was also released on Soma.

Our Where There's Life album was released in 1998. I had performed the vocals, in the studio obviously, but now I had to perform live and I still wasn't sure how to do it.

I felt nervous, but I was ready. Around that time, Funk D'Void and Ewan Pearson had released their albums and were already performing live to promote them, so I tried to take my inspiration from them and how they went about it.

My first-ever Envoy gig was that year, very close to Battersea Power Station in London. To top it off, loads of people I knew were stood in the front rows. 'Oh my God,' I thought, '*He's* here, so is *she*, and *they*'ve even turned up.' I was a bag of nerves!

We started the set and everybody was shouting at me to turn it up. I kept thinking 'Why do they want me to turn it up?' It felt loud to me plus it was already at ten on the amplifier. All I can remember, though, is hearing people having conversations during the whole of the set.

I finished, walked off the stage and all I felt was disappointment. I didn't feel good at all and what really annoyed me was the fact that I was just stood behind equipment.

Remember, as a kid I loved to act, and I wanted to incorporate this into my live sets. Never again would you see me behind a laptop, or stacks of equipment. I wanted to perform and have a stage presence, be exciting and create a show.

It was from that night on that I was determined to change.

It was still a new and emerging music scene, as was the culture. I have to admit, in the beginning, I didn't know what I was doing, or how it would go down. I really thought I was just blagging my way through and that one day soon somebody was going to realise. Perhaps a negative review would label me an imposter and call for me to be taken down and removed from the scene.

The next gig was at The Arches in Glasgow, with the Soma crew. I remember doing a soundcheck and just knew that it was all going to go down well. I was so excited. The sound engineer was great, telling me not to worry and assuring me that if there were any issues he would be right behind me to sort them. He just told me to give him a signal if something was wrong, or if I needed to turn it up.

The time came to perform, the club was full and it was going off. Everything was going well, until I took to the mic to sing. As soon as I started singing, a huge wave of feedback came screeching through the speakers from the mic. It was so loud, a huge piercing sound, and I just thought 'You've got to be fucking kidding me!'

This was only 15 minutes into the set and there were still 45 minutes left to perform.

I have to confess that I came off raging and wanted to murder the club's sound engineer, especially after him being so confident that there was nothing to worry about. But before I could find him everybody swamped me telling me what a storming set they had just witnessed, which I could hardly believe. I was still furious with the sound problems, but eventually my mates talked me down. It was a real baptism of fire, the whole performing live thing.

We started to travel more with bookings, things were evolving nicely and then a manager came knocking. We were performing every week, meeting other artists from the scene, and it felt good. I was more involved in the scene and started to feel a real part of it and, inevitably, started to see and experience a bit more of the wild circus that was touring the world in its superstar-DJ heyday.

One highlight from around then featured worldwide superstar Carl Cox. Carl used to run a night on a Thursday in Oxford Street, London.

On the back of Envoy's recent rise and success, we were asked to perform. But before that, we were also asked to go on Kiss FM with residents Colin Dale and Colin Faver. We'd followed Kiss since the illegal days and I used to listen to that show religiously with Simon. It was a big thing for us in those days, when there was no internet and hardly anywhere to hear the kind of tunes to take you to the Outer Limits. We'd tune in to every show without fail and then go around the record shops at the weekend trying to
173

find the best records they'd played that week.

I always used to tell Simon that one day they would be playing our tunes on the show. So to be invited on to perform on that very show, with those two legends, was a very big thing for us. It was more than we could have dreamt of, working away with a minimal set-up and no cash in a small flat near Peckham in the early days.

Afterwards, we went to Carl's night, where we were also doing a live set. It was actually Carl's birthday party. Jim Masters, Carl's right-hand man at the time, was stood on the door. You weren't allowed in unless you took a drop of the narcotic-laced concoction he had.

God knows what is was, but everybody in that club was hanging from the roof, we were all completely smashed. It was complete madness – all the better for being a school night. I'd already seen some sights as a raver attending the acid house parties, so I was quite prepared for whatever generally ensued. But this was something else and it was full of producers and DJs, a few of my heroes even.

Other top times were spent touring – special mention to great times in Dublin with the D1 crew and wild gigs in Amsterdam.

They really had that deep house sound nailed and I always heard mind-blowing tunes there that I'd never heard before, with none of the break-to-endless snare roll cheese that was killing the good name of house in the UK.

My first big festival-style gigs were in Holland as well – the Lowlands festival and a Queensday gig on a stage in the middle of Den Haag, which was mental. A crush of tens of thousands of people as far as the eye could see in all directions, firecrackers going off left and right. It took over half an hour just to force a path through the wall of people from the edge of the square to the stage, which was no more than 100 metres away.

We had some great years, although I recommend you don't sniff vodka!

Then I did a world tour with Slam – The Alien Radio Tour. Envoy was Envoy, and I thought that was great, but Slam were on another level. Better hotels, longer sets, roadies to help with equipment – it was proper.

One weekend, with Slam, my outlook just changed dramatically. We performed in Munster, in Germany, on the Friday before flying off to Istanbul, in Turkey, for a gig the next day.

We were on the same line-up as the Chemical Brothers and Basement Jaxx, and over on the other stage was Robbie Williams, Oasis, etc. It was all pretty surreal. I would be backstage in the toilet and be stood peeing next to Paul Weller and Noel Gallagher. It all went up a gear and it was a little hard for me because I was alone. Although I was with Slam, it was Carl and Simon that I had grown up with, as Envoy, performing and sharing our experiences.

Still, the gig went great and all I remember was disappearing with two of the beautiful dancers for the rest of the night. I saw the rest of the band at breakfast the following morning but I just keep my head down and said nothing.

The down side to that weekend was the journey home. On the coach from the hotel to the airport I was sat with the Chemical Brothers and Luke Slater, both artists of whom I am a massive fan. It was great to be able to chat and hang out with them. At the airport we did the usual Duty Free shopping and everybody was in good spirits. I felt great. Here I was hanging out with my heroes, having a drink and laughing together. 'I've made it,' I thought.

But then I couldn't find my boarding card and suddenly started to panic. It was nowhere. I was in a real state and hearing the final call for our flight, with instructions to head to the gate immediately, did nothing to help. Of course, everybody else had their passes and were ushered through. I was left on my own, having been told no other flights were available until much later that evening.

There I was, with long dreadlocks and coloured skin, standing in Istanbul Airport all alone and in a real panic, while inside my head I was replaying scenes from Midnight Express.

A few airport officials approached me and took me into an office. Knowing I had misplaced my boarding card, they demanded that I purchase a new flight ticket. I was really scared. They didn't speak any English and I couldn't explain myself properly.

After such an amazing weekend it was all fast becoming a horror story. I had to use my entire weekend's wage to buy a new ticket and had the pleasure of sleeping on an airport bench until the flight left later that night.

Then I went to the check-in for my new flight, only to be greeted by a representative who told me they had found my boarding card for the flight for which I was originally booked. I was not impressed, to say the least. So I boarded my flight and was sat next to a mother and her screaming baby for the entire three-hour flight to London. A perfect comedown.

176

After returning home I was totally fed-up. I put the television on and fell asleep. I woke up in a bit of a daze, after some weird dreams, and thought Die Hard was on. As I started to come round and wake up I saw a plane fly into a building in New York – it was September 11th, 2001.

That had to be my most surreal weekend ever.

I never would have thought, right back at the beginning all those years ago, that the scene would have lasted and evolved the way it has worldwide. I felt so lucky to be involved and still do as I'm living it years later.

Unfortunately, in 2013 I began to experience a cramp sensation in my arm and a pain in my hand. I didn't think too much about it and just put it down to repetitive strain from lumping large monitors around the studio. I then started to walk with a limp and thought it was maybe to do with wearing new shoes. Again, I just carried on.

One night I was at a party with a mate and I suddenly wasn't able to dance. My body just didn't want to move and that's when it finally kicked in that there might actually be something wrong with me.

When we returned home my mate and I started researching online what the problem might be. We were looking up the symptoms and suddenly Multiple Sclerosis came up. That was enough to make me go to the doctor to check it out.

I was given an MRI scan and it turned out that I had a problem with the discs in my back. They said it wasn't too serious because it wasn't pressing against my spinal cord, but that it did need treating. It was enough for me to cancel all my artist bookings and future projects for that period of time and to enter hospital for an operation.

At the time I was in the middle of touring with Ben Sims and it was heartbreaking to have to cancel it. I'd been on a bit of a break creatively and it felt good that Envoy was on the way back. But all that changed.

I was admitted to the hospital and the night prior to my operation I was given a piece of paper to sign. It was a disclaimer regarding the operation about what might go wrong. I asked what could possibly go wrong because I thought it wasn't too big a deal. That's when I was told that the surgeon would be going in through my neck. I just hadn't realised how serious it really was. It was too late to back out and, as things turned out, the surgery did leave me with a few unwanted complications.

The problematic disc was removed but it has left me walking with a limp and permanent nerve damage in my feet and hands. I haven't been able to play the keyboards and standing up to DJ was impossible. These two things are probably the two things I love doing the most and it really did affect me mentally.

I began to go full recluse and didn't reach out to my mates or the techno community. I went completely the opposite way and began to feel extremely sorry for myself, had a complete shutdown and felt embarrassed that I was in such a situation.

People thought that I was dead, basically, and it was a very difficult time. To be honest, I still haven't really come to terms with it.

Eventually, I resurfaced and began to reach out here and there.

I spent quality time with Simon and his family down in Brighton, and declared myself alive to a few people. I needed to reach out and feel the love from my mates. Nowadays, I'm starting to feel inspired to start living again. Although the pain in my hands continues, I have learned to manage it a bit.

Fortunately, I can just about do enough to lay down some stuff in the studio again, and I'm certainly in a much better place than I was a few years ago.

I'm really looking forward to new Envoy projects, so watch this space.

Positive thinking!

JAKE THE RAPPER

Jacob Dove Basker, aka Jake the Rapper, is American, born in New York, but spent a lot of time across northern America. He moved to Europe in 1990. More on that in the interview below.

With a love for punk, and having already performed with several bands, Jake began rapping in 1992. A jazz-rap combo was created – MC Eye and Blind Jazz. He even joined a hip-hop 'training camp' called Trainingslager. Here, Jake learned to freestyle and not long after that his collaboration with beatboxer Mark Boombastik and Felix Kubin created Jake's other band, Anaerobic Robots.

A more professional, in-depth life within the house and techno scene began to grow quickly after moving to Berlin, where Bar 25 played a prominent part in Jake's musical education.

Berlin was soon warming to this loving bundle of joy and Jake's DJ career grew until appearances all over the city became a regular fixture before he progressed to spreading his vibes worldwide.

I hadn't pre-arranged anything with Jake regarding an interview but I simply introduced myself to him backstage. He was very gracious, compassionate and a joy to be around. We spoke after his set and it felt as if I had known him for years. There was a very positive aura and a great bonus to the day. Cheers Jake!

Jake touched upon why he moved to Europe, life in Germany, the pressures to perform and an unforgettable Goldie experience.

I moved to Germany in 1990, mainly because of the first Gulf War and George Bush. It was a political move and I wanted to get the hell away from what we all now know to be true.

In 1990 I was watching underground documentaries on how George Bush was doing cocaine deals with Daniel Ortega, the Nicaraguan President.

I was like 'That's not true,' but it *was* the truth. That's the weird thing. A year before I left they didn't have the internet, so they had to make a documentary but no one would broadcast it. They had to go from underground theatre to underground theatre, and charge admission to help support the film. Even me, as a total lefty, I watched the film and thought 'Is that true?' There was a signed document between Bush and Ortega, more coke was being demanded while the 'War on Drugs' was going on. And so that's the reason why I left.

There's a documentary out, on the History Channel I think, which tells all of this terrible shit.

I went to Hamburg in Germany for the next 15 years. I was a punk, and into my rap back then.

Techno and house was born in America but Germany really rocks the world for the socialist. For example, the toilet cleaner in a German club could also be the DJ an hour later. Everybody pulls on the same rope to make the party happen, plus DJs could bring themselves down a couple of notches. It's not amazing just because of the DJ but because everybody is working on it and they all share the same mentality.

Live and let live.

Back in 2002 a group of friends of mine opened up a club called Click. I had been fighting against everything that had a straight beat because I really liked my broken beats. Musically, I was into everything that had a story.

Music is story-telling for me. I didn't understand what other purpose music served.

I was then exposed to this club and I would hang out there. I was loudly exposed to house and techno but for a while, not just for the usual 15 minutes. I felt like 'Not you, too.' I was losing myself and turning to the dark side.

I had previously been DJing, and I liked the 606 and the 808 stuff, but for me I needed the hip-hop and a broken beat. The straight beat was boring.

Then I realised that momentary boredom is how time freezes and all of a sudden eternity can open. You are in this moment, making a connection with the people there, and suddenly music serves a deeper purpose. You have to go to a club to experience that.

I heard techno on a cassette but when you hear it in a club there's an epiphany. You stop in time; you are creating a certain eternal moment where you are all here, right now. But where do we go from here?

I was like 'I need to be involved with that.' But I was a rapper. Rap music is telling a story and you lose yourself in the artist. But at the warehouse raves you didn't even look up and it didn't matter that you couldn't see the DJ. It was like being cleansed, like yoga. But I didn't get it. It's a different dance too and I used to mock it.

But I then lost myself in that moment at Click. I started to write raps for techno and house, and 15 years later I'm still doing it. What is rap? Rap is poetry, it's beautiful and limitless. But it became testosterone laden with show-offs and it was not my scene any more. I'm about peace, love and unity and this is my scene – the house and techno scene. I don't really know where rap is going any more.

When you're on the dance floor, you don't want to be talked to. Okay, maybe a sentence or two, but you then get your head down and feel the music.

I've been doing this a long time. I'm 50 and I'm trying to figure out what to do next because I have no financial insurances. I have put everything into what I love. What I love is what I do and I support two kids with this.

I was doing this transgression from story-telling to techno at Bar 25. I taught them a lot about performing and telling stories, and they taught me a lot about how to go deeper within you. I have the Bar 25 stamp tattooed on me because it was such a seminal moment. I was like 'Wow, I've found myself.' I discovered so much about myself and humanity, who people are and what we do.

When my wife was seven months pregnant, she came to Bar 25 before it closed. My two worlds together, but one was reality and the other an escape into the universe.

It was my birthday and I wanted to do a ladies' night, so I booked 10 female DJs. I also dressed as a woman but you really don't
183

want to see me in drag! Remember, my wife was seven months pregnant at the time and she was dancing with an entourage around her to stop people bumping into her belly. She had a ring of friends surrounding her.

It was one of my most memorable nights as a DJ.

You have to have your little egg of attitude as a DJ and have a love for partying. I'm always ready for a gig a couple of days in advance. I'm prepared for it and ready to go but promoters can kill that. You know, like this is wrong, or that's not working etc. But I don't like that, I like it how I want it and perhaps feeling a bit grumpy because of it. Then you have to go out there and perform. Sometimes it's hard to be professional all the time, with a hard shell on your back, thinking 'I'm not going to let them get to me.' When you are at your least you have to give your most.

I'm not a mystical guy but I don't always get what I'm supposed to be doing. What is my job exactly? I'm here to play some records for you but any fucking asshole can do that. Am I controlling the room?

You know what really separates the wheat from the chaff as far as the DJ goes? It is not whether they can play a great set and rock the house when it's full, but rather they can die a thousand deaths when it's not exactly right. They can feel like it was the most humiliating experience they have ever had, thinking 'I suck, I'm a terrible person.' I'm the DJ and I've ruined everybody's night. But the next week I want to do it all over again.

It's the getting back up and pulling yourself together, and the realisation that I have to keep doing this, despite the week before hurting my ego.

I've played in empty places and a poor workman always blames his tools. I couldn't really hear properly and I had problems with the sound, but it's all energy. You are trying to control the room and you feel good. You could start with five people and end with 15 people, and that would still be great.

Today, I started with 40 people but ended with five. It can be hard. What did I do wrong? Sometimes you can be over-prepared. I thought Wooferland was old-school house, so I prepared an old school set, different from what I'm normally playing. I wanted to be funny – I like humour in my sets – but you have to be so confident and if you're not confident you lose the crowd. That's the moment you realise 'Fuck, I've lost them.' I would be personally hurt and it would be hard not to feel hurt. Maybe five of them leave to get their coats, and you think you should play what you think they want to hear, instead of the other 50 still on the dance floor.

It's a very gentle dance between riding the razor's edge, pondering and being too much of an artist.

Red Robin was one of my favourite DJs. He said that DJs are alpha-sissies. An alpha-sissy is the idea that you're like 'I'm the awesome dude that's going to be playing the music tonight.' Then you get up there to play and you have no idea what to play, plus you're nervous and shy. That's what happened to me for a long time – about 10 years – but it's exhausting sometimes. Like this gig today, compared to two weeks ago where I had an amazing gig, and it was just so much fun.

There's a book, which a friend of mine sent me, and now it's been quoted in the TV show Barry. It's about the four agreements.

One of the agreements is to do your best. Don't try and do more than your best, especially as an American. That's a limitation I have had to learn and appreciate.

In America, it's always like 'Do 200 per cent, give more than your all.' There's no such thing as giving more than your all. If you are trying to do more, you're making a mistake. That really helped me with my DJing. You have to suss out the situation real quick, otherwise it isn't going to be that great. Every time I DJ it has to be superlative, the best set I've ever played. I have to keep improving. Maybe I have a cold or I'm too drunk – or not drunk enough – or I have problems at home, wrong audience for my music etc. It could be any one of a thousand things. You have to assess the situation and put yourself 100 per cent in that place. If you reach that, it's much more open rather than this fake-ass attitude of 'I'm the best,' you know. It's a long way to fall from there, you know what I mean? Instead, be like 'This isn't 100 per cent, but that's what I am aiming for.'

So, I've learned that, but it's not always the DJ's fault. Today it hurt a little bit but five years ago it would have hurt a lot more. It was a totally foreign intuition. The guy before me was playing techno, the guy after me played harder techno, and so what did they want me to play?

They have booked me twice, once at the winter party in the Paradiso, and now at the summer festival. When I played Winter Wooferland, I played nothing but old tracks, and I was like 'Cool, I know what they want to hear.' Easy gig. Today I was pulling out old tracks, but without the dynamics, and people were like 'Oh, okay, bye.'

I saw a DJ once on social media, who actually apologised to his audience. Most DJs are like 'I played the most amazing set, I rocked it last night.' Totally fake-ass. It's only the shiny parts
186

they want to mention.

Everyone wants to be a DJ because they only hear about the shiny parts. But it can be ugly, too.

I feel naked and exposed as a DJ, but I've been on stage since I was 14 years old – in punk bands, as a rapper and as a DJ. There is nothing more pure and naked as house and techno music. I feel as if everybody can see and feel what I'm feeling. If I'm not into it, they won't be into it. You have to be prepared for that; it's fragile and it can break. If it's broken, your ego is broken and you still have to go on, keep playing, there's still two hours to go. And they could be the longest two hours of your life when, at the same time, nobody thinks you're cool. I would always ask myself 'Why am I doing this?' but then you pull yourself together and escape the crippling self-doubt.

That's something that most artists go through. A large portion of self-doubt is only natural when dealing with a large part of creativity. Despite this, DJing is still fun, even when less creativity is involved and it's a more sensitive bubble in a sense. You're like 'I'm the DJ and I'm here to play some records for you and make you move.' When you are performing live you have your sound and that's it. But as a DJ you are naked, without your shield. I don't know how other people react but I know I'm strong and can climb back up after being demolished and derailed. I'll just brush myself off and do it again.

Some DJs these days are all about cabaret. People don't realise it but they are going to a cabaret.

There's a festival in Poland called Garbicz Festival and it's one of my favourites. It's not really about the music, but more about the attitude. It's situated in the forest and is super-relaxed and mellow.

I was really nervous because I was playing the main time, right after Ricardo Villalobos. Unfortunately, the stage I was on was the kind of Instagram stage, more about the glam. Everybody's like 'I know him, I know her, blah blah blah.' But over on the Forest stage it was very deep and everybody was into the music, and that's what separates those two areas.

It's a whole different job DJing when you're fighting an uphill battle. To start with nothing in an empty hot tent and then fill it is great because they feed off your energy. A DJ is also a scapegoat, especially with bad programming.

I've played in Russia and Istanbul, for example, where there is this clear hierarchy of 'You don't talk to the barman or the doorman because they suck. We are the DJs, we are the elite.'

No!!!! That doesn't make a nice party, you need unity. Or rather unity and a certain level of respect. When people party in Berlin for the first time, they learn that lesson fast. You don't know who you're being a dick to – they could be producing your next record or doing the artwork in a month or two. You can't allow ignorance and arrogance; there is no room for it. I'm Jewish but I've raved with Palestinian dudes and Muslims, especially in Germany. The clubs and the drugs have opened a lot of people to a lot of things. It's definitely political, but beautifully political.

In the scene in Germany, there's more acceptance for somebody to step up from nowhere and become someone.

I've got tons of friends but as a DJ you are often alone. I don't travel with an entourage or anything.

In all these years, I've only ever missed two gigs due to some reason or another. I can still get really nervous, despair playing a thousand gigs. I envy people who are totally relaxed, like American Reggie Watts. He's just so smooth.

In 2007 I played at the Melt! Festival in Germany. Goldie was also playing and arrived from a gig in Belgium to discover his record bag was missing. He was asking around backstage for a laptop and I told him I had one he could borrow. We went into this little cabin together and he put his stuff on my laptop from a USB stick, but he didn't know Macs that well and accidentally erased my set-list. I gave him a 'Jake' t-shirt, which he put on. When he played he was yelling into the mic: "Jake the Rapper saved my bacon." He really was a super-sweet guy.

He actually left all his music on my laptop after his set. I had his entire set and more on my hard drive, stuff that I probably wasn't allowed to have. There was an entire MP3 folder with all the stems for Inner City Life. I felt like doing a bootleg but I was too honest. I did think for a moment to do it and send it to him to see if he liked it, though.

Back in the Love Parade days I was still quite unsure of where I was between techno and hip-hop, grunge and all of that. It's hard for me because I love all kinds of music and it was hard to get a set together that had some thread and basslines. In 2006 I was invited to play on a truck and that was the last parade in Berlin. I was playing vinyl in those days but it was hot and the other DJs were more experienced and using CDJs.

I had my favourite records, I put one on, turned around and it had turned into a bowl. I hadn't seen this before, so I put another one and the same thing happened. The turntables were so hot that every record melted almost immediately. I was like 'Fuck, how

189

can I cool down the decks?' I put a few coins on the needle to weigh it down and so it could still ride the bumpy record. In reality, I should have already made the jump from vinyl to CDs.

It was amazing to be there, with amazing energy. I could have played dog farts and the crowd would still have gone wild!

DJ DIMITRI

You have to go all the way back to the summer of 1988 to the beginning of a phenomenal career for Dutch DJ Dimitri. It was at Club Richter where he was handed the very first of his many DJ residencies.

It was around this time that he started to play at The Roxy, a club that, sadly, eventually burnt to the ground, but not before it played a major part in the career of this Amsterdam favourite.

In 1992, Hi-Tech Soul Movement – Dimitri's famous club night and long term residency that attracted clubbers from all over the Benelux – was born at The Roxy.

The 90s proved to be an extremely fruitful decade for the then rising star. Another successful residency followed at popular club night Chemistry, he was crowned best club DJ in the Netherlands four years in a row and in 1996 he was voted fourth best international DJ.

After 23 years of performing, running a label and promoting parties, Dimitri took the decision to retire. After a career of nightlife activity and playing around the world, Dimitri made the switch from DJ to becoming a volunteer to work with mentally disabled children who were based on a farm.

This shows you just what a big heart this guy has. From fulfilling people's weekend desires with groundbreaking residencies and DJ sets for years, he decided to offer his support and passion to those most in need. I salute you, Dimitri. Very decent of you.

In the meantime Dimitri still maintained a love for the scene, hardly surprising given his glittering career.

In 2009, on the back of installing a new studio, the thought of performing to a crowd again was very appealing. The love had never left him and the buzz was back, so on June 30th, 2010, the legend took to the decks again.

Dimitri, who continues to perform on a regular basis, spoke about a certain road trip to Milan, playing at the wrong club, stolen records and a lot more.

You know, I've been through so much. I've had 30-plus years as a DJ and so much has happened to me during my career that I don't know where to begin.

Back in the day, when I used to play vinyl, I think somewhere between 1996 and 1997, I played at Awakenings, a Dutch techno party, at the Gashouder in Amsterdam. I arrived and put my records in the DJ booth and the DJ before me was still playing, so I thought I'd go for a walk around the party until it would be my turn to start playing. I headed back to the DJ booth and noticed immediately that my records were missing. I asked around but nobody knew anything. They had only been stolen just before I was about to play so, regrettably, I couldn't play my set.

Rocco, the Awakenings promoter, was really embarrassed and apologetic. He was so pissed off this had happened at one of his parties and it even made national news. It was in the papers, on the news, and announced on national radio that I had been the victim of a cruel theft. The Dimitri sound was so well known at the time and they even managed to mention that in the record bag were acetates, which are exclusive one-off vinyls of which I was the only person who had copies. If anyone heard these tracks being played or knew anything they were urged to please contact the studio or me as soon as possible.

A day or so later I got a call from some shady character from Den Haag and he told me he knew where my records were. He asked me to meet him in a McDonald's car park. I told Rocco and he wanted to come along, so we both headed for the car park and met the people as arranged. It wasn't that easy, however, because they weren't prepared to hand over the records unless I paid a ransom of more than 1,000 guilders. Fortunately, Rocco paid as I guess he felt kind of bad as it was at his party that they went missing. Funny thing is, though, that there were more records in the bag than when it was stolen!

It was a good thing is that I got my records back – at least on that occasion.

There was another time, in the late 90s as I recall when I was driving home from a gig in Germany. I made it home, went to bed and the next day, when I went to the car to get my stuff, I noticed my records had been stolen from the boot. Two boxes this time, somebody had got really lucky.

I never did get them back but I was contacted on Facebook by someone who had bought one of the missing records and he actually sent me a picture of it. It's an acetate exclusive only to me at the time, and it had my writing on the sleeve, so he thought it could be mine. It was, but I no longer play vinyl so I asked him to send me a digital version of the track. Thankfully he did so I can finally play that tune again.

Incidentally, it was later discovered that most of my missing, stolen records were being sold at the Waterlooplein market in Amsterdam.

In the early 90s I was playing in Germany and I drove there with a friend of mine. I don't know where exactly, but it was either Frankfurt or Dusseldorf. I found the right street where the club was located but noticed it was full of clubs.

We found a parking space and then my friend and I headed down the street with my record bags in the direction of the club. At least, that's what we thought, and we headed straight for the entrance. The security people could see I was a DJ because I was carrying my record box and they waved at me and ushered me through the crowd and into the club. 'Great,' we thought, 'we're in, now let's party.' I headed for the DJ booth and because I was carrying records people willingly moved out of the way to let me through.

So there I was, in the booth, sorting my records and ready to start playing. My set started and after only one record someone came up to me and in a booming German voice told me I was in the wrong club!

Unbelievably, I had managed to walk into the wrong club, walk past security and other personnel and enter the DJ booth. I even started spinning my records, only to find out I should have been playing next door!

When I was booked to play in Milan it was my first gig abroad. I had never played outside of the Netherlands before then.

There I was, excited to be playing abroad, when I found myself in a car heading to Milan with these guys who were connected to

194

the promoters over there and had an entire book page full of LSD with them. I was already annoyed that we were driving all the way there and back, and now I discovered the car was also loaded. Anyway, we made it to Milan.

We arrived at the party and these guys were handing out the acid to everyone and, not surprisingly, everybody was freaking out. The good thing was that they were freaking out to my music!

That wasn't the end, though. Not long after the party finished we drove home, all the way back to Amsterdam, and the driver, clearly under the influence, was convinced the motorway was being invaded by sheep. It was a memorable road trip, to say the least.

Another time I remember flying to Naples and I was booked to play in a valley somewhere. Just one problem – my records did not turn up. Unfortunately, this was a fairly common problem back in the day.

So there I was at the party, 10 minutes until I have to start and still no records. I nervously asked another DJ who was playing if I could borrow some records from him. He didn't mind and let me look through his box, and I recognised some of what he had. I was able to put enough records together for my set and I started to play.

It was going well but I was constantly being interrupted by the guy whose records I had borrowed. He kept coming up to me, saying he was loving my set but asking me what record was playing. This happened several times and I eventually told him that they were *his* records that he had let me borrow from him earlier! I only played the B-sides, so perhaps he had never played the flip side before and that would explain how he didn't recognise his own records.

I used to hunt high and low for my vinyl back in the day, finding some real gems! I was playing in London at the Soundshaft and had been record shopping earlier that day. One thing that really bothered me was when people would ask me what tune I was playing – name, label etc. I might have spent hours searching for that tune and wasn't really happy that someone could now go straight into a record store and get a copy. To avoid this I'd put a label sticker in the middle of the record. I had loads of Strictly Rhythm stickers and I would put one on the middle of the record to disguise its real ID!

The owners of the record shops in London were amazed at how many requests they would receive for Strictly Rhythm tunes I had played previously in the Soundshaft as none of them actually existed.

During the 90s I toured the US many times and I had a residency at Twilo in New York. On one particular tour, I was playing in Gainsville, a really nice student town in the middle of Florida. During my set I played a really great track with this great melody. I'm not sure where it was from but it almost started a riot. Somebody came up to me during this particular track and told me to stop playing it because the melody was the same melody used by the student basketball team from Miami – Gainsville's arch-rivals. Man, they really love their basketball.

I was the first to book Carl Craig in Holland, and Europe actually, as it was his first gig outside America. He played live in the Roxy at my High Tech Soul Movement night. This was right back in the beginning when Carl was still a local Detroit boy and before he became an international star. He was really anti-establishment and did everything his way. At the end of his live set he kept the music playing and just walked off the stage, through the dancing crowd and gave them all the middle finger. We became good mates, played various parties together and the Detroit boys took me under their wing. Great days.

Many years later, in 2014, I played with Carl in New York at Mysteryland. We did an interview together for ID&T and Carl said that both Derrick May and I were his mentors. That was really special. We are still very close and have been ever since the early days.

Derrick used to book me in Detroit and I was usually his only guest. He would organise parties on Broadway in the old theatres that were shut down. That was really special for me, being from Amsterdam and spinning alone with Derrick all night.

All the Detroit producers would come down and we had a great time.

JIMPSTER

Jamie Odell, aka Jimpster, is boss and founding member, along with Tom Roberts, of critically acclaimed record labels Freerange Records and Delusions of Grandeur.

Being a DJ myself, and with a taste for all things deep and with a sophisticated groove, Freerange Records is definitely a stand-out label. Consistently top-quality releases, but always with a great colourful cover design. Freerange tracks always stood out on the shelves in the record shops with their eye-catching sleeve designs.

Messages From the Hub was his seminal vinyl release that helped cement Jimpster as a respected artist back in the late 90s.

With two decades of experience within the scene, and countless remixes and 12" to his name, Jimpster's tracks can often be found in the sets of many a leading international artist today.

With regular gigs in the world's major cities, Jimpster is very much in demand, as are his productions, and he is certainly a purist when it comes to underground house music.

Great music and great DJ sets, this charismatic DJ is certainly on the top of his game.

Jamie spoke about early gigs, touring and the unfortunate theft of his records.

Enjoy...

My first professional DJ gig was in London back in 1990 or 91. The party was called Inspiration. The warehouse raves had recently started and I was playing with a promoter friend of mine. It was in Hackney, or to be more precise Homerton, a really dodgy area of the borough, where nobody wanted to go. It's actually where the Freerange office is nowadays but the area has gentrified and is nice. Back then it was pretty rough.

Even before we got inside my partner, who I run the record label with, was mugged in the queue to get in. These guys just came up to him and said: "Give me all your money."

Colin Faver and Colin Dale were playing good quality underground techno in the main room. I was playing in a smaller room, the VIP room perhaps. It was my first proper gig and I didn't have enough money at the time to buy a record box, so I arrived with my records in three open crates.

I played, the gig was great and had about 50 people in the room dancing. It all became a bit crazy and at about 6am I went back to the decks to collect my records and go home. I found the open crates but just one problem, they were completely empty. Clearly, someone had stolen all my records.

I spent the next day ringing everybody I knew asking if they saw or knew anything, like whether they had seen anything suspicious or perhaps even knew the identity of the thieves. Of course, nobody said anything. So that was my first experience at a gig – losing almost my entire record collection there and then.

I was only 17-18 at the time and I was much younger than everybody else. I was just learning. I was buying my records from the commercial record stores at the time, rather than the specialist record stores. It was the time when the music was crossing over, like the release of Seven Stars from Amsterdam outfit Quazar, for example. There was a lot of Dutch and Belgium stuff, especially the R&S Records releases.

I spent the next year pretty much replacing all the records that were stolen. It was like a mental note, and slowly I was able to buy everything again. It still really hurts and since then I have lost two more boxes of records, on both occasions when I was travelling to and from gigs.

It actually happened twice in Spain and I was never reunited with them. Fortunately, as it turned out, they went missing from the return flights, or in transit, so at least I had already played the gigs. But that was small consolation.

I contacted the airlines, who said they were unable to locate them. Nowadays, the guys aren't interested in vinyl, but back in the mid-90s and even a bit later, a DJ with records was worth something.

There was even a third time, which was the funniest. My records were lost and I was still to play the gig. I was calling the airline to see what was going on and three hours later they finally arrived. They were missing for ages but thankfully they said they had found them and were going to send them to my hotel. It was one hour before my gig.

The record box arrived and I opened it fearing the worst and thinking a lot would be missing. The box was unlocked and somebody had written 'These records are shit' on the top of the first record cover in the box. I just thought 'Wow, that's bad, they didn't even want to steal them.' They must have just opened it up, had a flick through and decided 'Nah, we don't want these.' Ha-ha.

I have a funny story about playing with Mr C. It was at a DJ Mag award ceremony, at which Freerange had won best record label. It was back in 2012, if I remember correctly. Because we had won a prize, they asked if I wanted to do a DJ set. It was a really weird gig, everybody was seated, so I was a bit anxious. It was full of industry people and the dance floor wasn't happening, while there were a few people standing around drinking.

Mr C was due to play after me and I had never met him before. I had about 15 minutes of my set left and Mr C came in and said: "What the fuck is going on?" He immediately turned everything up and the mixer was in the red, but everybody did start dancing. I was being super polite and just trying to be a professional. He came in and was like bish, bash, bosh, volumes up, in the red, and they started to dance!

I played first in Amsterdam in 2003 and every time I go there I have an amazing time. The night kind of goes on forever and I go to all these different places and have no recollection after the event. That's my lasting impression of Amsterdam – one club after another club and you just keep going until it all becomes one big blur.

Because I have a family, travelling is probably the hardest part. Wherever I play outside of Europe, I pretty much go in and straight back out. I played recently in Hawaii, just the one gig. It took me 24 hours to get there and I only stayed for 12 hours before heading home on another 24-hour flight.

Even when I play in Australia I only go for one or two gigs before flying straight back – in economy class, of course, which doesn't really help. But that's what we do. They say the DJ is paid to travel and play the gig for free. I would say that I probably see more of the inside of airports than the clubs.

I'm getting older now, but 10-15 years ago I would always go out and experience the local culture and food. I'd stroll around for a bit and see something of a new city I hadn't been to before. But in Hawaii I only managed two hours of sightseeing before having a sleep and flying home. My wife's often on the phone telling me to go out, have a drink, meet people, but I had no cultural experience in Hawaii at all.

We've had parties shut down before and normally in Eastern Europe. I remember a couple of times in Montenegro or Kiev, places like that, where it's completely on the edge and often with corrupt police.

I played at the Papaya Playa Project in Tulum, on the Caribbean coastline of Mexico's Yucatan Peninsula. I had played in Mexico before but this party was really kind of crazy. The promoters were crazy and they told me we had to go to this after-party in the middle of nowhere by a cenote, which is a deep natural well or sinkhole. The guys insisted I go with them and I was promised it would be worthwhile. It was about three hours after I played, I was feeling good and we bundled into a car.

We literally drove around for about five hours, trying to find this cenote, which was supposed to be 15 minutes down the road from where we were. I was being super polite because I didn't know these guys personally. I had no idea where I was and just sat there being very English. But all I was thinking was 'Where the fuck are we?'

We were driving down dirt roads and every now and again we

would see headlights heading coming towards us. But we had no idea who it was.

I didn't know where the fuck we were going, things were getting more and more intense. My phone was about to run out of battery, too.

Just as I was about to lose my shit with them, the guys found the spot and it turned out to be about two miles away from where we started. It was paradise, in the middle of nowhere, and we stayed for the next three days!

DJ ROMBOUT

Rombout Wagenaar has been a member of the Amsterdam underground for over 20 years. With residencies and sets all over the city, Rombout now works alongside girlfriend Kiki Toao. Together they are founders of The Shamanic Movement, which combines shamanic ceremonies, music productions and fun-filled, back-to-back DJ sets.

I remember Sunday nights in The Vaaghuyzen, a cafe that, sadly, is no longer an essential part of any cool Amsterdammer's weekly ritual. Rombout was a long-standing resident and his sets always closed the weekend off in fine style or, in some cases, kept it going until Monday night.

Rombout spoke about playing and touring in Thailand, Amsterdam gigs and much more.

Enjoy...

From all the illegal parties where I've played and partied I really can't remember too much. It's all just a blur but there have been some memorable gigs that I do recall.

The funniest moment for me when I'm playing is when people want to order a beer from me. I mean, there are no glasses, no bottles or anything that looks like I'm a barman – I'm the DJ! But some people are just too wasted to work that out.

Women can also be really weird. On one occasion I finished my set and this girl came up to me and said: "You are coming home with me!" I replied, with wide eyes: "No I'm not, I don't know you and I have a girlfriend, so thanks but bye."

Lots of weird things happen during gigs but there are also a lot of top moments. Nice talks behind the decks and backstage, so nice that sometimes you even forget you're at a party and then realise hours later that you're just backstage, chatting and having fun.

I was often booked to DJ the closing slots, the last DJ of the party. One time was at the Stubnitz boat for Sub Utd, which was open until 9am.

I had to close from 7 to 9am, followed by a set at an after-party, then an after after-party, and then it was time to start DJing in the Vaaghuyzen, where I was the Sunday resident DJ. Sometimes the days just flow into each other, but it's always a funny time.

There was a time when I slept and woke up in time to go to an after-party at Vaaghuyzen. I had to start playing at 8am so I had a coffee and a croissant on the way, and I was easily the most sober person at the party. The Vaaghuyzen was so smelly, everybody was wasted and I learned that you don't really have much of a connection with the people. Being sober, you're on a completely different level. They were still there from the day before, whereas I had just woken up and it was totally weird. I don't think I'm going to do that again.

The last time I played at Dance Valley was for Vaaghuyzen, when they had a tent set up on the mountain top area. I was backstage at the artist tent, which was almost the size of the festival itself, where we picked up our passes and wristbands before driving us in a golf cart to our location to DJ.

I was sat in the golf cart and I was sharing it with DJ Spider Willem and his sidekick. He always had his right-hand man to carry his headphones and records. Willem was so hyped-up and he was taking it out on his sidekick. Everything that was wrong was the sidekick's fault and if they were late that was also down to him.

Willem looked at me, saw my artist wristband and asked me if he could be taken to his location first. He explained that he was a bit late and had to start playing in 15 minutes. I was fine with it and said it wasn't a problem. Willem then turned back to his sidekick and began screaming at him again, and also demanded the poor driver hurried up.

We arrived at his stage, dropped him off and the driver turned to me and told me that this always happens with some DJs who think they're big-time. It seems they are always moaning, while acting like divas and the personal assistant is always the bitch.

We invited Finger Lickin' crew to play at a Sub Utd party at the Odeon during Amsterdam Dance Event one time. It was the final party that Simon and I did together as Sub Utd.

The night that Finger Lickin' played, if I remember correctly the manager decided to steal a bottle of whisky from the bar towards the end of the night. The bar staff saw this and wanted to kick him out there and then. He started saying he was the artist's manager and because of that he couldn't be kicked out. He then pushed Simon into the club's staff and tried to hide the bottle in a banner that we had just taken down and was rolled up. The Odeon was already a bit of a student place and they weren't happy. We weren't allowed to leave until the bottle appeared.

The accused manager and his English entourage then started to act tough and it was all getting a bit loud. Finally we all left and sat outside on the benches on the square, which were usually occupied by alcoholics, and funnily enough the bottle of whisky magically appeared.

On Queensday, a national holiday now known as Kingsday, I was always running through the crowds with my record box going from gig to gig, but only to arrive at a party and find out there was NO party, absolutely nothing set up. Speakers not hooked up, maybe a loose mixer and that was it. People were just sitting around smoking joints, too stoned to organise and set anything up.

The first time that I played in the main room of the Paradiso, for Sub Utd, was when my dad was in hospital. He was actually having major surgery at the exact time I was playing. My mum called me to say that everything had gone well, which was a relief. One side of my head was thinking of my dad in the hospital and the other side was thinking about me playing in Paradiso for the first time, especially the main room. It was the first time I had played in front of so many people.

Thailand was amazing. Together with my girlfriend, Kiki, who is also a DJ, we did a tour of Thailand in 2008. We had managed to prearrange six or seven gigs before we left.

We played first in Bangkok, then flew to Phuket and played there. The organiser in Phuket really liked it and arranged for us to go back another time when we were able to stay for four days. After Phuket, we flew back to Bangkok to DJ at the Hilton Sukhumvit, located in the business district. It was the most chic hotel I've ever been to or seen. We had a suite as part of our payment, which was really nice.

After Bangkok, we went to Koh Phangan to play, plus the full moon party. It was 2008 and they were into the goa and psy trance. There were mainly European tourists there and to them trance was dead. People really wanted to hear more techno and house, and that's exactly what we played. We arrived at the perfect moment. We played at this really nice club somewhere for 10 hours straight and people elsewhere started to hear about us, so by the morning the place was full. They really loved it and we also went on to play at both the Backyard Club and Shiva Moon, among others.

Everybody goes to the Full Moon parties. They drink the buckets, piss along the beach and fall asleep in the sand. The music is really shitty – it's really bad – but there are some nice party people there and they know how to behave. Surrounding the full moon party, there are clubs for the locals that many don't see and also for the people who are in the know. The music and the people are much better in these places.

Gigs were either in a club, the beach, up a mountain or in a jungle with the monkeys. It really was amazing and the people were very nice. They really took good care of us and were very hospitable, making sure we had everything we needed. We met a lot of people who return every year and a great many who now live there.

When we had almost finished our tour they told us there was one place where they couldn't get us to play, but that they really wanted to take us there. You could only get there by boat. It was a resort with a bar that became the club from Saturday morning to Sunday evening.

We were warned about drugs being sold, which obviously wasn't allowed, so they told us only to get stuff straight from the bar

208

instead! Everybody was on holiday and in full-on party mood. Everybody had the same stuff they had acquired from the bar and they were dancing in the sun, running along the beach and cooling off in the sea before heading back to the dance floor.

In the morning you could hear the monkeys howling in the background. It was a really amazing experience, something that you just don't get in Holland.

OLIVER KUCERA

*I first met Oliver back in the early noughties when he was
playing backstage at the Awakenings Festival, long before his
name was known internationally. He already stood out then as an
original artist, fresh and full of love for what he was doing.*

*Our DJ paths crossed a couple of times, notably at the Corona
DJ tournament semi-final in Holland, in 2005 if I remember
correctly, after I had been invited to compete.*

*I won, but it was Oliver who went on to international stardom. If
you have seen him perform then you would know why!*

*It is always a pleasure to be in this happy chappy's company, and
his live sets always deliver.*

*Oliver talks about his health, family and an unforgettable
experience with the Czech riot squad.*

Back in 2005 I was booked for the Dance Valley Festival, near
Amsterdam. The gig was on the Saturday but on the Friday I was
still lying in a hospital bed after a week of being treated for my
Crohn's disease.

Most people in my life know that I have Crohn's disease. It's
pretty well known that I live with this, it's a part of me. Around
2012 it got pretty bad, it was my fault as I was always putting
pressure on myself and keeping on the go. It was a tough time
but I always had my family's support. For the last 15 years I've

been standing on stage performing, and they have always supported me and believed in me. I did have a three-year break around 2009. I just felt I needed a break and to have some time off, but it wasn't long before I was ready to get back to the music.

But back to 2005 and my Dance Valley gig. I was actually annoyed that they wouldn't let me bring any of my studio equipment into the hospital, so instead I had my headphones on and sat in my bed arranging some things with Ableton on my laptop. I was making beats for my live set and I just thought, come hell or high water, I was going to play this live set whether it killed me or not.

In order to discharge myself I had to sign a release form. When I left I still had all the bandages on, while the IV drip was still hanging out my hand. I was planning on going back to the hospital after my gig, so I decided to keep it in. We even stopped off to get the 909 on the way. I played the set and packed away my equipment. It was raining really hard, a proper torrential downpour and it was actually knee high in most places. When I walked backstage I collapsed, but luckily my brother found me and we left.

In 2007, Chilean DJ Carlos Rios and I were booked for a gig in the Czech Republic. At the time we were performing back-to-back live sets, after originally performing together at Awakenings in Amsterdam. The organiser, Rocco, asked me to perform back-to-back with this other guy who, at the time, I didn't know, but it turned out to be Carlos.

We just clicked. He was industrial sounding, I was funky and banging. He was such good company. Our sets were pretty successful, and we started to be booked together a lot.
211

So, off to the Czech Republic. We ended up in this mad little place, with about only 150 people present. The residents were playing, plus the two local DJs who had booked us and were actually really good DJs.

Our time came to play and after the second song the main lights came on and a SWAT team came charging in. We were in the middle of a drugs raid. I saw M16s and other guns; it was like something out of a movie. One armed officer screamed at us, in Czech, to get down on the ground, and I just said: "Ummmmm, okay," and sat on the ground. The music was still playing, so I just reached up and pressed the space bar to stop it, put the fader down, and the armed officer just gave me a nod, like he approved or something.

Everybody was searched, five people got busted and the SWAT team left. The lights went off, the music was back on, and we managed to finish our set, which went on for an extra two hours. Someone from the crowd went around and collected money from everybody on the dance floor, and gave it to us like a tip. It wasn't much but the thought of it was funny.

In 2016 I was booked for Techno Culturae, a party near Bari in Italy organised by ATProject and their friends. There were about 400 people there from all over the region. David Meiser and I were the headliners. That was my first booking outside Holland and I performed without a laptop – just hardware.

I started my set and after about 25 minutes everything that could go wrong went wrong. I was having sync issues and found out that I had wired two FX units the wrong way, which was making certain things I had planned almost impossible. For some reason I just had a 'Fuck it' moment and went on with the set actually rewiring the units on the go, ha-ha. After two hours, the tempo was at 148 BPM, and everyone was screaming wildly, hanging over my gear and going crazy. Everybody was calling me The Destroyer afterwards.

In 2014, together with my brother George, we started to build a recording studio in Diemen, where I finally had my own space to be creative after so many years. Our older cousin helped with the rent for the first year and half, and things were definitely on the up. A lot of magic has happened in there since then.

I'm currently with Djax Records from Eindhoven, Holland, for my solo music. My first release was my Spaceprobe EP, on vinyl, plus I also did a remix for Miss Djax, the label's boss, called The Fog, which she originally released back in 1998 and has recently re-issued for remixes. That was released in 2017. I'm just happy Miss Djax likes and supports my music!

In 2015, Roxy Tripp and I started collaborating together. Roxy is a British conceptual artist and music producer. Together we are known as Unknown Archetype. We were recently signed to R&S Records and our debut record, the TRIPP EP, was released in January 2017.

There will be more to come but for the time being my solo stuff is being put on hold and the main focus will be Unknown Archetype. I can say that I'm happy with where I am at right now – but I can't wait for what is still to come.

SAN PROPER

San is an enigma but in the nicest possible sense. He's unique and has a very original approach to both his music and how it is performed. If you have seen San Proper performing either live or as a DJ, you may say he's eccentric. Fair enough, but a San Proper set is largely unforgettable.

Often incorporating an instrument or two into his DJ sets, a shirtless San is always lost in music and is a joy to see.

I've been lucky enough to know San for many years and have shared the decks with him a few times at Vaaghuyzen, although that bar is sadly no longer with us.

San's productions are very original, always with a unique sound or two and after going on to build a great international career he deserves every bit of success.

San spoke about gigs in Russia, changing a tyre in Georgia and a certain TV interview.

I remember one particular occasion in Moscow; it was back in April 2015. I had flown in early from somewhere else, I honestly can't remember where, and I was really sleep deprived. I was booked by ARMA17 to perform live at this crazy festival called Outline – the coolest festival, coolest organisation and coolest location ever.

I wasn't due to perform until early the next morning and with no sleep I was fast becoming an irritant to everyone. I changed into what I call my Diva mood – a Grace Jones diva!

Nobody was safe, not the stage manager, not the organisation, nor my management – nobody! The stage manager, especially, was really pissed off with me acting out, as you do from time to time.

Eventually I fell asleep backstage, to the relief of many. Apparently it was only 20 or 30 minutes before my live set was due to start and my management were a little concerned to say the least.

I woke up in what I can only describe as a concrete holding cell and it really freaked me out. To be honest, if you had seen the backstage you would probably say it was beautiful, chilled, a nice place to be, but if you were looking through my eyes then it was a different story. I literally thought I had been arrested and dumped in jail. I was still sleeping in my mind but I was awake and couldn't work out where I was – a fucking freaky moment!

I was thinking 'Oh San Proper, what have you done to yourself, how are you going to explain this to your mum and to your friends…..YOU ARE IN JAIL!' I really couldn't remember anything; where I was, if I was performing, day, date, time etc. My mind was blank – but I was due to be back on stage in 10 minutes, performing LIVE!

Suddenly, this really angry woman came in, placed a line of cocaine on the table and told me to 'DO IT NOW!' It was actually the stage manager who I had been harassing all night for a little something. She finally obliged, much to my delight. I started to think that this couldn't be jail but an asylum, perhaps, with a beautiful blonde dishing out lines. 'Am I crazy enough to be in an
215

asylum?' I thought, while my mind tried to comprehend what was going on.

Suddenly, my mind started to kick in, my senses switched on and I started to reassess the situation. I noticed this little gap at the top of the concrete wall in front of me. I stood on a chair and, to my surprise, I saw a party, a really big party with loads of people. 'I'm not in jail,' I thought.

My memory had now fully kicked back in and my mind was alive again. I realised I was actually in Moscow about to do a live show with my manager, Derek, on drums. So I made my way out of my cell, jumped on stage and had the best live show ever!

The relief of being free and not behind bars was overwhelming and you could hear this in my set. I kicked ass and Derek kicked ass – it's what we do and I'm seriously thinking of taking a power nap before every gig from now on!

I like to perform in cities around the world where the house and techno scene is going through a rough patch, whether financially or politically.

One such gig was in Kakheti, Georgia, in 2013. I arrived at the airport and I was expecting to be picked up directly and taken to the festival but after about 20 minutes I heard a message in broken English over the PA system asking me to go to the information desk. Being the nervous guy I am I usually ran away like Forrest Gump if I was being told to report to somewhere in a foreign airport but on this occasion I went to the nearest information desk. I'm glad I did because they told me that my pick-up was going to be late because of a flat tyre and that I should just relax and wait. I decided to take out my laptop, make some music and have an Ableton jam at the airport while I waited for my ride up the mountains.

A short time later my driver arrived, I jumped in and we headed
to the festival. It was then I noticed just how bad the roads were
in Georgia, with dirt tracks up mountains. It was really fucked –
just like my journey. The roads were full of police cars, vastly
outnumbering normal cars. They were everywhere. I was told
every youngster in Georgia wants to be a cop because it's the
only job that pays. The only buildings I could see were police
stations; they were surrounding me and the other civilian
buildings were clearly suffering from many years of decay.

Suddenly the car suffered another blow-out as we negotiated a
dirt track up a mountain. Being a hardcore motherfucker, I lent a
hand and together we managed to change the tyre and carried on
up the mountain to the festival site.

I have to admit that in my eyes it seemed a pretty unsuccessful
party for the organisers. The mix was totally wrong; too many
police and too few party people. It wasn't a good ratio, maybe
300 people partying and 700 police policing. A crowd of 300 is
cool, I like that, but they were surrounded in a circle by an army
of 700 strong police officers. The crowd was dancing though
until 10am, even though the alcohol was limited and there were
no drugs. But it was the police who were first to feel the effects
of such a late night and by about 7am all you could see were
these cops passing out against the trees and holding on to one
another, while the music played and the crowd carried on
dancing.

Suddenly, a swarm of white butterflies in their thousands flew
out of the trees and bushes. I was stood in the middle of all this
like some freaking twilight zone. The cops were all passed out
against trees and the music continued pumping with people going

217

crazy and the air filled with a thousand white butterflies. One of the best moments I have ever experienced. It was an amazing spectacle; strange but beautiful.

I do remember another time at a festival when I was with Derek, my manager. We were just acting up, jabbing one another all weekend, just two boys having fun.

A little later, en route to see my hero Theo Parrish perform, I was stopped to do an interview for national television. I was trying to be all intellectual about electronic music, saying intelligent things and, suddenly, out of the corner of my eye, I could see someone coming towards me. As I turned to see who it was all I could see was a blur and I felt this huge, and I mean HUGE, punch in my ribs – straight in the liver! I couldn't talk and I was bent over gasping for breath but somehow I managed to continue my interview. I even offered an explanation for what had just occurred and told viewers that the culprit was not only my manager, but I had it coming as I had been punching him all weekend, and it was his revenge.

I still made it to Theo Parrish, though, and while I may have been a little breathless we still had a great night.

VEZTAX

Slavko Stojkavic, aka Veztax, was originally responsible for the European breakthrough of his fellow Slovenian DJ, Umek, in the mid-90s after some underground gigs in Amsterdam, before rocking internationally renowned Awakenings, and later Dance Valley, back in the day when they actually booked proper techno artists.

We met in Mazzo back in 1995. Slavko and I spent many a time on Amsterdam dance floors back in the day before he became the DJ he is today. I have been fortunate to spend quality time with him and his family in Kranj, Slovenia, on several occasions.

Thanks to Slavko's generosity, I was able to combine the different holidays with a few gigs in different cities. I'm also blessed to be able to call him one of my best mates, a brother for life.

After spending so much time with Umek, Slavko was positively inspired and took to the decks himself. His first set of decks were from Japanese firm Vestax, hence his choice of artist moniker.

He has his own record label, Vezotonik, and many releases under his own name. Techno legend Dave Clarke is a big fan!

He continues to perform and promote parties in his beautiful homeland of Slovenia and DJs across Eastern Europe.

Slavko spoke about his time on the road between war zones and the difficulty in actually making it to gigs, embargoes and stolen amplifiers.

I remember many years ago being held at the Croatian and Slovenian border for about seven hours. I was going to play in Pula, in Croatia. At the time we had lots of problems and it seemed the customs guys always seemed to want to add to our pain. They would stop everyone, ask for some papers and wait to see if anyone actually had authority or permission to cross into Croatia.

We were going to the fortress Fort Bourguignon in Pula for our party, and our cars were packed with turntables, mixers and all the rest of our equipment. The serial numbers of each product always had to be noted when travelling across the border in order to prove the equipment was ours.

Annoyingly, we had been fined before because we didn't have the right paperwork.

What happened was that we received a document, which contained all our details and was good for a year. It allowed access across the border but our document had expired so we were all fined, about 50 euros each, and they confiscated all of our equipment for about seven hours. It was a long wait!

On the way back I had to wait again at customs. I was just driving through, papers in hand, but didn't say 'Hello' to the officers – so they pulled me over. My car was full of equipment and they just wanted to show who the boss was.

What a pain in the arse!

When I lived in Amsterdam I organised parties at the place where I lived. Rijks Hemelvaart was an old military complex but by then it had been turned into a community squat after being squatted in 1989.

We always hired our equipment and never had a problem, except on one memorable occasion.

It was the end of the party and we were all unplugging equipment, cleaning up etc. The sound system was being collected and so we were putting it in one place. Some of the equipment, including three amplifiers from the upstairs room, was already stored and ready to be picked up. We walked to the other rooms to get the speakers and other equipment and in that time, maybe five minutes maximum, somebody had managed to steal the three amplifiers that we had hired and drive off the site.

They left the speakers, which were too large and heavy, and Mark, the guy with whom I had organised the party, and who was putting the money in to rent the equipment, sadly lost thousands of guilders, the Dutch currency in those days.

We often had problems bringing DJs into the former Yugoslavia. The craziest road trip I ever went on was when I was going to play in Belgrade, the capital of Serbia, back in the late 90s.

At the time my good friend Mario lived in Amsterdam but he was in Serbia visiting his father and sister. He asked me if I could play at Marko Nastic and Dejan Milicevic's event. He also asked me to bring some new and used techno records because there was an embargo in Serbia at the time. You couldn't get new records anywhere and absolutely nothing was allowed in from the outside world.

'Why not?' I thought, so I packed records for my set and also took along another record bag full of spares and new records, plus a
221

rucksack full of clean clothes for the journey home. My plan was to drive to the train station and jump on the train to Belgrade. I thought it would be pretty easy.

My friend Bojan picked me up the following morning at 6am but he was 10 minutes late and unfortunately I missed the train. The train was heading first to Ljubljana, the Slovenian capital, before heading to Zagreb, the Croatian capital, and then on to Belgrade in Serbia.

The plan was to drive to Zagreb from Ljubljana and then board the train. But we were late again, so I managed to miss the same train twice!

There were no more trains, just one a day, to where I wanted to go. I had to be there, in Belgrade, to DJ later that night.

So I decided to take a different train to the Croatian and Serbian border. Well, it was actually about three kilometres before the border that it stopped and a few kilometres from the nearest town or city.

It was a small station, very quiet, and I was still a very long way from where I needed to be, plus I had two full record bags and my rucksack to carry.

I found a guy at the station who offered to help me get to the nearest town or city; just somewhere I could find a taxi and continue this horrendous journey. He agreed and he drove me somewhere – don't ask where – but it was really terrible. There was nothing, no public transport, no taxi or anything. I was in the shit.

Some local people, thankfully, arranged a driver for me but I did have to wait until the driver finished his meal before he would come and get me.

Anyway, he drove me to the Croatian and Serbian border, and there was three kilometres of no-man's land between the Croatian and Serbian borders. The driver refused to drive over and it was clear he had absolutely no desire to drive into Serbia.

Without any choice, I had to get out and walk the long distance with my records – two full bags of them – and the rest of my stuff.

I made it to the Serbian border but I still had another four kilometres to walk until I reached the nearest city. I sat down, had some bread and water that a local lady had kindly given me and I started talking with a police and customs officer who asked how much I was getting paid for the gig. I told him that only my travel costs were paid, that was the arrangement.

"What do you mean they pay your travel costs? You're walking!" said the officer, at which point we both fell about laughing.

It was time to continue my journey to the nearest town but I had to take another walk as nobody would drive across the border at the time because of the ongoing war. Eventually, I found a taxi driver who would apparently drive me to Belgrade. He was going to drop me at a petrol station a few kilometres from Belgrade, so scared was he of actually driving into the city. He said he couldn't go to Belgrade because he was from another town and it would be bad for him, as a taxi driver from another town should not be taking business from the locals.

I had to call Mario and tell him what was happening and he sent a taxi from the club to pick me up from the petrol station. I finally arrived at the club at midnight, exactly 18 hours after I left home that morning. I had taken two trains, three taxis and had walked six kilometres with two full record bags on my shoulders before I could say I'd arrived.

Outside the club, Mario was waiting for me with Marko and Dejan. They were so happy that I had made it and grabbed my bags and took me inside. The club was absolutely packed and I spotted water was dripping from the ceiling. Finally, it was time for me to play. Marko and Dejan asked me if I wanted to play back-to-back, one turntable each, because they were so keen to listen to the new records I had brought.

I put my first record on then the next DJ played his. When I took my record off a third DJ played his record before it came back to me. When I grabbed my second record from my bag and turned round both the other DJs had taken over the decks and pushed me out!

I wasn't angry, because if you had seen their faces you would know how happy they were to hear new records. Perhaps on a different party I would say something but these guys were my friends so I allowed them to continue. I gave them all a hug, the crowd applauded and they played every single record, the A side, the B side, whatever – they were just sooooo happy!

The crowd were loving it because they hadn't heard new music for ages because of the embargo. Everybody was buying me beers and rolling me joints. I really couldn't be disappointed because they were all so thankful to me for coming, despite the issues I had getting there.

So basically I had travelled, often by foot, for 18 hours to get there with new records for them all, and all I managed was to play one record!

I stayed for a week to have a bit of a holiday with my friends and it was a really nice time. Then my wife called me and said I had to get out of Serbia immediately because NATO were bombing the country. She was really panicking because the borders were going to be closed and no one could travel freely, meaning I would be stuck in Serbia for months.

I took her advice, headed home and thankfully it was a lot easier than the outward journey.

Within 12 hours of me returning home the bombing started. That was – and still is – the craziest time I've ever had.

TYREE COOPER

Tyree is a house legend; absolutely no disputing that. Growing up on Chicago's South Side, he was soon gaining recognition for his house and hip house DJ sets all over Chicago before becoming the international star he has been for decades.

Turn Up The Bass, featuring the one and only Kool Rock Steady on vocals, from 1989, was a track that absolutely drove my dad mad. I'd play that track and many others repeatedly up in my bedroom. What an absolute stomper and it still sounds sweet today.

Being at the birth of such an influential and inspirational time for the underground house music scene worldwide, Tyree Cooper and Chicago were a recognised force in the growth and education of house music.

Tyree loves Amsterdam and this is what he had to say.

I had previously been to Amsterdam for work and TV commitments back in the day, in 1998-99, but I had never been in a coffeeshop. Sounds strange, I know, *me* not being in a coffeeshop, but that shit is true. At the time the promoters took me to the Red Light District, not to any of the coffeeshops.

I didn't know what a coffeeshop was but I knew all about smoking weed, and it was a few years later that I actually visited one for the first time.

In 1995, the hottest summer I can remember, I drove with my German friend Choco to Amsterdam. We arrived at about 8.30pm and headed to the first coffeeshop we saw.

I could not believe that you could buy anything you wanted off a menu. Why hadn't anyone told me this when I was in Amsterdam in '88-'89? If they had done I would have never gone to the mother-fucking Red Light District; I would have been smoking my weed and chilling. I wouldn't have started a fight with taxi drivers either, but that's another story!

The following day, we headed to a coffeeshop called Grey Area. Our chauffeur had mentioned this shop to us, saying it was run by some American guys.

We arrived on the street and I couldn't believe it. There were two white American guys, Jon and Steve, in Amsterdam, doing what American white boys would be doing in America – but they were doing it legally.

I was so impressed at how down to earth and cool they were – no prejudice, nothing like that. I gravitated to them and I would hang out there every day. Every time I was booked for Amsterdam I always hung out at that shop. They were always very decent to me.

In 1996 I decided I'd had enough of flying to Europe from America all the time and I moved to London. Not long after, I thought I'd try Amsterdam. I was good friends with Jon from the Grey Area – we had kept in communication via the phone – and also Mladen, who I originally knew from Germany. He owned Torso Clothing and later Foodism, a restaurant that was situated right next to the Grey Area on the Oude Leliestraat.

227

We would talk about Amsterdam and I decided to move to the Dam from London. To start with, Mladen and his wife helped me out. I'd help looking after their baby and they'd let me stay with them.

Every day during my time living in Amsterdam you could always find me in the Grey Area. I even wrote a couple of my Dance Mania tracks in the shop, that's how dedicated I was to the Grey Area.

Mazzo was another place I enjoyed. I was friends with DJs Angelo and Steve Rachmad, who were Mazzo residents.

I think my most memorable booking has to be the unforgettable weekend I spent at Glastonbury in England but, again, that's a story for another day.

One of my most memorable, but not my best, experiences in Amsterdam was back in 1996-97. The music at the time was separated from other music, like drum & bass, trip hop, house, ambient etc., but at this particular party the music was so intertwined.

I was after this girl I had met; I was really horny and wanted me some pussy. She asked me to go to this club with her and when I asked her what music was playing she said it was goa. "What the fuck is goa?" I asked. It was the new sound in Amsterdam everyone was getting into and it was really psychedelic.

We walked into the club, Trance Buddah if I remember correctly, and I felt this euphoria. I felt like I was on a trip even though I hadn't taken anything. In fact, I only smoked weed, tons of it of course, because that's all I take. I had never heard this music before and I was immediately in a psychedelic world. It was dark and weird, and me being a brother from Chicago's South Side, I decided to roll a joint to see how it would affect me with this music.

Now, there's no place on earth that I could not feel comfortable smoking a joint. Until, that is, that day in that room, where I started to feel real sick. I had already smoked a ton of weed that day but the effects of smoking in that club with the lights and the music made me wonder how anybody could dance. I was stood there looking at them all and I was tripping. I couldn't believe what I was experiencing. I was actually tripping and that's the experience I had. It wasn't good, it wasn't bad – it was a trip. I had no expectations of the night but my whole world changed and my equilibrium was really fucked up.

When I walked out of the club, I was trying to get my senses together and all I remember was telling myself to make a mental note – don't fuck with goa and don't fuck with that glow-in-the-dark shit. Those glow-sticks really traumatised me.

I couldn't stand those motherfuckers for a long ass time. Every time I saw one, all I could think about was being back in that room, where it felt like I was in a 1970s Jim Morrison and The Doors-type movie. Fuck that shit! Anything goa, or psychedelic, or glow-in-the-dark shit....it's a noooooooooooooooo.

Also, you know, I was thinking how crazy it was to try to get me some pussy while I was tripping.

SAYTEK

Joseph Keevil, aka Saytek, is a UK artist specialising in quality underground house, acid and techno. He's a live act too, which means no two sets are the same. It's total improvisation and outstanding creativity.

I've been a fan of Saytek since his early releases on the wonderful Wiggle label and his rise, in my opinion, had been no great surprise. Recognised record labels such as KMS, Bedrock and Soma, to name but a few, know a tune when they hear one and he has produced many amazing tracks for such labels, plus many, many more.

A real talent, he keeps it underground too. Between being a father to two boys and a loving partner, he also finds the time to run his own label, entitled Cubism.

International legend and UK megastar, Carl Cox, is a fan of this charismatic geezer, so much so that he added Saytek to his and fellow techno producer Christopher Coe's new label, Awesome Soundwave. Alongside major bookings worldwide with Carl and becoming a regular feature within Coxy's techno family, Saytek is proving himself to be a well-travelled and accomplished performer.

A bouncy, positive bundle of fun, Saytek is forever reaching new heights within his critically acclaimed career. Long may it continue.

I spoke with him just prior to his gig at Awakenings ADE and despite the noise backstage he was able to pull a few goodies out

230

of the bag.

He touched upon live acts, travelling and having a hand in partly destroying London's ecosystem, ha-ha.

Enjoy...

I'm from Reading, in England, and after living in London for 20 years I've just moved back to my home town.

All my crazy experiences are back in the day but my mind is a bit bland these days. A lot of shit went down in those days but I don't have any recollection of those moments. Nowadays, I'm too serious, but back in the day I wasn't.

This is not something I'm proud of, okay? But back in 2002 my mates and I organised an illegal outdoor party in the middle of Hackney, in London.

We actually managed to make the local newspaper the next day. Apparently, due to the party and its location we had destroyed an entire species of mushroom. Not magic mushrooms, fortunately!

I wasn't happy because it definitely wasn't my aim to destroy the ecosystem. I was devastated and I don't think I slept for about three weeks worrying about it.

There have been many occasions at illegal parties when the police have come charging in. I would always talk to them and try to persuade them to keep the party going.

There were definitely some funny stories and experiences back in the day. I used to talk to plants a lot, especially at after-parties. You would always find me talking to a plant and when people asked me why I would tell them: "I thought it was you."

I was quite famous for eating grass as well.

I had only just started doing live performances when I had a gig together with Mr C. At the time I was using an old desktop computer and the soundcard was so big that it actually wiggled its way out of the computer during my set. This meant that I was left without a computer to finish my live set.

This was one of my first big gigs and I had Mr C dancing behind me. What the fuck was going on? I was stood in the DJ booth and I had to take my computer apart while I was playing music from a drum machine. I managed to put the sound card back in, reboot it and start all over again.

Thankfully, it never fell silent but it did get a bit loopy in places for a while.

When I was playing in Ibiza a sound engineer unplugged my entire live set-up three times during my set. He was really stoned and he was actually trying to plug someone else's equipment in. He stunk of hash and I kept on telling him: "Please don't do that." I had 700 people dancing in front of me when he unplugged my stuff.

Boom, bang….silence! I was using a Roland MC 909 at the time and it felt like it took about 20 minutes for all the samples to reload. It was probably more like three or four minutes but it felt longer when I was stood in silence. The dance floor was full but silent. Everybody was screaming: "Come onnnnnnnnnnnn!!" I was like 'For fuck sake' but this bullshit happened three times

232

during my two-hour set.

I had a gig in Croatia recently but the nearest airport to the venue was in Italy. The organiser and his friend were picking me up at the airport but, annoyingly, my luggage didn't arrive.

And obviously, being a live act flying with loads of hardware, I couldn't do the gig. Or at least that's what I thought.

The airline told me my luggage would be arriving on the next plane, which wasn't due to land for another five hours, and we were three hours away from the gig.

I waited and they waited with me. We were stuck at the airport together, completely in the middle of nothingness, with only a couple of cafes and not much else.

We were hungry so we went to a cafe. We hung out for a while and we did actually have a good laugh. Basically, we were waiting around for another six hours for my lost luggage to finally arrive.

When my luggage did finally arrive, it was probably the happiest moment I've ever had. I could see my bag in the distance and it was sitting on the floor, all alone in this airport.

I was so happy.

One time in Goa, I managed to disappear for three days. You know, just doing the things you do in Goa. I was completely lost in the jungle.

I didn't arrive back at the hotel until three days later and my missus at the time simply said: "Where the fuck have you been?"
233

I was actually half-naked with no shorts on, just in my underwear. I didn't even realise that at the time, I was so out of it!

VINCE WATSON

Vince is a very busy man. A husband, father of one, lecturer, DJ, media composer and one of the world's finest techno producers. He also has a monthly radio show on Pioneer DJ Global Radio, as well as gig after gig in some of the world's most desirable locations.

Having begun his career in the hardcore rave scene, under the Technosis alias, Vince has progressed through the underground scene and is still very much a sought-after producer with a great reputation. With releases on Cocoon, Poker Flat, Planet E and BBE, he has built a solid reputation in the international techno scene.

Originally from Scotland, Vince is now an Amsterdam resident. He is a lecturer at the Conservatorium Van Amsterdam and I think the students there are in safe hands. Who better to learn from than one of the best?

Vince spoke about his Russian experiences, cheeky thieves, memorable gigs and life on the road.

Enjoy...

My most memorable gig was not at a festival or a massive gig, or anything like that. Instead, it was actually at Yellow Club, in Tokyo, Japan.

It's a legendary club, but it's now closed and has become

something else, unfortunately. When it was open it had the most detailed, personalised sound system. This was way before Funktion-One or anything else – it was just incredible.

I think they had tried to model Yellow on The Ministry of Sound in London, you know, the booth etc. at first, and it was unrivalled, particularly for Japan, a country known for being really precise for its sound and everything. Even on the other side of the world there was nothing to compare to it.

I was fortunate enough to play there in 2001, when I was booked to play a house set, which wasn't long after my first album was released. It was one of my first big gigs outside Europe, after playing at many smaller, less decent-type clubs and venues, and I was just so excited.

I had heard about the club but had never experienced playing on a system such as that. It wasn't so much the power, but more the clarity.

And when I actually got the chance to play on it, *it was just immense!*

I kind of regard that as the gold standard, so anywhere I go now I kind of look to see which clubs and promoters are trying to reach that standard. There are a few who are able to pull it off but most of them can't. Either through finance, or the way it's set up, or simply sheer laziness.

But, to be honest, I would play in front of any sound system. I don't turn down gigs for that reason, but the sound is very important to me, and it's the first thing I enquire about when I've been booked.

There is a little bit of preparation involved. For example, if it's a really detailed sound system I can incorporate a lot of effects and things like that, and a lot of bottom ends. If I was playing on a tinny system, and square box systems, none of these things would be possible.

I try to get my sets perfect for those clubs that in my opinion have that gold-standard type of environment. As you may have gathered by now, I'm very particular about my sound and the Yellow system really stands out for me.

My ethos is to spread the music as much as possible and to let others decide whether it's good or not. Maybe, at some point in the future if I have too many gig requests, I can then look to choose from who's involved and the system they use. Then I can either think 'Okay, I'll do those,' or if I don't think it will make my sound any better, maybe I won't.

I was a resident at Tresor, in Berlin, for seven years. In 2010 when I played there, the sound wasn't so great, but now, when I go back, it's amazing, so powerful...not quite Yellow standard though, but it's getting there. It's a Void system that they have, a kind of Funktion-One system.

There are some really great clubs out there. I've had some amazing gigs over the years for various different reasons, played on amazing systems, but nothing, as far as I'm concerned, has come close to the warmth and sound I experienced at Yellow. I always try to be creative and reach that gold standard, too, when I'm in the studio but sometimes happy accidents can occur, like with half the solo in Mystical Rhythm.

The reason that track works is because there's something really strange in it that you can't quite pinpoint. Not just because it's melancholic, but the fact that the solo has mistakes in it, which I deliberately left in because when I took them out it just didn't sound right.

Most producers who release organic music will often rely on an element of chance with some of the programming because if you're too strict and sterile with the programming you can tell at the end, when it becomes monotonous. You've got to have a bit of jazz in there – not the genre, but the musical jazz you can express when creating music. Jazz music is actually laden with mistakes that make sense, and notes that don't exist.

I've had my fair share of problems when travelling from gig to gig, but it's part of the job.

Back in May 2017 I was playing in France at six o'clock on the Saturday morning, and once I was finished it was then a three-hour drive to the airport. There was only one flight to Amsterdam so it was pretty important that I made it on time as I was playing later that day, at 3pm, at the 909 Festival.

I landed in Amsterdam at 1pm and there were no queues, so I managed to make it home at 2pm before leaving for the festival and playing at 3pm. I did cut it fine, but this sort of thing happens all the time.

Another time, I was playing the Friday night in Greece, before having to fly to Glasgow for a gig Saturday night. Unfortunately, though, a volcano had just begun to erupt in Iceland.

So, with this in mind, I flew from Greece to London Gatwick with the intention of transferring to an easyJet flight north of the border. It was then that they announced all flights had been cancelled because of the ash cloud from the recently-erupted

238

volcano. It was a total disaster but I don't give in easily. I tried every possible way to get there. The last resort was to go by bus, a journey which would last many hours.

The bus left Gatwick and went to Ipswich, south east England, then headed to Hull, which is on the east coast. From there it travelled across to Leeds, in Yorkshire, then to Liverpool in the north west, and then finally on to Scotland. But we even stopped at Edinburgh before reaching journey's end, Glasgow, to complete a 14-hour nightmare trip. It was the worst bus journey you could possibly imagine – and by the time I got there I had already missed the gig.

The only other time I missed a gig was when I was living in Glasgow. I was playing with Derrick May at Loveland's Queensday party at Hotel Arena, in Amsterdam. The previous night I was playing in Cardiff, the Welsh capital. The gig was fine, no problems.

The following day I was due on the last flight to Amsterdam. Upon arrival at the airport I discovered KLM had announced that my flight had been cancelled. They insisted that they would get me to Amsterdam, and all I had to do was get to London Heathrow which was a six-hour bus journey away.

I made it to Heathrow but soon discovered that my flight, which was supposed to have been delayed to wait for us to arrive from Cardiff, had already left for Amsterdam.

What a total shambles!

We were then informed that KLM were not going to offer us any overnight accommodation or compensation. I wasn't having this and began to tell them about the gig that I was missing and the fact I was also losing good money. They listened and not only arranged a hotel for me, but also got me on a flight home to Glasgow the following day.

On another occasion, when I was playing in Ibiza. I was booked to play at Richie Hawtin's Enter, at Space. I was flying with Vueling, who I considered to be the worst airline in the world, and when I arrived in Ibiza it soon became clear my bags hadn't arrived.

I had everything packed for my live-set, which was a special one-off type gig that Richie had requested after hearing my Serene album, which I released on Radio Slave's Pyramids of Mars label. Richie had asked if I could perform an ambient/electronic version of Serene, with synths and drum machines too, in the Mind room – a more experimental room. I was really happy and over several weeks I began to plan, create and prepare my set. Serene was actually a difficult album to make and to then create a one-off set from it, as requested by Richie, was anything but straightforward and demanded a lot of time and effort.

Back to Ibiza and my missing bags. I went to the desk and they apologised for the mess but told me my bags were in Barcelona. This was still morning time and because I wasn't due to play until the following morning I wasn't too bothered. I thought it would be okay. But the airline representative then told me that the earliest my bags would arrive was the following afternoon. Let's just say my mood changed.

I told them this was totally unacceptable. I said I didn't care which airline they used, but those bags had to be here by that evening at the latest. She said she would try her best.

I went to my hotel and later that day I received a phone call from
240

Vueling telling me that my bags had been located in Barcelona and were on their way to Ibiza with British Airways. They said they expected them to arrive at midnight but by 2am I still hadn't received anything. I tried ringing Vueling but no one answered. Time was running out and I had to leave for my gig at Enter.

I had some equipment in my hand luggage but was still missing some vital stuff. After arriving at Enter, Richie, his promoter, and I began phoning around everyone we knew in Ibiza to try to borrow some bits and pieces. After two or three hours of frantic calling I managed to arrange a TR-8 – a performance rhythm machine – but minus a plug! Nobody on the island could arrange a power adapter. At the time, the TR-8s were brand new and the power adapters were proprietary, which meant it wasn't a standard voltage and completely useless to me.

I had no drums, no synths, but I did have a few midi keyboards, and I did have Richie standing next to me and he totally loved it. He said he was amazed how I'd managed to pull it off despite having so little in the way of equipment. It's actually one of my most memorable gigs, not because of the shit that happened but because of how inventive and creative I had to be during my set to keep everything interesting.

Ibiza and Enter is just one story about my live equipment not turning up. There have been many more occasions when my records never arrived and I even had records stolen from my box during a gig in Turkey.

I was booked for a festival in Istanbul earlier in the day and then a second gig in Ankara later that night. After the festival, my girlfriend and I were driven to Ankara.

During my set I kept looking for a certain record but couldn't find
241

it, and it was really starting to annoy me. This continued throughout the entire set and I just couldn't work out where it was. I had played it in Istanbul earlier, now it had completely disappeared. After my set finished, the organiser came up to me and explained what had happened.

One guy was distracting my girlfriend, whilst another was dipping his hands into my record box whilst I was playing. They caught the guys responsible and my records were returned, but it wasn't until we'd arrived back in Istanbul after the gig that I realised they had stolen my brand new digital camera too!

I also had a camera stolen in Amsterdam, during Queensday, when I was playing with Billy Nasty and Dave Clarke.

After my daytime set, we didn't have much time to get to Schiphol Airport so it was a huge rush from one gig to the next.

Being rushed, I stupidly put my fee, which was in an envelope, into the front pouch of my record bag, along with my camera. I usually take my record bag on as hand luggage, but because the flight was so busy I was told all bags must be checked in. We were in such a rush that we didn't question it and boarded the plane.

When my bag came out on the luggage belt in Brussels, I could see immediately that the front pocket was open and my money and camera were gone.

Since the late 90s I've played many times in Russia, mostly live, but I did DJ twice in Moscow and Ufa with records. On both occasions, after flying home and waiting for my bags, I noticed that my record bag had not only been opened but had clearly suffered some damage.

242

There's actually a funny story about the Ufa gig back in 2013. Ufa is the capital city of the Republic of Bashkortostan, situated quite far south in Russia. I was picked up at the airport by what appeared to be some gangsters in a limo. Everything seemed to be a bit dark, a bit shady. They drove me to my hotel, where I checked in, and then on to the club where my original outlook dramatically changed.

After arriving at the club, the promoter told me, in Russian via a translator, that I wasn't just there to play a gig, but that I was also there to introduce, on stage, winning DJs at the DJ Awards, an event which was actually being broadcast live on TV. This was news to me. I was totally unprepared but made my way to the stage, where I stood in total shock and bewilderment.

I was handed a microphone and an envelope, just like you see on the television, and I was to read out the winning DJs, then do a half hour live set, followed by a half hour DJ set. The funny thing was that the names were written in Russian.

I was reading out all the names wrong, but after each one a Russian guy would take the mic and pronounce the name properly, so the whole concept of me doing this was totally pointless.

I was paid an absolute fortune for that gig and I flew Business Class. The guys just didn't care. It was such a low-key production, though, with no lighting and only about 50 people in the audience. They tried so hard to make it right, bless them, but it was just like amateur hour.

The after-party was good, though. They were cracking out the straight vodkas, with the local gangsters milling around with guns on show. I have to say, if anyone from Ufa is reading this, I had such a great night and I really enjoyed it despite my initial shock.

The Russian club scene is loaded with interesting characters. I've really enjoyed nights in Moscow, especially at Propaganda and Shanti, a Himalayan tea bar and restaurant. The very first time I played there I walked in and just saw loads of people lying around, spaced out on this special tea they were serving. I felt a little out of place, as I had a bag of banging techno records ready to play, but this was just the way Shanti did things and they actually booked a lot of big names to play there.

You can travel all around Europe, playing the same cities and clubs, but Russia is always different.

I like that.

NATHAN COLES

Nathan's career has taken him all over the world. Mr Coles was also responsible, along with Mr C, for the creation of the tech-house genre which shook the underground foundations worldwide. And continues to do so.

In 1994, together with Terry Francis and 'Evil' Eddie Richards, Nathan created the legendary Wiggle parties. From gangster hangouts in Hackney, to meat factories and various fields across London and the UK, Wiggle has cemented itself into the British and international underground and has recently celebrated its 25th anniversary. Here's to the next 25 years!

Before Wiggle, Nathan was also behind Heart & Soul, The Funny Farm and the Release parties, together with fellow tech legend Mr C.

The brains behind record labels Wiggle and Is This Music, Nathan has also released over 150 tracks to date, under such guises as Get Fucked and Two Right Wronguns, together with Asad Rizvi, and as The Delinquents with best mate Terry Francis.

With DJ residencies stretching all over the globe, including a decade at London's award-winning Fabric, Nathan is now residing in Ibiza. He continues his role in the scene, but is also the go-to man for high-class villas in Ibiza. Love Ibiza Villas – check them out, simply stunning.

I had a very enjoyable and unforgettable weekend in Brighton with Nathan in the early noughties.

Nathan had been playing earlier in the evening at Concorde 2, alongside Terry and Eddie at their Wiggle night. I was playing afterwards at the after-party, but this wasn't just any old after-party. After the club closed, the organisers took the decks and speakers from the club and we headed for the seafront. This party was bang on the beach, playing out towards the sea, with a huge cliff as our backdrop. The sound just bounced off the wall and smothered everyone in blissful after-party vibes on sunny Brighton beach. Fatboy Slim isn't the only DJ to have rocked the beach, albeit we had a smaller crowd.

I opened the party, playing out towards the sea, with the morning sun supplying the heat. It was an absolute pleasure. Nathan played afterwards.

One guy was enjoying himself a bit too much. He was dancing but looked like he was having a fit. I'd say he was in his late 40s, early 50s perhaps, with a toothless grin. This fella was really freaking out. He seemed harmless and nobody was too concerned, at least not until the jerry can of diesel went missing. I looked over at him and he had a cigarette in one hand with the jerry can in the other. He started swigging from the can, knocking back the diesel, and shaking his head and laughing uncontrollably. A few of us rushed over to him, removed the diesel, and thankfully he didn't go up in flames.

He remained at the party but did calm down a lot after a few choice words.

Nathan is one of the scene's most lovable characters, always with a beaming smile. He never disappoints and I'm also honoured to be able to call him my mate.

Nathan spoke about his time on the road, memorable gigs, an indecent proposal and an unforgettable honeymoon etc.

Enjoy...

Most memorable gig and why? That's a tricky one, because I've had so many. But I can recall my most memorable tour – The States we got into Tour – together with fellow DJ and good friend Terry Francis. We were performing under the name Housey Doingz.

This particular tour was in North America, back in the mid-90s. We had managed to arrange in advance with Muzik, a British music magazine, to document the tour for a forthcoming edition of the magazine. Fortunately my wife Louisa, who was also on the tour, was able to get involved and managed to do the write-ups for Muzik.

No major incidents to report, but we just had the funniest of times. The usual farting competition in the hotel, among others, but the fact we were all together and having so much fun was a great experience and one I'll never forget.

Playing in Mexico was also pretty memorable. I played there for the first time back in the early noughties. I was playing at Playa del Carmen, near Cancun. There was a party in the jungle, right next to a lagoon where the locals were cave-diving. That was a pretty incredible experience and a truly amazing place to play. The scenery was fabulous and I was expecting a dinosaur to walk out.

Over the years I've been lucky enough to play in Carmen several times, both in the jungle and at the local festival.

Another memorable gig that comes to mind was when I played in Tel-Aviv, in Israel, back in 2003. Not because of the gig as such, but because of what happened afterwards.

After the club closed I went back with the local resident DJ and his mates to his house, where the party continued. He eventually fell asleep, his mates left and so I walked back to my hotel. I was staying at the Hilton, but there were three Hiltons on the same street – which one was mine?

It was situated on the front, somewhere near the beach, and I had to walk along this huge promenade. Well, I was actually stumbling, with two huge heavy record bags over my shoulders – the good old days. I really had no idea where I was going but, fortunately, I bumped into a local guy and his girlfriend. It looked like these two had also been out all night as well and they were in some state.

Anyway, he was massive and I thought he could carry my records for me, and he did!

They showed me where to go and walked me to the hotel, while at the same time insisting that I go to his house for food. That wasn't going to happen because all I wanted to do was go to bed.

Finally, we made it back to the hotel and I invited them both in for a drink as a way of saying thank you for directing me and helping with my records. They declined the drink, explaining it was apparently a holy day and alcohol was forbidden, but they both still came up to my room.

It wasn't a massive hotel, and we were stood shoulder to shoulder in this really tiny lift. As we approached my floor, the lady turned to me, with a full-on snotty, runny nose, and asked me if I wanted to fuck her!

I just simply replied: "No thanks."

The guy, who I thought was the husband or the boyfriend, turned to me and said: "You can fuck her sister instead, she has got massive tits," while gesturing with his hands to indicate just how big. I politely insisted that I was fine, but thanked them anyway.

We made it to my room, dropped my bags, but I really needed to go back downstairs to the bar. I really needed a drink after the indecent proposals. So off we went, back down in the tiny lift, no offers of sex and sat in the bar, where it soon became obvious that this couple were only interested in money. I gave them what I had, thanked them and off they went.

Get Fucked live in Scotland was another great gig. We played the live set and were invited to hang out at the club after closing. Obviously, we stayed but decided it would be best to first pack up the equipment and put it all in the van. We had pretty much brought the whole studio with us, and it needed a clear head to organise and re-pack it all in the van.

We took our equipment out to the van, responsible boys that we were, and returned to party on with the rest of them back inside the club.

Earlier that night, we met a chemist at the party who had a homemade concoction, which he called something like 2CBD, or 2BD, I can't quite remember exactly. He was dishing it out to everyone and the after-party was in full swing. Everyone was going for it but it soon became a very messy adventure.

An hour or two passed when we all headed for someone's house. We left the club and we were stood outside, completely spangled, and noticed random boxes on the street.

After a closer look, we recognised some of them. We'd only gone and left our entire studio in the road outside the club next to our van. Amazingly, though, it was still all there.

Another funny memory of that night included a giant chocolate chip cookie.

There was a shop nearby that had a special offer on chocolate chip cookies and had made these huge 30" cookies for a promotion campaign. They had been dumped outside the shop by the bins, and we found them when we were walking back to someone's house.

We were all tripping and this was so bizarre, and we were all simply amazed by the giant cookies!

They stayed with us, and even took them back to London on the plane, where they even had their own seat.

Schiphol Airport in Amsterdam was the scene of another funny moment returning home after a gig. I was on a connecting flight, and changed at Amsterdam. While waiting for my flight I was in the bar, of course, and met some guys who told me they were camel jockey trainers. They told me that they basically starved the jockeys and then strapped them with gaffer tape to the camels. I'm sure it was all bullshit but it sounded funny.

The time came for me to board my flight. Unfortunately, I'd somehow managed to mix up my boarding number with the gate number. I turned up at the gate, which was actually my seat number, and thought 'Strange, where is everybody?'

I missed the flight, booked a replacement, and headed back to the bar for more and cracked on with the camel jockey training boys.

Another airport story involved me boarding the wrong plane. It was Oslo, if I remember correctly. I was sitting on the plane and I realised it was full of Italians. All I could think was that *they* were on the wrong plane because we weren't flying to Italy.

An air steward was frantically walking up and down the plane counting the passengers and he must have done this four or five times. He was shouting out in Italian, and then it just dawned on me, that I was the problem – I was on the wrong plane. This was right when Europe started experiencing terrorist troubles, so God knows how they had managed to put me on the wrong flight. I looked out of my window and I could see my flight was at the gate further down, so I quickly departed and boarded my scheduled flight without any delays.

After my marriage to Louisa we went on a honeymoon – but with a difference since I had managed to arrange some gigs during our planned stay in South America.

We flew via Charles de Gaulle Airport in Paris and we were almost flattened by a section of the airport roof that collapsed. We had just seconds earlier walked through that particular part of the airport, and heard the huge crashing sound behind us but couldn't see it. People were screaming, running in all directions but, thankfully, all the passengers were able to board their relevant planes.

We were heading for Argentina and the beginning of what we

hoped would be an amazing, unforgettable honeymoon.

We touched down in Buenos Aires, only to discover that our bloody clothes were missing and, to top it off, the airline had also lost my records. We basically had nothing. Not the start we were hoping for, what with the collapsing roof at the airport and now this.

When the promoter had booked me previously, he'd always put me in a four or five-star hotel. But not this time.

We were put up in a very basic, shitty hotel and remember this was our honeymoon. Louisa's wedding ring had a diamond in it, but it broke and the diamond fell down the plug hole in the shower and was lost. My bag of records still hadn't turned up, nor had our clothes. I managed to borrow some records for the gigs in Argentina and, fortunately, my bag of records and our much-needed clean clothes had arrived at the airport in time for us to fly on to Uruguay.

We headed to Uruguay having been reunited with our stuff. Not long after arriving at our hotel there was another incident when the roof of the hotel collapsed into the outdoor swimming pool. Unbelievable.

We rented a car but I crashed the bloody thing, and then Louisa and I came down with severe salmonella poisoning.

That was some honeymoon!

Thankfully, it was time to fly back to the UK. There were issues with thick fog, so we had to wait and fly via Brazil on the worst plane I've ever been on. Louisa and I were sat at San Paulo Airport with severe salmonella poisoning, but managed to crawl to a hotel before our flights were ready to depart for the UK.

The ironic thing was that we turned on the television in the hotel room and watched a movie about a couple on a bloody honeymoon where everything goes wrong!

I have to say our experiences pissed all over those in the movie.

Finally, we were heading back to Britain, still with salmonella and on a very busy flight. We were in our seats, with one seat spare next to us. Suddenly the largest bloke I've ever seen boarded the plane. Lou and I both looked at each other, the only spare seat left was next to us, and yes, you guessed it, he headed right for it and squeezed his large frame into the unfortunate chair. We were a sweaty, salmonella-ridden mess, with the added bonus of being squashed together the entire flight. Lou wasn't having it and, to her credit, managed to get him moved. I needed the toilet every two minutes and I would never have made it being squashed up with old matey-boy.

The adventure wasn't over just yet. After touching down and being extremely relieved to be back in the UK, we waited for our luggage only to be told that my record box was missing – again!

253

DJ JURIAAN

My brother from another mother, Juriaan is one of Amsterdam's most underrated artists. Juriaan is a technical wizard who always leaves a dance floor begging for more.

From initially rocking Amsterdam's Mazzo in the mid-90s, Juriaan has gone on to enjoy European DJ success, although in my opinion he should be playing more often in the Netherlands, especially Amsterdam and its techno scene. Take note, promoters!

I enjoyed a road trip to Salzburg back in 1998, if I remember correctly, together with fellow Amsterdam DJs Bart Skils and Juriaan, and Slovenian DJ, Veztax, who was living in Amsterdam at the time. We were booked to play at the Cave-Club, which was a club built inside a cave, as the name suggests. My girlfriend at the time, Roberta, also came with us.

One outstanding memory of that weekend is of Juriaan being reprimanded by the local police.

After the club closed we headed back to our hotel and Veztax was driving. We needed to withdraw some money and Juriaan soon spotted a bank, complete with a cashpoint. We pulled over, at which point he jumped out and sprinted across the street to withdraw some money. Nobody thought anything of it, until the blue and red flashing lights pulled up swiftly alongside us. They immediately gestured Juriaan over and began screaming at him in German Austrian. It turned out that he had jaywalked, which was strictly forbidden. He was being threatened with arrest and we all fell about laughing, as hard as we could. We made it back to the hotel, thankfully with no arrests.

Juriaan spoke about early squat parties, road trips and an entertaining boat trip etc.

Enjoy...

I was really into the early acid house and rave scene, and the first record I ever bought was Android by The Prodigy.

I was living in Utrecht at the time, with my parents and younger brother, Mathijs. It was 1991 and I was playing at squat parties, friends' birthdays and wherever we could organise parties.

One weekend, back in 1993, I was playing with my mates at a squat party in Utrecht. I was always the one that was known for playing a harder style, usually 130 BPM – beats per minute – without any compromise and because of that I would play the last set of the night.

When I listen back to those tapes now, the tempo is so high and with good intent, but I think it was too fast. I've evolved over the years with my music choice and I think it's because of my age. I now prefer more sophisticated slower sounds – but still techno.

I finished my set and when the guy who lived at the squat had had enough he asked everyone to leave. We were all stood in the car park and everybody was still really high. The party always seemed to continue in the car park in the old days with booming car sound systems. One of my mates told me that there was a warehouse after-party at a secret location elsewhere in the province of Utrecht. They wanted me to DJ but he told me very late because he said everybody was already at the party.

He was about to leave but his car was full and I was left all alone in the car park with my bag of records. But it was okay as he said one of his mates was on his way to pick me up and drive me to the party.

Suddenly, in the distance I could hear a car that was clearly going way too fast, followed by a loud booming techno bassline coming from the open windows, as it was summer time. I could see it getting closer but didn't think it was for me. But it came flying into the car park and headed straight for me, skidding and stopping within inches of where I was stood. Immediately I saw who was driving, I recognised him and realised he was my chauffeur. My lift to the party had arrived.

The driver who came to collect me was a good guy, who would do anything for his friends, but he was also known as someone who did not always operate within the law in the Netherlands, although he came across like a teddy bear that would never hurt anyone.

I smiled, picked up my record bag and told him I was happy to see him. As I went to open the front passenger door I found it was already open and I just assumed he had done it for me. But once I was in he immediately started to drive away and at the same time asked me to hold the door with two hands. I thought nothing of it because I was wasted and just did as I was told. After a couple of minutes I asked why I had to hold it and he calmly replied: "I've just stolen the fucking car. I had to break the door to get in!"

I'll never forget his face when he told me but because we were on the highway I decided to say nothing, although I felt really uncomfortable. Finally we arrived at the party, without any incidents, and we looked at each other, nodded, and we have never mentioned it since then.

I played another hard and fast closing set, which was great by the way. It was a really great party. It was already deep into the following afternoon before I left to return home and I decided that using my free student travel was preferable to clinging on to a car door with two hands in a stolen vehicle.

Around the start of the millennium, during the summer, we organised a boat party with a bunch of very good friends. The boat belonged to the parents of a friend of mine and her father had agreed to be our captain for the weekend. He was the only person allowed to sail the vessel and for a very good reason – he was the only sober person on board. He didn't care, he had a great time. He wasn't there to keep an eye on his daughter, like at a kids' party. We were a close group of friends and her father just let us get on with the party, for three days. We actually had the boat for the entire weekend and all the equipment, including the turntables and sound system, was provided by the guests. Some things were hired, but the majority of what was needed was supplied by the group of friends. People bought their own food and drinks, and we had enough of everything to last until Sunday.

Much to my surprise, a DJ booth was constructed as the boat began to set sail. The drinks were beginning to flow, everyone was enthusiastic as they anticipated a great party and it was perfect weather to be on a boat. We didn't know the route we were initially going to take but eventually there were several suggestions as to where we should go.

We hit the river IJ behind Amsterdam Centraal Station, where we found ourselves alongside a massive cruise ship that was docked there. By this time we had the DJ booth up and running and the techno was booming out of the speakers. The people on the cruise ship were standing on the top deck and when they heard us approaching, much to my surprise, they started to dance and wave at us.

We had a problem with the wind. The slipmats from the turntables blew up into the air and landed in the water, so we decided to stay in that area for another 30 minutes before heading for more open water.

On the first night no one slept. We kept the music going all night and by this time we had docked, somewhere near Veluwemeer, so the captain could sleep. I eventually fell asleep on the floor and woke up next to my good friend DJ Dano, the hardcore Amsterdam legend.

Once everybody had eventually woken up, we had coffee and a swim. By this time it was early on the Saturday night and we all enjoyed a barbecue next to the boat on the island where we had previously docked. We took turns to DJ on the boat and with no one anywhere near us the music was blasting and everybody was in high spirits.

On the Sunday morning, and after two intensive days of fun and laughter, the mood was still nice. By that time we were almost three hours from the river IJ so we sailed back, music pumping, with the last of the drinks going fast. This actually helped with the cleaning. Nobody minded getting stuck in because we were all so wasted. Everyone was involved with absolutely everything from start to finish and there was a great spiritual feeling of togetherness. It was a really wonderful experience with my very good friends.

Back in the late 90s I played every second month at Radost FX in Prague, in the Czech Republic. Most of the time I took the coach there and back. I was paid a fixed amount up front and to try to save some money I took the bus from Amstel station in Amsterdam. I wasn't looking forward to the 18-hour journey, but at least it meant I would have more money to spend on beer!

The good thing about those gigs was that I always a managed to have a week-long holiday because there was always accommodation and food provided. Transport wasn't a problem either; they took me everywhere I wanted to go.

But for that particular trip I didn't prepare as well as I should have done. We made it to the German-Czech border, where the Czech border police felt the need to board our coach. I was sat at the back and watched as the police stopped and spoke to everyone as they slowly walked towards the back where I was. They asked for my passport and where I was travelling from. I told them Amsterdam and explained I was a DJ on my way to perform in Prague. They looked at each other and told me I had to go with them to their office. The coach driver then had to get off and locate my bags in the baggage area. He wasn't happy.

I took my bags and the policemen immediately said they were going to search them. Stupidly, I hadn't anticipated a search, so there was still some weed in my bag, as well as rolling papers. The look on the policeman's face changed when he spotted the weed. There were two officers, one good and one bad, in the room with me. Every time the good cop left the room, the bad cop would be very loud and aggressive and kept asking me where the rest of it was. I was stunned that I even had that amount on me because it wasn't something I would normally overlook. When the good cop came back into the room, he would apologise for the other officer's attitude. It was freaking weird.

My record bag was searched record by record, which took ages. I was also strip searched, but I had nothing on me. After an hour or so, I was taken back outside and I assumed we were going to continue the journey to Prague. I was met by the other passengers, who were standing outside the coach with their bags, while the police were actually on the coach and were beginning to strip it to look for weed and possibly other drugs. It looked like the police were fresh out of school as they eagerly looked for something that wasn't even there!

This lasted for about four hours and for the whole time everybody had to stand where the police said and not move. Not surprisingly, I was Public Enemy Number One for the rest of the trip.

Eventually, we were all allowed back on the coach to continue on our way and we made it to Prague, albeit a lot later than we should have done. It was a huge relief, and for my fellow passengers no doubt, that we finally made it safely to our destination.

Another amusing travel tale occurred when I was booked to play in Barcelona back in 2006. I decided to fly and was accompanied by my Spanish friend, Andres, who was one of the organisers of the gig. We departed at 8am and being very excited about the trip we started early on the beer. As it turned out, a little too early!

We were too busy in the bar to even think about using the toilet. Then, once we were on the plane, we ordered more beers from the stewardess. But then we started to experience turbulence and things went from bad to worse. We were told to fasten our seat belts but right at that very moment I felt an uncontrollable urge to pee. Andres was sat a few rows behind me and he was in a similar predicament, but he was really sneaky and used his empty beer can before placing it on the floor.

Meanwhile, my seat belt was pressing on my bladder. I was turning white and sweating, and I really felt like something was about to burst. I took off the belt, despite the stewardess telling me not to, but I couldn't wait. I told her I was sorry and that if she reported me, and I was fined, it wasn't a problem; it would even be worth it. I continued on my way towards the toilet at the back of the plane.

Because of the turbulence I was falling into people and without noticing I even knocked over the can of urine that Andres had put on the floor. Once I was in the toilet I was being thrown all over the place and my head kept banging on the walls. On my way back to my seat I apologised again to the stewardess and I then spotted Andres laughing really hard. He explained what had happened with the can he had used earlier but, incredibly, nobody seemed to notice.

When I returned to my seat a few rows in front of him both Andres and I laughed all the way to Barcelona!

LEFTFIELD

With their certain legendary status, this band always rock. The ultimate live band to shake you from head to toe, Leftfield are always on the edge of something new, and incorporating it into their signature sound.

Sure, their albums feature harder, slower creations, and that unmistaken dub approach they produce so well, but the Leftfield sound is recognisable at 100 paces, or across a muddy nutter-filled field.

Having experienced the Leftism tour of 1996 at Amsterdam's Paradiso on April 13th 1996, I can confidently say that a live gig has not blown me away as the sound system did on that particular night. Mind-blowing; more on that in the interview.

Many years later Neil Barnes and his new-look Leftfield took Leftism back on the road and again shook the Paradiso's foundations on December 3rd and 4th 2015, but without that somewhat original, controversial monster sound system.

I'm not even sure if a venue ever allowed that system to be plugged in again! Very controversial, but it really had to be heard to be believed. Simply amazing.

To be sat at a table discussing one of my favourite albums, Leftism, and its unforgettable tour, with the man responsible, was a memorable moment. I'm just not sure Neil felt the same way. Ha-ha.

Neil was suffering from the alcohol effects from the previous

*night's gig, while I was just out of hospital. But we did,
thankfully, manage something.*

*Neil isn't the only member of the family with a life in music. His
daughter, Georgia Barnes, is an electronic music producer, and
ex-drummer for spoken poet Kate Tempest and Kwes. Her artist
name is Georgia, and she was nominated for BBC Sound of
2020.*

*Neil touched upon the early days and the legendary Leftism tour
from 1996.*

My early influences were punk rock and jazz, stuff like that;
reggae, obviously, and John Carpenter too. My first band was
called Elephant Stampede. I always thought they were a funny
band and I was the lead guitarist.

We, as Leftfield, were also into our club music and it was the
type of music that made us dance. It felt like it was the right thing
to do. It was also the music we would play as DJs.

Paul and I really liked what Jon Lydon did, and we thought
working with him on Open Up would work. It was a natural
progression for Leftfield, working alongside somebody who had
an edge to them. I loved Jon and saw Public Image Ltd in
concert. They were also a big influence on our sound. A lot of
those bands, in those days, would really fill you up with their
sound, whereas nowadays it can be too polite. Those early
influences definitely inspired the Leftfield sound.

Paul Daley and I started playing congas and percussion down at a
club called Violets, which was quite a funny scene, in London.

The club was more of a poetry club and was run by the Sandals – a London-based acid jazz quartet. One thing I do remember was the exercise routine that would start in the middle of the night and that would really crack us up. Everything would stop and Derek Delves would get on the mic and he managed to get the whole crowd doing exercises. They were funny nights.

Our first-ever live gig as Leftfield was in Amsterdam at the Paradiso in 1996. It was the beginning of the Leftism tour and that will always be a favourite memory of mine, alongside the hot, sticky, mess as we walked off stage.

That gig was an incredible moment. The fear, mixed with panic and pleasure at the same time, created an epic moment. It felt like our baptism, as we chucked ourselves into the unknown, and it's been like that ever since. Even today, as I walk up to the stage, I have the same feeling as day one.

We're using a line array system on this tour, the Alternative Light Source tour, rather than the now legendary Funktion-One/Point Source system we used in 1996 on the Leftism tour. In terms of speaker boxes, there's probably less now because it's a different type of system plus it's a different way of delivering the sound.

There are a lot more controls these days regarding regulations for sound systems. There are so many laws around that actually stop us from playing as loud as we could. We tried to offer an experience, a feeling. That was the market we were trying to tap into and I suppose we still do; that was the whole point to it all really. In the past, people have been amazed at just how loud it was and to be honest our sound man in those days was probably deaf. Nowadays, we use somebody that can actually hear; it does help.

I do remember one soundcheck before a gig from the Leftism tour, when we played up in the north of England. It was so loud that this enormous panel, a steel grill if I remember correctly, fell from the ceiling above us! Fortunately no one was hurt. There were also cases of plaster board falling down from other venues. The Brixton Academy, in London, was particularly unimpressed with the bass-shaken plaster falling down.

The memories from that gig are a little messy, with a lot of cleaning too. I do remember a big chunk falling on Billy Nasty's head whilst he was DJing. The venue made a thing about the system being too loud and banned the sound system from future events. That system really became a part of folklore – and rightly so.

I remember a gig in Japan during our second tour and before we went on we asked them to put the lights down low. They turned everything off and it was so dark. As we walked on, I simply fell off the stage into the dark abyss below. I've always been worried about falling into the crowd during a gig, but on that particular night it was a pit. Luckily, we've never had to cancel a gig due to health or injuries. As the walking wounded we've always managed to get through it. We're consummate pros, you see!

Glastonbury was an amazing event back in 2000. I remember looking out at 45,000 people and being terrified. Our sound crew were also pretty nervous because we never imagined ourselves performing to so many people, so that was a really big moment for us all.

When we recorded Not Forgotten back in 1990, the whole thing was produced on tape. It was all chopped up into bits to do edits because Paul was also editing Not Forgotten's remix. Basically the whole room was full of tape and we had to try to find certain

265

bits of tape to stick on to the right bit of music. Accidentally, bits of tape were stuck on backwards and happy accidents would happen.

We discovered de-tuning samples was also a fun thing we would do in the studio. Nearly everything we did was an experimental moment, with something happening you didn't expect to happen or had actually planned.

Top of the Pops was an amusing thing to do. We decided to do it as an experience and thought it was something we should try. But even as we were doing it we were regretting our decision. We performed Original, with Toni Halliday. It was recorded in a small studio and we had to sit through other artists' performances. We were sitting around all day waiting for something to happen and then we got our two minutes to perform. I remember Duran Duran being there and to be honest they were pretty embarrassing.

MC P-PHOLL

"The best MC I have ever worked with," are the words of 808 State's Andy Barker after they performed together in Amsterdam for Wooferland.

Paul Weber, aka P-Pholl, is recognised as one of the original artists to have emerged from the Dutch dance scene, going all the way back to 1987. In those days Paul was very much into his dub and reggae, and this apparent inspiration is clear to hear in his vocal delivery.

Many an MC can hold a microphone and say something, but the art is knowing when to shut up!

With expert smooth delivery, in his own unique way, Paul has earned the chance to MC on the world's biggest stages alongside the world's leading artists.

With residencies at two of Amsterdam's most popular club nights, Chemistry at the Escape and Earth at the Paradiso, to hosting Tomorrowland's main stage, P-Pholl has an extensive CV and is still very much an active part of the electronic music scene worldwide.

Paul spoke about travelling, performing in Russia, sharing the stage with icons and more.

It's funny because my best friend Rogier, who is sadly no longer with us, told me I should start to MC professionally. At the time we were just kids and I thought 'No way, nobody wants to listen to me, you're mad Rogier,' but he was right. Not long after my career started I was performing at the Lowlands festival in the huge Bravo tent with DJ Dimitri. All I could think of was Rogier and how it was such a massive shame he couldn't be there with me. Especially because he had predicted this scenario many years ago.

I originally started as an MC in my teenage years with doing reggae, dub etc. plus a few jam sessions. I was also part of a small acid house act back in 1989 called The White House. There were two guys behind computers – the old-school Atari – with some studio equipment alongside a rockabilly-type dude with snakeskin boots. He also had an Elvis quiff and he was on the electric guitar with yours truly on the mic.

As my career developed I had many bookings across Europe, as well as bookings together with DJ Per and the Earth organisation. One gig really comes to mind.

It was back in 2005 or 2006, if I remember correctly, in Moscow. There was me, DJ Per and a couple others performing in this club full of beautiful women, who were accompanied by rich dudes in wrong suits. These rich, but badly dressed, Russian men would buy up all the VIP tables at parties and basically invite all these beautiful women to join them. The rich guys paid for everything but in exchange for extras and benefits.

I say women but they were probably still teenagers. However, they were always beautiful, dressed up and always alongside the rich dudes.

These girls would never be able to afford the tickets, so they would get into the party for free thanks to the money men. But these guys always wanted something in return.

At this particular party, the dance floor was surrounded by VIP tables. I spotted these two fat, ugly bastards, who on a normal day would be ignored by any woman, but they were surrounded by these beautiful women just because they were splashing the cash.

Now, Per and I weren't wearing trashy, shiny suits coming from Amsterdam. We just looked casual, we were playing nice music and the girls were interested in this. They would come over to the DJ booth, want to hang out and have some contact with the DJs, MCs etc. The problem with this, though, was that the rich dudes paid a lot of money to be there and would simply tell the club security to ask the girls to go back to the VIP tables immediately. These guys saw these girls as their possessions, but the girls wanted away from all this bullshit and to hang out with some Europeans who had some style and respect.

Fucking ridiculous, what a crazy place.

Travelling can be a hassle. There's nothing worse than hanging around at an airport waiting for a connecting flight and when you finally arrive, most of the time you're driven to your hotel. Then you maybe do a soundcheck at the club, go back to the hotel, head out for food, return to the club, go back to the hotel and then to the airport and fly home. Maybe even on to another booking somewhere else in the world!

Singapore was crazy too. Not the party but the amount of travelling in such a short time. That was back in the early days of my career, 1996 – 1997. I arrived at the airport, was driven to the club, did my gig and was driven to a hotel for a two-hour sleep before I was back at the airport and heading home to Amsterdam.

269

That trip really broke me; I was fucked.

With some bookings, though, I've managed to plan ahead and make a holiday for myself, like Mexico for example, where I managed to have a 10-day holiday after one gig.

These are the rewards for sitting at airports for hours and hours without sleep.

This brings me back to Russia, where I – and it happens to every non-Russian to be fair – was held at the airport for hours and hours for interrogation. My MC equipment is always intriguing for the customs officials but especially so in Moscow. I always carry my equipment as hand luggage and when I had to open it in Moscow the customs officials were in a state of shock-horror seeing all these cables, processors etc. among my stuff. I don't speak Russian, they don't speak English, so it's really difficult to explain what everything is used for and why I was travelling with it. They took me away for interrogation and to investigate me and my belongings further. I'm sure they thought I was a spy. In the end everything was fine, but it was two or three hours later before I was allowed through. Irritating.

Another time, in Ukraine, Per and I were being driven back to the airport after our gig, probably around 8am, and Per was a little tipsy. We arrived and walked through to check-in and customs, only to be stopped en route by two customs officials. Per was told he couldn't fly because in their opinion he was too drunk.

He was not drunk at all; most of it was due to tiredness – and a little alcohol, ha-ha. But these guys, little bastards to be precise, had a way of manipulating all the foreigners, not just us. They told the promoter who gave us a ride to the airport to pay a fine of 25 euros and they would then let him aboard the flight. It wasn't much but if we had refused their demands they could have easily just held us there for a day or two.

In reality these guys earn nothing from their jobs but they can triple their income, possibly more, in one day by manipulating those vulnerable foreigners into paying fake fines.

In the scene, you have DJs who don't appreciate the MCs and vice-versa. If a DJ would prefer to play his set without me MCing over the top, on moments etc., that's fine with me. I don't have a problem with it. In my opinion it's always about the DJ and his music, not about me.

Often I'm booked by the organisation, not the DJ, so we share the stage, but I don't want to perform if the DJ doesn't want it. So, sometimes, there can be a little issue because the promoter wants value for the fee he's paying me. But I don't really get involved. I'll just do an intro and then an outro and take a two-hour break.

It is really important as an MC to forge a good relationship with the DJ, if possible, so they trust you to do a good job and not just shout 'Make some fucking noise' at every opportunity. Jon Digweed is a good example of this. I have performed with him in the past and he's not really one for an MC through his set. But he has always liked and appreciated my style, and just lets me do my thing. For me, that's probably the biggest compliment you can be paid and I really respect him for that.

I did, however, have one run-in with a massive international Dutch DJ from the trance scene.

Back in 2001 I was performing at the Rotterdam street parade Fast Forward. It's a parade with trucks and sound systems going

271

from one part of town and through the centre before ending up at the site where the party continues. I was hosting the trance stage, but it's not my first choice of music, nor second or third for that matter. But I'm a professional, so I'll do it. There must have been thousands of people in front of the podium, what a sight! The DJ started his set and I had already prepared a nice little introduction about him and his record label etc. So I waited for a break in his first record to start to MC.

Now, I do this for a living. I do my research and will always be professional, regardless of the DJ, but this one moment will live with me forever. I'll never forget it.

There I am, in full flow introducing the DJ with a customised intro, when I look over to the DJ booth and I can see this Dutch superstar trance DJ gesturing with his hand, moving it back and forth across his neck, mouthing the words 'Shut the fuck up!' I found this really disrespectful, especially in front of so many people. He could have just asked me to stop or gesture in a non-threatening way. I know trance music is not very suitable for MCing, so my idea was to just do an intro at the beginning and an outro at the end of his set.

I was so pissed off, especially because I had prepared a little something to introduce him, so I marched over to the DJ booth, stepped inside and told him I'd been involved with house music since the day he was still listening to Milli-fucking-Vanilli and that he was a rude, fucking clown!

Funnily enough I was hosting a trance party in Amsterdam at the Melkweg a few years later and Tiesto was playing, plus the international superstar Dutch DJ I previously mentioned.

Tiesto doesn't like MCs either but does like a short intro at a time of his choosing, usually two or three records in and during a big break. He came over and introduced himself to me and he asked if I could do an intro for him, I agreed and everything was fine. I appreciated him taking time to say hello and together we arranged a little intro at the right time. The other DJ – yes, that one from before – liked what I did with Tiesto and came over to me to ask if I could do the same for him. "Here's my mic – do it yourself," I told him. Ha-ha!

I might have had a run-in with a Dutch DJ but all fellow MCs in Holland are one big family. MC Marxman was always very decent and respectful towards me. He got me involved with some parties, plus the Dance Valley festivals in the early days and my career seemed to take off. Kevin – MC Marxman – was the Chemistry MC at the time in the Escape in Amsterdam during the mid-90s and when he left I took over from him as resident MC for the next eight years.

MC Conrad from England is one of my heroes, a real inspiration for me. I was lucky enough to be invited to perform at a Logical Progression event in Amsterdam back in 2011. I was MCing with another DJ before LTJ Bukem and Conrad took over. To share the stage with those two legends was a dream come true.

I feel the role of the MC has changed over the years. For instance, back in the day, an MC and a DJ would perform together as a kind of duo but in recent years the superstar DJ wants all the credit and the MC is often unplugged or turned down low by the DJ and given only very limited time to do their thing, if at all.

There are some events I've been involved in and the MC doesn't even get a mention in any promotion or on the flyer. What the fuck? I'm there performing for 12 hours. Show some fucking
273

respect.

Other organisations couldn't be more gracious in the way they advertise and promote the artists performing at their event. Tomorrowland are great, they always make an artist profile with all the links to your relevant pages online. That's how it should be. But in all fairness the MC role is becoming less and less, or at least not being used to their full potential. The crowd is there for the DJ, not the MC, which is fine to me. Our scene is all about the music.

I've even had people give me the middle finger at parties. I was hosting the Cocoon stage at an I Love Techno event in Belgium. I was performing alongside Richie Hawtin and it was going off. The vibe was great, music was amazing and I started to freestyle over the music during this big bass break. Richie was loving it and so was I, but as I turned to the crowd there were some kids in the front row telling me to 'Shut the fuck up' with their middle fingers in the air. I'll never forget it! You simply cannot satisfy every person in the audience; it's a thing you have to accept the moment you step on a stage. It gives you an elephant skin.

The best compliment you can receive as an MC is when, at the end of the night, they tell you that they thought the voice they kept hearing was in the record. Sometimes when I'm performing I'm stood behind the DJ or in a spot that isn't obvious, and the crowd can't see you but they can hear something.

For me, there's nothing better. I know I've done a good job when I hear people say that because it means everything fits, like it's part of the record. That's a good MC!

BILLY NASTY

Billy is a legend of the highest order, in my opinion. Despite his choice of football teams, he's a top bloke! Arsenal, by the way.

The first time I heard Billy play was at the Dance Valley Festival in 1995 and he immediately became an Amsterdam favourite. He was often booked for Mazzo, the legendary club my mates and I frequented every week, and various other events throughout the Netherlands over the decades.

My most memorable Nasty experience? It's got to be Leftism live in the Paradiso, Amsterdam, back in 1996. Billy was supporting Leftfield and played after their live set. It was the combination of an immense sound system, amazing, huge flashing bright white lights from the stage and Billy's choice of tunes that provided an intoxicating mix and the hairs on my arms still stand to attention whenever I relive that night.

Billy continues to rock dance floors worldwide and is a walking, talking techno institute. Head honcho at Tortured Records, Billy's techno flavour continues to serve up treats globally.

During our interview, Billy touched upon his early days, Amsterdam, a particular compilation mix photo shoot and touring with the mighty Leftfield.

I have been buying records since I was 13, over 30 years ago, and I first bought a set of turntables when I was 16 – before house music.

In those days I was into funk, rare-groove, hip-hop, and I was influenced and inspired by the likes of KRS-1, Public Enemy, Eric B etc.

It was around 1988-89 and the beginning of the acid house explosion when things started to change. I'd had my decks a few years by then, I'd mastered the art of mixing and it enabled me to leapfrog above other local DJs. I felt like I had mastered the craft, I was obsessed with precision and water-tight mixing, and acid house became my new sound and direction.

Being a smoker, I'd often visited Amsterdam when I was around 17-18, but it was only really a couple of years later that I started coming over as a DJ.

I first came to Holland as a DJ back in 1993 and Mazzo in Amsterdam was the first club that I played. Paul Daley, from Leftfield, had already played there. He knew the guys well and highly recommended it – especially as I was a big smoker at the time!

I was really intrigued about Mazzo. I'd heard a lot about it and I asked Paul if I could join him when he was next playing. He spoke with Cellie, who at the time was the resident DJ and all-round Mazzo chief. Much to my surprise, Cellie had heard of me and liked the music I was playing, so he offered to pay for a flight and hotel for me. But because it was Paul's original booking and he was on the flyer, I wouldn't receive any payment for playing but instead be a surprise guest. Fantastic! I was happy with that.

So, Paul and I both played at Mazzo together and the place just exploded. What a night! That was my first memory of Mazzo and there were many more to come.

Mazzo was the club that in those days, the early to mid-90s, was booking all the best underground UK talent. DJs like Darren Emerson, Fabio Paris, Paul Daley, David Holmes etc. were regularly rocking Mazzo. It was a great introduction for us as artists to such an amazing city like Amsterdam.

The Roxy, with Dimitri and his international guests, was probably Amsterdam's most recognised club but Mazzo had its own way of doing things and quickly built a very positive reputation in Amsterdam, especially among the British tourists who were pretty much guaranteed an underground British DJ or two during a Mazzo weekend.

Mazzo, for me, was MY generation. The days of Cellie, Carlijn, Steve Rachmad etc., amongst others, was a really great time for me. A massive help in my career and many great friendships made.

It was from those early trips to Amsterdam that I met Murph and Ricardo, two brothers that went on to form Dance Valley, as well as MC Marxman, Niels and Punan etc. and many more people from the early days with whom I'm still good friends today.

I played the first Dance Valley in 1995, then the second the following year and I was booked for the third edition. But my girlfriend at the time was pregnant with my eldest daughter and we were expecting her arrival the same week as Dance Valley so it was really touch and go whether I would make it or not. Florence was born on August 6th after a 30-hour labour and Dance Valley was August 7th, the very next day. We arrived home in the early hours with our beautiful new baby daughter and I had to leave less than an hour later to catch my flight to

Amsterdam.

With everything that had just gone on, no sleep and a brand new baby daughter to look after, I thought it was best to cancel so I called the Dance Valley boys and gave them the good news...then the bad news. What's really great is the video footage from that day which shows MC Marxman informing the crowd that I couldn't make it – and then telling them why! The whole Mainstage crowd was cheering at the news I'd become a dad for the first time.

Nice moment, despite missing the gig, and I've been back at the Valley a few times since. I had a Tortured tent one year and played their 21st anniversary in 2015.

In 1996-1997 Vincent McDonald, owner of Screaming Pixels and a photographer for music magazine Muzak, approached me when I was working for the Ministry and told me that he was a massive fan. At the time he was streets ahead of everyone and asked to do a photo shoot with me.

We had a good chat and I agreed to a few photos but I wanted a concept. We spoke about my gigs, speeding about in cars, nightlife etc. and he thought up a concept relating to my role as a DJ.

At the time I was working on a compilation called Race Data E.T.A and I sneaked a few racing car samples over the top of some of the tunes. That inspired him to create this racing driver image, complete with oil on my face and data cables coming out of my head. Knowing I was a vinylist, he used the platter of a Technics turntable in the background and set it amongst some clouds.

It felt good – I had the music and he had the photography skills. There was no CGI in those days, just a computer and a lot of know-how. He did all my early work and all my press shots. We got on so well I asked him to be godfather to Florence.

Back in the early 90s the Leftfield boys were good friends of mine. They still are and they would often come into the record shop, Zoom Records in Camden, London, where I was working. It was around this time that I also started to do some work with their Hard Hands label. We really connected and they asked me to support them on their first tour.

It was 1995 and the album Leftism had just exploded around the world. They were also nominated for that year's Mercury award so it was really going off for Leftfield at the time and it was great to be a part of their forthcoming first tour – the legendary Leftism tour!

The Paradiso gig in Amsterdam in April 1996 was the very first night of the tour and with me already known in Amsterdam from Mazzo it was great to have some local support to help with the nerves. Leftfield, on the other hand, were really nervous because it was the first time that these new cutting edge speakers and amps were being used, which produced this amazing 360-degree surround sound. And get this, the tour's sound guy, who had previously toured with Thin Lizzy and Led Zeppelin, was actually deaf!

No bloody surprise they were feeling nervous. This guy was a real Rock 'n' Roller, so what he thought was loud was *stupid* loud!

It was so loud that people were asking for their money back. People were holding their ears, stomachs, whatever, because the
279

bass just blew people away.

Before the tour began we were in the studio in London testing the system. There's a sweet spot, like the apex, in the middle of the room where you hear everything, but if you were stood at the back of the studio, in the bass-trap, it would bring your fucking dinner up.

For years everybody was complaining that sound systems weren't loud enough and for the first time ever there was a sound system that virtually blew people away! Still, to this day, Maz from Paradiso and many others still tell me how legendary that night was and that nothing has come close since – more than 20 years on.

Unfortunately, there's no pleasing everybody because the other DJ playing that night wouldn't stop complaining about it. Unbelievable. Wherever you were that night, you couldn't escape the music. Even if you were hiding upstairs under a table the bass still got ya!

Back then what we were doing was really cutting edge and wherever we have played that particular gig has always had legendary status. The Leftism tour really WAS legendary and because of that we always received an amazing reaction wherever we played.

My first Queensday [now Kingsday] in Amsterdam was an unforgettable experience. I had already worked with the Dance Valley boys, Murph and Ricardo, and they had booked me for their Queensday party in the Melkweg. They also had a coffeeshop, 222, where I'd spend a lot of time blazing away, and on this particular occasion I had my records with me for the party later that evening in the Melkweg.

Being Queensday, the city was rammed, absolutely heaving. Because of this Ricardo wanted to take my records to the Melkweg earlier in the day to avoid the crowds in the evening. And he wanted to take them on a boat through the Amsterdam canals! I was not having any of it. Absolutely no way. My records stay with me. I told them to pick me and my records up from the hotel before the gig but they wouldn't have it. "It's too busy, Bill, to walk through the streets with your record box," they kept saying. So, to shut them up, I agreed and handed over my records nervously. Just a couple of weeks earlier, Sven Vath had a box of records stolen and I wasn't happy with the arrangement.

Rightly so, I was really nervous.

I was introduced to the guy who was put in charge of delivering my record box to the Melkweg and I told him that, no matter what, I would be getting paid that night and I would be claiming double what we had agreed if anything happened to my records. I also mentioned I wouldn't use any other DJ's records either and it was his responsibility to look after them. "And don't let anyone fucking touch them," I reminded him.

I'd been drinking and smoking all day, so I said goodbye to my record box and went back to the hotel for a disco-nap. I agreed to be picked up at 2am and start playing at 3am.

Sometime before 2am I got a phone call in my room from Murph and he said: "Bill, there's a problem with your records...." I immediately thought they'd been stolen but Murph said they hadn't – they were wet instead. "What do you fucking mean they're wet?" I replied. He wasn't keen to talk over the phone so instead he came to the hotel and explained exactly what had happened.

The boat they were using should only have been carrying four people but 12 or 13 had jumped aboard and sunk the fucking thing. Everybody's overboard. The boat's sinking from all the water and my fucking record box is bobbing up and down in the fucking canal! And while all that was happening, I was asleep in my hotel!

They managed to get my records to the Melkweg, with water gushing out of the box and saturated sleeves. Ricardo wasn't too happy with the situation because he knew how anxious I was at being parted from my records. He took it upon himself to sort out the mess. Murph came to the hotel to update me on what was happening.

We left the hotel and headed to the Melkweg, which on a normal day is only 10 minutes away, but with it being Queensday it took us 45 minutes. We arrived and all I could see were my mates in a back room trying desperately to clean and dry the sleeves with hairdryers, while others were frantically wiping the vinyl. What a carry on. MC Marxman was trying to reassure me that the records were fine – but the sleeves were fucked!

Being Queensday, the streets were full of market stalls selling just about anything and Marxman – all credit to him – rushed straight to the nearest one selling second-hand vinyl and bought the whole fucking lot. He simply tossed the vinyl away and replaced the second-hand pop, folk, rock and country sleeves with my techno records.

I really couldn't believe what I was seeing. My sleeves were now Nana Mouskouri, Bon-Jovi, The Canary Island Trio, Tina bloody Turner and so on, with banging techno for vinyl!

Normally, I'd look through my records and recognise the sleeve but I had to look in every sleeve to see what record it was. Everybody was waiting for me to explode, but I managed to keep it together.

It's funny, because so many people have asked me about my records falling off a boat. They think it's the bloody Titanic or QE2, not a bloody four-man boat on the canals of Amsterdam. Well, now they know!

Sometimes there are obstacles in life and you just have to get over them and I often found that a bit of background drama actually made me play better. You won't catch me throwing a tantrum. I'm always eager to perform and, especially when the shit hits the fan, I'll always give 100 per cent.

It's in such moments that you earn your respect and my friendship with the Dance Valley boys just grew and grew. I quickly became a regular in Holland, and Amsterdam especially, over the next 20-plus years. I even moved to Amsterdam for a few years and I really see it as my second home.

In 2001 my record label Tortured put on a party in Amsterdam, again at the Melkweg, with Adam Beyer, Umek etc. Ahead of the party, the Melkweg asked me if I could contribute something. A souvenir perhaps, of myself or my label – something they could use in their glass cabinets to promote the party. I thought back to the time with the boat and my records getting a soaking, so I gave them the wet, soiled record box which had previously been seen bobbing in a canal – and they put it on display in a glass cabinet with a short story.

Brilliant. I love Amsterdam!

I can pretty much tell you that if Paul Daley hadn't told me about Mazzo all those years ago, then I probably wouldn't be where I am today. It's all down to him, cheers Paul!

Over the last 25 years or so there isn't a country in which I've performed more than Holland.

ARON FRIEDMAN

Not only a DJ and producer, Aron is also a music journalist. He has written for Resident Advisor and VICE, as well as transcribing for ID&T, the Dutch giant with enormous worldwide recognition and responsible for events such as Thunderdome, Mysteryland, Sensation etc.

Along with fellow Amsterdam DJ Eric de Man, they are known as Spaceandtime. They started producing together back in 2015, with releases for labels Krooks and Capsule. Their debut EP is called Desert Breath and features their first release, 85 Miles.

I first met Aron back in the early noughties when I was asked to play at Traffic. Techno was Traffic's preferred genre but had a second room for deeper, house type music, which is where I played.

Aron was a Traffic resident and co-promoter, along with promoter Daan Spoek and fellow DJs Boris Werner, Lauhaus, David Labeij and Bart Skils. They would often rotate from party to party and play in both the main room and second room, which was actually the cafe within the Melkweg. I played several times in the cafe and I absolutely loved it.

Mono and Household were other club nights which they all co-promoted and supplied the music for great nights within Amsterdam's historical nightlife. They certainly knew what they were doing, because they have all since gone on to bigger and better things, and nowadays are all internationally recognised artists.

For the interview, Aron spoke about his early days and introduction to Amsterdam's hedonistic nightlife, unexpected gigs in New York, first gig in Berlin, a certain Bulgarian road trip, co-promoting and a mescaline adventure.

I was 17 when I first experienced the nightlife Amsterdam had to offer. Together with my mate, we used to go to the Melkweg on Saturday nights to the Dance Arena. It was always a good bet that you'd hear some pretty decent music, often a mix of house, rap, hip-hop, techno etc. At 17 we didn't know any better – and we loved it.

There was one night, though, when we queued and eventually made it to the entrance, only to be told that our favourite night was not on that particular night! "Aaaarrrgh, damn, what are we going to do?" we said. Instead it was some night called Timemachine and because we had never heard of it, and it was not what we were after, we left.

I had already heard about the drug ecstasy and how people were dancing all night long, everybody was friendly and loved up, and this really intrigued me. My mate had connections with the kids in the year above us at school and he said he could arrange something and that the older kids go to the Timemachine parties in the Melkweg.

Aha, Timemachine you say?

Soon after, we managed to arrange some ecstasy pills and we made the plan to go to the next Timemachine. It was going to be our first time experimenting with anything like this, as we had never taken ecstasy before. Was I going to like it, would it like me, would I dance? My mind was anxious but it felt quite exciting at the same time and a new experience awaited us all.

We thought we'd take one E each on the way to the party and after some time we all decided it wasn't working, it wasn't for us and was nothing more than a complete waste of money. We were taking a tram into town and we were a little late, so we had to run to catch it.

BOOOOOOOOM, there it is. It's working!!!!!

We all, instantly, came up and the ecstasy was well and truly flowing. We had to try and keep it together on the tram and all I could think about was screaming with sheer joy because of the feeling I was experiencing!

We made it to the Melkweg and into Timemachine for the first time, and we were well and truly hooked. Quickly becoming regulars, we absolutely fell in love with it. The music, the people, the atmosphere and even the ice lollies – we had arrived! I even smoked my first joint at these parties, given to me by an old hippie in the cafe/chill-out area. I wasn't sure if it mixed well with ecstasy but the old dude said it was a perfect mix so I puffed away, and away, and away, and he was right!

I didn't want to go home at the end of the night, so we all went back to our mate's attic and chilled up there. His mum was pretty cool and she didn't mind us all congregating upstairs.
It was the following morning that I experienced a come-down for the first time and on top of that my mum wasn't very happy with me as I stayed out all night without telling her. We ended up having an argument and I spent the night in the nearby park after walking out. I wish I hadn't – it was pissing down.

I was so under the influence of the music and the people we'd seen at the Melkweg that I felt it was up to me and my friends to try to introduce a house music scene at school. There were a few gabbers but no one really took any notice of house, techno etc. We had to change this. Alternative rock was just too popular for my liking – the kids needed educating.

This was the first time I felt connected to a culture, so I convinced a few people to come with us the next time we went to Timemachine and, all of a sudden, a group was formed. We started going each week to various parties at the Melkweg, HQ for example, and all the other hard-house and techno events. It was vastly becoming our stomping ground!

There was a guy at school a couple of years older than me, Lauruz, later called DJ Lauhaus, who was already DJing. I used to watch him and I really got into it. I started to take an interest in the other DJs, knowing the record names, artists and labels, and felt like I wanted to do that. I asked my mum for a loan to buy myself a set of decks, a mixer, speakers etc. She obliged and I am truly thankful to this day. She could see that it was an obsession and I think she was just happy that I was obsessed about something productive.

I'm still obsessed today.

I moved away from home not long afterwards and I moved in with Daan Spoek. It was there that I turned my bedroom into a club with a disco ball and a DJ booth, whilst his room became the chill-out room – a very hazy chill-out room.

After some time the various parties at the Melkweg became a little repetitive for us and we felt like the purists of the scene. We had the urge to do something new and different within the hard

288

house scene. The Melkweg gave us the old room and we put a party together called Pumpers

The name didn't really work, to be honest. It was a play on pampers, the disposable nappies, with similar design but all the Dutch locals would pronounce it as poompers, obviously not our original intention but it was too late to change it as the flyers and posters had already been produced.

I had only been playing for seven months and I was already playing at my own party in the Melkweg together with Lauhaus and a couple of others who, after two parties, decided it wasn't for them and walked away.

For our first party we wanted to book a DJ from England called Dave Randall and local hero Danny D but we weren't sure if we could afford it and whether we'd sell enough tickets to pay his flight, hotel, fee etc. Fortunately, the owner of a coffeeshop – yes, the type selling weed – where I was working offered to finance the party and everything went according to plan. I had already decided I would play first, being the least experienced DJ on the line-up, and I had a plan.

I had managed earlier to get hold of a large supply of pills and before I started to play I had a panic attack thinking the club would be empty and that nobody would want to listen to me DJ. To combat my fears I asked my mate to give my supply to everyone outside for free. I thought it would be an investment, the perfect way for people to discover this awesome new DJ.

I was so nervous that my hands were shaking and I couldn't look up at the crowd because I was just too nervous, really panicking! Once I had done all my mixes fairly well, I thought 'Fuck it, I'm going to have a look' and as I peeked at the dance floor the
289

heaving mass of clubbers started cheering back at me because I had finally looked up from the decks. It felt great and made me think 'What was I so worried about?'

That was my very first gig, one I'll never forget.

In 2002 I managed to arrange my first international gig in Upstate New York. My father lives there so I would go and visit him for up to six weeks at a time and thought perhaps I could combine business and pleasure while I was in town. I knew there were a few local promoters who were regularly booking Dutch DJs, so I made it my mission to contact them and arrange a gig for myself.

I got in touch and they said they were busy organising parties in Syracuse, New York, and it wouldn't be a problem for me to play. OH MY GOD, my first international gig….and in New York. Suddenly my entire holiday was focused around this gig.

Finally the big day arrived and I had to find a way of getting there. Usually, I'd ask my dad because I didn't have a licence at the time. But for this particular occasion I didn't think it would be very cool to have my dad drop me off for my gig, so I decided to take a train and almost missed my set because the fucking thing was delayed for three hours!

I had all these ideas of how the club would look, the DJ booth and all. I was really starting to get excited by the prospect of DJing in another country.

So I made it to the club and I was stood outside. Full of nerves and excitement, I decided to make my way inside and much to my surprise it turned out to be a fucking amusement arcade. Boom, straight back down to earth with a bump.

The arcade machines had been pushed back to make a dance floor, which was empty because there was nobody there. On top of that, the lighting rig was a few coloured bulbs you'd see at a poorly decorated wedding do, set up next to the traffic light display.

There were a few candy ravers who insisted on giving me my own personal light show. Regardless of their good intentions and altogether loveliness, I was still disappointed with the entire scene.

Despite it being a quiet night there was some sort of turf war going on with two local gangs. Not long after I started playing I was ordered, in no uncertain terms, to "Turn the fucking music off…NOW!"

One gang member had drawn his gun on an opposite gang member and the place froze for what seemed a lifetime. It was probably just a few seconds to be honest but it was a hairy moment for me to say the least. I was then told to turn the music back on. Everything was okay and they had put their guns away. It was quite a normal occurrence apparently.

At the end of the night everybody was going to a party elsewhere. It turned out to be just 15 minutes from where my dad lived so they dropped me off at a petrol station along the way and, after some time, my dad picked me up.

My first international gig was a bit of a disappointment but a great memory nevertheless.

In 2012 I played in New York City but this time it was a themed party and everybody was dressed as characters from The Great
291

Gatsby, 1920s-style. I felt like a gangster from Boardwalk Empire.

It was a good night, pretty surreal with all the costumes, and after closing we went to an after-party at someone's apartment elsewhere in New York. What a place it was, an incredible apartment that must have cost several million dollars. It was very lavish, with gorgeous women, costumes and a party that seemed full of swingers – where the fuck had these people taken me?

It was actually a really cool atmosphere, despite my original concerns, and I really enjoyed it. The one thing that did irritate me was the bloody braces and trousers I had to wear. Don't forget, it was Gatsby style, not my regular Saturday night outfit, because it felt like my balls were constantly being pushed into my stomach. Ouch!

Most afters I've attended often have a source of music, whether it's a DJ or computer. But at *this* party the owner had a huge stage built in his lounge. Honestly, it was big enough for a full band, DJs, speakers, the lot. Let's party!

The party was in full swing, if you pardon the pun, and the homeowner came over to me and asked if I'd like to see his dungeon. What the fuck? A dungeon…at a party…in his house… Jesus, what's next?

He took me across to the corner of the room and there was this small door in the wall-type thing. He pulled on it and it opened up into, yes, you guessed it, his freaking dungeon. It was fully furnished, well-kept and really clean despite all the S&M action. It was even equipped with hooks from the ceiling for people to hang from.

What struck me the most about it was the homely IKEA hook systems with his neatly arranged sex toys. In his impeccable Brooklyn accent, he elaborated. "So on this wall we have awl the metal and on this wall we've got awl the leather," he drawled. What I did find slightly disturbing was the helmet in the corner, which looked like an 19th century diver's helmet, except without any windows to look through. I guess it just locked completely shut over someone's head. When my friend Jim asked what all the cameras were for, he replied: "Oh, those are just, uhm, for security reasons."

Bulgaria was another interesting experience. A few Amsterdam friends had recently bought a bar on the coast and were starting to organise parties featuring Dutch, and in particular Amsterdam, artists. They named it the Totally Romantic Bar, which would not exactly have been my first pick but I felt it was okay.

The name should have started to ring some bells, and all I could think about was what was going to be next and why I did this to myself. We already knew in advance that they would take care of the travel expenses, all food and sleeping arrangements, but no money for DJing. At least we didn't have to pay anything.

They had a complete programme planned for a total of three weeks. Many Amsterdam artists were booked for different days and it was being promoted all over Bulgaria but, despite all the promotion, it was empty as only a few people had turned up. My mates, Boris Werner and Lauhaus, were also going out there to play but at a different time than me. I was with a bunch of people I didn't really know that well. To be honest, with hindsight, I probably wouldn't have gone, but at the time I was just looking to play as much as possible. The offer to play elsewhere in Europe, especially Eastern Europe, was very appealing to me and my mates so we did it, but on different days unfortunately.

293

During one night, while I was asleep, there was this huge rumble and the hotel started to shake. I really panicked. It must have gone on for about 20 or 30 seconds but felt much longer. Robert Powlson, the other DJ I was sharing the apartment with, was standing on the sofa screaming hysterically. We had just experienced an earthquake. Being right next to the sea, he thought there was going to be a tsunami and so did I. We were still pretty wasted from the party earlier, so finding out what an earthquake was like and fearing a tsunami was pretty terrifying. The adrenaline was flowing, neither of us could sleep any longer and the following morning we went back to the bar. The local Bulgarian barman kept telling us how he'd never seen the sea look so wild before and how he feared something awful was going to happen. Was a tsunami going to happen after all?

We made our way to the top of a mountain, just in case, but the tsunami never came, much to everybody's relief.

The following day, two of the DJs that I had travelled with were playing in Romania and I decided to go along for the experience. It was supposed to be a five-hour drive to the location but it ended up taking us 14 hours. The Dutch crew were driving but they didn't have much experience on these roads and one guy, Robert, had previously been in a car accident and his mental trauma was getting the better of him. He was freaking out the entire journey and his girlfriend, who was driving, was freaking out at him. And we were in the back freaking out too. We had even left a petrol station without paying as none of our debit cards were working and no one had a credit card.

After stopping briefly, the driver wanted to swap so she slept on the back seat with Robert, and another DJ, Tommy Kornuijt, took over the wheel while I read the map. By the way, Tommy has
294

ADHD, so it was far from being the perfect driving scenario on the eastern European roads.

I was still wasted from the previous few days and I had the task of reading the map and directing us. At one point Tommy didn't know where he was, I couldn't read the map and a lorry was heading straight for us. We were in the wrong lane and I was in hysterics screaming at Tommy to move out of the way. Instead, Tommy smacked me in the face, because I was screaming so loudly at him. Fucking crazy. Robert was screaming from the back seat, I was screaming in the front seat and Tommy was trying to punch me, with the lorry's headlights getting bigger and bigger. Fortunately, Tommy swerved out the way just in time.

After some time we made it to the party but because we were so late it was already empty, although a few crazies were still going strong. One guy really took a shine to me, no idea why, and kept telling me how I was his special Amsterdam friend and how he wanted to give me a special time.

"Stop right there," I said. "You've got the wrong impression." Just as I uttered those words he buried his little Romanian head in my chest and kept telling me how he wanted to give me a special time so I could give him special music. Okay, I was beginning to understand this guy. He wanted to give me some drugs, so why didn't he just say so? But what he sold to us as ecstasy turned out to be Romanian herbal pills, whatever that meant. In any event, our trip was hilarious and full of colours. Once the ceiling started melting, my friend Wouter Smit and I had to go out for a walk to chill out, ending up in a huge dilapidated factory where we saw in the corner what we thought was R2-D2 from Star Wars. The Romanian party people had a good laugh when they saw us coming back with our new little friend because it was actually nothing more exciting than a bin on wheels.
295

After some time, probably a day or so, we headed back to Bulgaria and the same crazy roads through Romania. Because it was daytime, we were stuck behind bloody horses and carts on the pot-holed single roads. We managed to find the petrol station where we had previously stopped without paying so we filled up and paid the extra. Good karma.

We eventually made it back to our hotel in Bulgaria and I have never been so happy to be home, or in the hotel at least. I passed out and slept for a whole day.

The entire trip was an experience and I was so intrigued by Bulgaria, which I found to be a really adventurous and beautiful country.

When I eventually made it back to Amsterdam I went to a smart-shop to find out what I had been given in Romania and it turned out it was mescaline.

2012 was a crazy year for Eric de Man and me. We had our first joint booking in Berlin, Germany, at Katerholzig during the summer and it's true what they say about the party in Berlin never stopping. Clubs stay open for days on end.

The place was full and they even had hand-straps hanging from the ceiling on the dance floor, like you would find on a tram or the metro, to help those feeling the effects of a weekend inside one club. I actually found those hand-straps most useful.

During our set a wasted German guy kept coming up to Eric and I, trying to ask us something we couldn't understand. Every time, he was too wasted to actually make sense. Then he'd try signalling with his hands to no avail. The fifth time he came back around, he smartened up, with a written note in German asking where he could find the front door. The poor guy had been trying to get home for hours, not knowing how to escape the club.

Only in Berlin!

CRAZY SHAUN

The ex-resident DJ from Amsterdam's Club Roxy, alongside Amsterdam legend DJ Dimitri, the UK's Shaun Sutton has been a permanent member of the Amsterdam DJ elite for many decades now. Often performing at Dutch old-school reunions and parties, Crazy Shaun is still rocking dance floors.

Shaun has been a good mate for many years and you never fail to have a quality time when in the presence of The Crazy One.

Shaun spoke about the hassle of road trips to gigs, annoying flights and a certain memorable Amsterdam experience.

In 1994 I remember playing in Stuttgart, Germany, for the Red Dog boys, where I was alongside several American DJs.

Flights were really expensive, so we decided to hire a car, and thought we could save a bit of money seeing as it was Christmas time.

After our gig we headed out for a few Christmas drinks with the promoters and the DJs before we headed back to the club we had been playing in earlier.

Eventually it was time for me to leave but I had consumed so much Bacardi that I rather stupidly decided to use the service elevator to exit the premises. Unfortunately, I somehow managed to lock myself out of the club after the elevator door slammed behind me.

I was stood outside and remembered that my jacket, which was still upstairs, contained both my passport and my girlfriend's driving licence, which I had to use for the hire car. It was essential we had it for the drive home and to show if we were stopped by the police.

I was absolutely livid but I was just too drunk to comprehend and decided to go back to the hotel. I guess I must have thought I would be able to collect it all later, after a sleep.

That never happened!

My girlfriend had recently bought me a new pair of white velvet jeans, which I had on, but they had become very dirty in the club, so I put them in the bath tub to leave them to soak and went to bed.

My driver later woke me up and I immediately remembered my jeans. I took them out of the bath but they were soaking, obviously. I had nothing to wear for the journey home, so I had to steal the bathrobe from my room and wear it all the way back to Amsterdam. It was quite a moment explaining the story to the girl downstairs on reception, although she found it hilarious.

I fell asleep in the car and when I awoke two hours later we were half-way to Munich, which was in completely the wrong direction. My driver had taken the wrong turn earlier at some roadworks, so we had to turn around and head back the right way. Not what you want with a stinking hangover and naked except for a bloody bathrobe!

The original plan was to hire a car in order to save some money but in the end our road trip was twice as expensive as the flight would have cost.

We were also quite lucky that the border between east and west was already down, as we would never have been able to leave Stuttgart without a passport.

We had to return the hire car minus our passports, which wasn't ideal.

Fortunately the Red Dog boys, Ali and Basti, who is perhaps best known these days as Tiefschwarz, had found my jacket and its contents, and the next day posted everything back to me, so it eventually ended well.

When I was going through a bit of a dip with my DJ career I was fortunately booked for an after-party in Amsterdam at a club called The Akhnaton, together with fellow British DJ and legend Nicky Holloway. The dip was over.

The following day Nicky had to play in Coventry, back in England, but he was loving it. He was pretty hammered but didn't want to stop. He was staying at the Hotel Okura and after the party we went back to his hotel room, together with a mate of Nicky's who had flown over from Ibiza to Amsterdam to see him.

Nicky had to leave, but he didn't want to, and this caused a bit of an argument with his mate, who left for the airport and flew back to Ibiza. I took Nicky out around Amsterdam for a few drinks and eventually, after a few more laughs, Nicky made it home.

I had a crazy weekend of gigs back in 1996. I had a gig in Haarlem, near Amsterdam, on the Thursday, which was followed by a gig in Oslo, Norway, on the Friday, before flying to Prague in the Czech Republic for two more gigs on the Saturday.

I made it home after playing in Haarlem and had a bit of sleep before heading to the airport for my lunch-time flight to Oslo. I got to Oslo, went straight to the hotel and had another sleep before I was picked up and taken to the club.

When the club closed I was taken out for an after-hours drink. We made it to this one bar and we were drinking everything and anything. I looked at my watch and my flight to Prague left in an hour. I got my bags and managed to find a taxi. We made a quick stop at the hotel en route to the airport. When I finally got there the security woman wanted to check my record bag and proceeded to search every record one by one. It was only with seconds to go that I finally made it on to the plane.

It was a huge relief because not only was I flying to Prague, where I had two more gigs that night, but first of all I had to change in Gothenburg, in Sweden, and also in Frankfurt, Germany, before finally landing in the Czech Republic capital.

I think that was one of the most horrible experiences I ever had in my DJ career. Not so much the gigs, or having to play, but how I had to travel from A to B to C to D, which was just fucking nasty!

Back in 1997 I was invited to play in Zurich, at a swimming pool party, the same day as the Zurich Love Parade. All the big names from Europe were playing there and it was something that really appealed to me. I had played a couple of times before in Switzerland, so I knew they had a really good scene.

I had been looking forward to it, especially because I was playing with Germany's DJ Westbam. We had spent the afternoon together, leading up to the evening when we would be DJing together at the pool party.

Westbam was also playing on one of the trailers from Basel's Future Bass Junkies. His girlfriend, who was also his management, and my girlfriend Peggy and I went with him for what was a very enjoyable afternoon.

We headed back to our expensive, glamorous hotel, before later leaving for the pool party, which was situated on the outskirts of the city.

We had been very well looked after. We had a limousine from the airport and another dropped us off at the party. It was a glamorous affair. Of course, we were with Westbam, who, along with main man Dr Motte, had played his part in the creation of Love Parade in Germany.

We made it to the party but thought it was strange that there were virtually no people there. The promoter had only gone and forgotten the fact that a rival party was set up right near the exit from the city's street parade. This party was enormous and had a very attractive international DJ line-up. Incredibly, the promoter had forgotten it was actually happening.

He was expecting about 2,000 people, but no more than 500 turned up.

All the people leaving the Love Parade were going straight to that party, instead of his party. So Westbam and I had to play to a rather small audience. Despite the small crowd, they were still having fun in the swimming pool with all the inflatables.

It's funny, because earlier in the day, when Westbam and I were being driven about, we actually saw the location of the rival party. We thought that was where we were playing so went to check it out, only to be told that the party further down the road, by the swimming pool, was where we would actually be playing.

Straight away, seeing where the exits were, we both had the same view that everybody was going to go there and not to the pool party.

The low attendance cut into the promoter's budget quite a bit. I remember reaching the end of my set, just before Westbam came on, and his girlfriend said to me: "I think you should go to the office straight away and ask for your money." I didn't think too much of it at the time. By the time I actually went, after Westbam had finished, everyone had gone and the office was empty. I should have listened to her and gone to the office when she said. She was a very wise woman because Westbam was paid and I wasn't.

We went back to our hotel and I decided I would find the promoter because he was also staying in the same hotel. The following morning we spotted him heading for the car park, so I went after him. He told me to call him later and we could discuss the money. He then jumped in his car and sped off rather quickly. I should have stayed with him, or made him stay. I spent the rest of the day trying to phone him but he never answered.

We were originally in the south of France on holiday and while I had made some money from various gigs it was running out rather dramatically. I was relying on the cash I was supposed to be getting in Zurich. That was going to budget the rest of our holiday. It wasn't looking too bright for us and Peggy was in tears. "How can they do that to us?" she said. Peggy actually knew his girlfriend, so we felt really let down.

After some thinking, we realised we knew where he lived so we decided to pay him a visit. We then discovered his girlfriend had been taken ill and was in a hospital in St Gallen, about 30 kilometres east of Zurich, so we headed there to see if we could find him. We drove to St Gallen and spent a lovely evening in a hotel, which we thought of as an extension to our holiday. With lots of detective work trying to find which hospital they were in, which was actually a lot of fun, we did eventually find the right hospital and even the ward she was in.

We went to her room and we were sat at her bedside. She had just had an operation, but was still very happy to see us. She was unaware of the problems I was having with her promoter boyfriend. It turned out that he was actually funding his parties with her father's money and while he was apparently quite a rich man he wasn't seeing any return on his investments and was also owed a fair bit.

The girlfriend told us to hang about because her boyfriend was on his way to visit her. His face was an absolute picture when he walked in. "Oh, hello, what are you doing here?" he asked rather sheepishly. "I think we need to have a chat," I replied.

We went for a walk around the hospital grounds and he agreed to transfer the money to me. Peggy and I were heading back to the south of France to continue our holiday the next day so we arranged to contact him from there to arrange the transfer.

Or so we thought. We tried, of course, but never saw or heard from him again. I never did receive my money and it was a considerable sum in those days, 1,500 guilders.

Looking back, I should have just sat on him at the hospital and refuse to leave until I had received my money. But because of the situation with his girlfriend and his big sob story from the party, I actually felt for him.

About two months later I received a phone call from a well-known Dutch DJ agency. They were after my experiences with this particular promoter and they were keen for some feedback. Two of the agency's DJs had also been booked by this guy, prior to the street parade. They too experienced the same scenario, albeit without a hospital visit thrown in. They had expensive hotel rooms, complete with turntables and limos but were never paid their wage.

Basically an action replay of what I had encountered.

AWANTO 3

Steven Van Hulle is a Belgian musician and an adopted Amsterdammer. Since the mid-90s Steven has been a regular fixture within the more alternative party and underground music scene in the Netherlands. With many guises, he is currently best-known as Awanto 3. As well as being a DJ, Steven is also a conceptual artist and music producer.

No longer an Amsterdam resident, Steven has moved his studio and home life back to Bergen aan Zee, in the north of the Netherlands, where he lived originally back in the day. His old elementary school was forced to close but the space has become a home for many different artists, which is where he now has his studio.

Alias Poeh, Alfabet, Steven de Peven are among the other aliases he uses, although Alias Poeh was a long time ago, I've not heard that one in a while. Rednose Distrikt is another name and project that he now shares with the Dutch DJ, Aardvarck.

Steven is a serial producer, with releases on Tom Trago's label, Voyage Direct, Amsterdam's Rush Hour records, and not forgetting Amsterdam's Dekmantel label.

Back in 1996, I was playing with Steven on Radio Static, live from Amsterdam's Rembrandt Plein. The show was called Rebels with a Cause.

I'll always be extremely thankful to Steven for opening the door for me and my DJ career within Amsterdam. He gave me a platform to perform, and we had some truly great nights in that studio.

In 1996 I underwent surgery around Christmas. Nothing serious, thankfully, but my sinuses needed fixing. I left hospital and went home on the Friday, and later that evening I was playing with Steven on the radio. Perhaps, with the benefit of hindsight, not the best idea, as my nose kept bleeding throughout the entire show. Not what you need when you're busy mixing.

For the interview, Steven spoke about a specific gig, a war zone and an unbelievable road trip.

After moving to Amsterdam in the mid-90s I met some local DJs, who were who playing around the city. Soon after, they asked me to go and play in Croatia with them. This was my first experience as a DJ on tour and it wasn't that long after the war in Croatia.

This experience changed my life completely because there were so many negative incidents.

We went by car on a road trip. Fellow DJs Steso and Steven Slim were in the car, along with our friend Mladen and a Croatian woman who was basically our tour guide.

I can't remember her name but she arranged our accommodation whilst we were there. Nor can I recall where we stayed, but I do remember playing in the club in Split. The club was great but after leaving in our car we were pulled over by the local police.

We were driving in the mountains and we were being monitored by the police. We were a bit eccentric, straight from the club, and the police suspected we might be drug dealers on a delivery.

We were all taken to the local police station, where we were locked up in separate rooms. Except for our tour guide, that is. She wasn't arrested and stayed to try to help us at the police station.

Each room had five officers. In my room, one officer told me to undress. I took my clothes off, completely naked and they told me to stand on the table.

They picked up my clothes and began searching them, looking for drugs. They were all sat around me and began discussing the best way of killing me! They were talking in broken English and it was already too much for me. I was naked on a table, fearing for my life. I had never experienced anything like it and the level of fear was off the scale. As experiences go it was humiliating and I couldn't comprehend what, or why, it was happening.

My friends were in separate rooms, being interrogated by five officers each. It was far and away the worst experience of my life.

They said my family would never see me again and pointed out of the window to a garden where they claimed I would be buried. "We don't care," said one officer. They were insisting that they would find drugs on me and not even the knowledge that I had nothing could counter my concern.

Their investigation lasted for about 45 minutes. It was extremely disturbing and I don't mind admitting that I started to cry. I thought that was it and it seemed certain I was going to die. In my mind, I was already dead, because that's what they kept telling me.

308

I was trying to make eye connection but they looked very cold and evil. It looked as though I could see war and pure evil in their eyes. It felt that they were still in the mind of dealing with prisoners of war. I was feeling and experiencing how it must have felt to be captured during combat.

The police officers appeared to be enjoying the moment. They could hardly have looked more pleased with themselves and seemed to be relishing the fact that their threats were sinking in, to the extent that I was convinced my time was almost up.

During all of this I could hear our tour guide talking to the police in a separate room. She was speaking Croatian but was crying for forgiveness. Extremely upset, she started screaming and shouting at the police, begging for mercy.

They didn't find anything. No drugs, nothing.

Eventually, some time later, maybe 30 or 40 minutes, I was told to get dressed. I thought this was the moment I was going to be killed and buried in the garden, just as they told me. I was led out of the room and thankfully clocked the others.

Then, suddenly, they released us. At that very moment my life changed. I was so happy. I had been fearing for my life but now I was free.

We left, jumped in the car, and drove to our tour guide's house. We sat up the rest of the night discussing our awful, desperate and unforgettable experience.

Fortunately, it actually turned out to be the best night of my life. It had looked like being the worst but the difference in emotions in such a short space of time made it the best ever. You could say I was relieved and extremely grateful that we had all survived such a horrible nightmare.

The next day we left Croatia, minus our tour guide. She stayed behind and we drove to Slovenia. Annoyingly, we were stopped at the border. Mladen had some weed on him and when the officials searched the car they soon found it.

We were all locked in a portable plastic toilet, like the type you see lined up at festivals. The four of us were inside but all I could think about was how hungry I was. Steven Slim became angry with me. In fact, he was so unhappy with me moaning about food when we were all locked in a toilet that he even struck me.

"You're fucking hungry? We are fucked!" he yelled.

To be honest, I no longer cared, especially after what had happened in Croatia. Surely, I thought, nothing could compare to that.

The customs search also discovered a concealed bag with what looked like white powder under one of the seats. We looked at one another, with 'We are completely fucked' written all over our faces. I looked at Mladen and said: "You have fucked us with your coke." But Mladen replied: "No, no!"

Suddenly a nice officer came over and said that he owned exactly the same car as the one we were driving. He said he would check his car and see if it had a similar bag in it.

He had a look and, incredibly, he said he had also found the same sealed bag with white powder under the same seat.

It turns out that the particular package contained a special white powder that is used to help extinguish, or at least contain, a vehicle fire, something that the car manufacturer would have installed. What a stroke of luck.

We were told to go, released without charge. Again, Mladen had a small fine to pay for being in possession of the weed, but we were not in any more trouble.

We drove straight back to Amsterdam, without any more incidents.

Whatever has happened to me in my life, as well as the crazy moments when I DJ, it is nothing that compares to the desperate, life-threatening war vibes we experienced in Croatia. Nothing will ever beat that.

If something happens when I DJ, like someone entering the booth when I'm playing and trying to fuck me up, like with the Boiler Room gigs, it really annoys me. But it doesn't matter. Fucked people who want to keep touching my equipment when I'm performing really pisses me off. Yes, I might get angry – but, really, it doesn't matter.

It's nothing at all. Nothing compared to my Croatian experience. To feel like a war prisoner, you feel and sense the death in your eyes.

For everything that I have, and for everything that I get to do, I am truly grateful. Every second of life, I am very thankful to be free, as free as a bird. To be able to play music, be respected by promoters, treated like a king, is very rewarding and hugely appreciated.

Everywhere I play outside of Holland, to be invited to wonderful festivals to play and to every country where I've been invited to perform, I feel blessed to have this opportunity. I feel like a King.

Whatever I do, I'm blessed, simply because of my Croatian experience.

I'm blessed to be able to play my music, to be invited to perform, for people respect my music, and for the fact it provides me with a living. I do still have times when I'm broke and have no food in the fridge, but I always know that somewhere in the world there is always something worse going on.

We have to be really thankful for what we have. Every second of our life we must appreciate.

Be thankful for your freedom – until you are locked up. Then, take my word for it, you are well and truly fucked!

BORIS WERNER

Having cemented his place in the Dutch history books with the longest-ever DJ set, Wip-Wap Werner is one of Amsterdam's more popular exports.

Traffic, MONO and Household are historic Amsterdam club nights which helped introduce techno to a growing audience and Boris was a major part of it all.

With residencies and appearances at some of Amsterdam's most prominent nights and events over the past two decades, Boris has grown to be a Dutch favourite. His profile overseas has also grown immensely and he is a regular member on the European DJ circuit.

With some big hits behind his name, Boris has produced on some of the biggest labels. After releases on Remote Area, Get Physical Music, BPitch Control and many more, Boris is now busy with his own label, Caught In A Bubble.

I have spent many a Saturday night – and Sunday mornings – chewing the fat with this charismatic geezer in the Dutch capital. Never a chore.

I was also fortunate enough to DJ many times with him and the Traffic boys at the Melkweg. And I do remember a really great night where we were DJing together, alongside fellow Amsterdam DJ and actor Egbert-Jan Weeber. It was a Household night at Club 020 back in 2004, but sadly those days are no more. It was one of my most memorable gigs. Great crowd, atmosphere and nobody leaving early. I miss those days.

Boris spoke about tours, early days, Ibiza and memorable gigs.

New Year's Eve 2000 was an inspirational evening for me. I was at my mate's place, he was having a party and he had turntables. I had never used them before but I was immediately hooked, and I knew then what I wanted to become.

Fast forward seven months and I had my first gig.

Bart Skils invited me to play at the AMP Catacomb Studios in Amsterdam. I also played on Thursdays at the Vaaghuyzen in Amsterdam, together with another Amsterdam all-star DJ Steso.

From then on, it all seemed to move pretty fast. I joined forces with local DJs Aron Friedman and Lauhaus, plus local promoter Daan Spoek, and together we began putting on parties at which I became a resident. Daan was working at the Melkweg, which helped with arranging a venue, and everything progressed organically.

At the time it didn't appear to me that it was actually something I could do for a job but, instead, just having fun. I never thought about the bigger picture until I got fired as night manager from Bitterzoet – that's Bittersweet in English. The venue was sold in 2006 or 2007 and I lost my job, as did everyone else who worked there. The new owner didn't want to retain any of the old staff. I just thought 'Fuck it' and I decided to focus solely on music and gigs.

At that time social media wasn't like it is today; there wasn't much hype and the scene was still quite underground. But of

314

course it kept on growing.

I remember driving to an illegal party organised by local Amsterdam DJ, Dimi Angelis, with my girlfriend at the time, Lotte. The party was close to the German border, near Arnhem somewhere. I had a flyer with directions on it but it seemed impossible to find until a certain left turn and there it was. We had no clue where we were but that was the exciting part. That feeling doesn't happen anymore. Parties these days are sometimes not very special but it's not like I don't enjoy them. It's just a different feeling and the unknown is now known!

Nowadays, Seth Troxler tries to recreate the unknown, which I like. He promotes that old-school vibe, which was always evident at his birthday parties at Pikes Hotel in Ibiza.

Carlos Valdes booked Seth a while ago in Amsterdam and he called to ask me if I wanted to show Seth Troxler around the city before the gig. He was playing at The Flex Bar but we met up earlier in the day and I showed him around. We did the usual, record shops and coffeeshops, and I remember Seth bought some mushrooms too.

We went to the party but, sadly, there was virtually no one there. About 10 people in total. I don't think Seth minded and he just ate his mushrooms during his set.

I always knew Seth would go on to have a successful career he has gone on to have. A lot of love and passion, great DJ, great guy. I couldn't be happier that he has become the artist we all recognise today.

I was doing a Boris 'Wip-Wap' Werner show at Studio 80 in Amsterdam. It was a while ago, back in the time when I was

315

playing marathon sets. I played a 10-hour set followed by an 11-hour set, which led to a 15.5 hour set, and at the last party I managed a 22-hour set.

The 10-hour set took place on 10-10-2010 and the 11-hour set was on 11-11-2011 but the date of the planned 12-hour set – 12-12-2012 – didn't work because it was a Wednesday rather than a weekend.

For those gigs I had some friends playing in the second room alongside the catering for the evening.

Years ago my girlfriend at the time gave me some capsules, which I just threw in my record bag and forgot all about them. Four months later, while travelling around Europe performing, I discovered that I still had two bags of 10 capsules in each, 20 in total, just sitting in the bottom of my record bag. They had been there since my last marathon gig at Studio 80. In that time I had also done a gig in America, but for some strange reason I decided to change record bags. Thank God I did. If I had taken my original bag, I would have been completely fucked. Thankfully, I never had any issues, despite the seriousness of what could have been.

But let's go back to my 22-hour set. The German DJ Karotte told me years ago that when you're playing these long sets it's essential you try to stay sober for as long as you can. To be honest, *they* were the longest hours. I managed five hours sober and in the beginning I wasn't sure how I would manage it, but I did. There was a fruit punch going around the club, with a little extra added to the drink, just to keep the dance floor shuffling. If I was there for 22 hours so were they.

Before I knew it I had passed the 15-hour mark but I was

surrounded by a vinyl mess, with records everywhere! I only actually played one record twice but it was deliberate. I had taken five crates of records with me but I also played some digital music.

As if 22 hours wasn't enough, after finishing my set I went to a friend's house for an after-party. I was sat smoking joints but all I could think about was the tracks that I *didn't* play. I was still in this loop of playing, but selecting records in my head.

I can't exactly remember which edition it was of those marathon sets but so many of my friends didn't want to leave the party. They actually had major arguments with their partners when they eventually made it home.

I only actually went to the toilet once during those evenings. I was so hot and I guess I managed to sweat it all out.

Studio 80 is sadly no longer and I haven't since found the right spot to try to continue those nights. I would like to do it again but I have the idea to do it outside during the day and finishing indoors. It's possible that one summer I will do it all over again. Maybe Thuishaven in Amsterdam, who knows?

Dutch journalist and founding Quazar member Gert Van Veen will tell you that it's the longest-ever DJ set in a club in Holland.

That's nice, but it wasn't my aim. It's the experience that counts for me, rather than the amount of hours.

Nowadays, when people ask me what I do, I don't feel it's that special any more to say I am a DJ. If I tell someone I'm a DJ and a producer, people often reply, for example, 'So is my little nephew, he's six.' I've been busting my balls for the last 20 years and now kids can become an instant DJ when they're not long out of nappies?

It's really easy to make music with a computer and the labour and effort no longer seem to be an essential part of it any more. Anybody can make a beat on their laptop, which is nice, but the creativity nowadays can be really hard to find.

Everything sounds the same. There are some dynamics but there are too many big breaks in the music. I certainly had some crappy records back in the day but it was my job as a DJ to make them work. Nowadays, there are buttons to do it for you.

Sadly, it seems the art has gone.

When I started out in the late 90s the scene wasn't established as it is today. We would go to illegal parties, Mazzo too, and the scene and music was still underground.

House music then started to be played in commercial clothing shops on the high street. The scene wasn't underground anymore; you could hear the music anywhere. Like with pop music these days, 70 per cent is made up of a house beat, often with a vocalist.

Unfortunately, it has become the norm nowadays. I want to put the anarchy back in the scene!

I'm really happy I was a part of the original underground scene, which I guess was probably the second wave after the acid house scene.

There was a time that my career and focus began to decrease, plus I was having no interest in my social media, which is quite important as an artist. I wasn't feeling the urge to produce either. I didn't want to be in the position that I *had* to produce music, just because I was a DJ, but nowadays it all seems to roll into one. Internationally it kind of makes sense, due to the fact so many people can do it. There are a lot of ghost producers too, who do the work. But the DJ's name promotes the music and just creates, in my opinion, pop music.

One night in DC-10, in Ibiza – it was in 2016 as I recall – I was playing on the terrace for Circoloco. I had been playing there since 2010 but never on the terrace. That was the place I had wanted to play for a while and finally I was there. For me, that was *the* place to play.

On this particular night, I remember I was super high on adrenaline and energy, plus I had a really good slot time. The whole party was banging.

It was really going off when suddenly a friend of mine suddenly tapped me on the shoulder. "I want you to meet Ricky Martin," said my friend. I was like 'Sure, that's okay' and we shook hands. He said he liked the music, and I said thanks before turning back to the decks. That was a super weird experience.

Also, in 2015 I was playing together with my mate William Djoko at The Secret Garden Festival in England, which was the scene of another weird experience. There was a tent on the site staging a sweaty lingerie party and you weren't allowed in unless you were dressed accordingly. My mate, Ed Karney, knew we were going to be at the festival and he actually bought us some lingerie to change into so we could get into the event.

I was going to wear it naturally but I had to put my boxer shorts on underneath because my balls kept popping out.

We went in and everyone was off their tits. I was sat on this piece of fence, smoking a cigarette and drinking from what appeared to be a jar of pickles, except it didn't contain any pickle juice. Everyone was taking pictures of me but I didn't care.

The next morning I woke up with a stinking hangover to find I had actually missed my flight. I had to leave immediately, jumped in a taxi and headed for Heathrow Airport to arrange a new flight. But after looking at social media on the way, I saw my mate Tom Trago had posted a picture from the party of me in the lingerie. I wasn't happy.

Motherfucker!!!

There were a lot of photos taken and to be honest it was probably the best of a really bad bunch, so it could have been worse. I was trying to convince myself it wasn't that bad but at first sight it was hard to swallow. Still, I wasn't happy.

In December 2016 I went to Australia to play for Circoloco in Melbourne. I had a gig, followed by a gig at an after-party, before playing in Perth the next night. I considered it to be an ideal opportunity to promote myself and enjoy a mini-tour at the same time.

So I left Amsterdam on the Wednesday and arrived in Melbourne on the Friday morning. During the day I took in some local culture and visited several places of interest with a girlfriend of mine who lived there. I wasn't even that jet-lagged when I arrived.

I played that evening, then the after-party, then travelled to Perth to play the next night. After the gig in Perth I was driven to the airport for my flight back to Amsterdam. I ended up doing a three-day tour of Australia, but considering the time difference over there, I never actually acclimatised in the three days I was there.

In total it was three full days of travelling and I was only there for three days, with a combined total of six hours DJing.

In retrospect, it didn't make any sense. It was an intense time and considering I went there to promote myself I haven't been asked back since.

I've had numerous weekends where I've played three countries in one weekend, usually starting on a Thursday or a Friday. One of those gigs always resulted in no sleep due to my travel commitments.

I once flew from Los Angeles to New York during a mini-tour of the United States back in 2017. I had been playing in LA then I headed off to another party where my reckless side took over, before leaving for the airport. I was flying to New York and I was convinced I was flying with United Airlines. I went to the check-in and there was nothing under my name. After a bit of searching, I discovered I was actually flying with American Airlines, which required me to be at a totally different terminal, and I had only 30 minutes to make it.

I was dehydrated, sleep deprived and high as a kite. I had to first go through a security check. I then asked the security people for help because I couldn't get it together while trying to catch my breath after my frantic dash from one terminal to the other. They told me where to go and that it wasn't a problem. I left and walked right through an emergency exit, which raised an alarm.

"SIIIIIIRRRRRRRR, what are you doing?" yelled the security guy directly at me. I thought I was going to be kicked out for the fact I was in such a state. But somehow, and I'm still not sure how, I was shown the way to go with a new ticket in my hand. But it got worse. I managed to lose my ticket somewhere between the check-in gate and boarding the plane. I didn't remember which seat I was in either. The flight was fully booked. I was asked which seat I was in and when I explained I had lost my ticket they suggested that I should just find an empty seat. I gestured to the other passengers that I was sorry for being late, but I don't know why.

I found a seat, jumped in and thought that was that. But when I sat back, ready to relax, someone said: "What are you doing in my seat?" Confused, I got up, grabbed my stuff and walked towards the back of the plane. The stewardess pointed to a seat and told me to sit down. As soon as my head touched the headrest I fell asleep and I didn't wake up until we were in New York.

After I woke up I could see people looking at me and they seemed to be annoyed. I was told that I was snoring really loudly during the entire flight. Funny thing is, it's not the first time I've been told that after a flight. The noise of the plane is really soothing, well to me anyway, and I never have any trouble falling asleep. Sorry guys.

Another time, when I was playing in Detroit, the day after the gig I went to TV Lounge and played a daytime Sunday set. I was given some LSD, but it didn't feel right taking it because I had to play. I was assured it was going to be okay so I went ahead and took it. Six hours later, after the party had long finished, I was looking for something to do. I was on an adventure and in the distance I spotted a casino, which I suggested we should all visit.

322

After 20 minutes I had won 600 dollars, so we left in a hurry.

We went to a friend's place but I had totally forgotten about my early flight the following morning at 10am. My mates were telling me I had to leave soon for the airport but all my stuff was still at my hotel.

I went back to the hotel, completely buzzing, but I discovered I had lost my key card. Reception needed some ID from me before they could issue a new card but I told them all my ID was locked in my room.

They decided that someone had to escort me to my room. She opened my door and I showed her my passport but she didn't leave. She just stood there, half-smiling at me. She was waiting for a tip but I said: "I think we are done here." I felt quite bad for the girl, actually, but I just grabbed my stuff and went back to my mate's house to continue the party before eventually leaving for the airport.

Everything was fine in the end and I slept like a baby. Probably snored all the way too.

In 2018 my family joined me at the Loveland Festival in Amsterdam. It was great to DJ and see not only my mum and dad, but also my two sisters, boogying on the dance floor.

Currently, I enjoy playing at Bret, which is next to Sloterdijk station in Amsterdam. It's constructed from red containers. It opened as a restaurant but they have parties there too. It's a place where everything just comes together. Everything makes sense, there's always a good vibe and it keeps moving on in the right direction. Everybody is just nice to each other, which seems to happen all the time. I'm always hyped-up to go there. It's crazy but it's hard to describe why. The music is just so on point and uplifting, none of that minimal house stuff.

It's good to see the other DJs too. They are much younger than me, playing sophisticated and mature music.

Recently, I have started a new label, Caught In A Bubble. I'm signing press and distribution deals as we speak. The name really makes sense to me because I have actually been caught in a bubble for some time. My first release is called Caught in a Bubble, funnily enough, and it features local DJ San Proper on vocals, guitar and bass. He came up with the name and was kind enough to give it to me to use. Ion Ludwig is also going to do a remix before I then have to master everything and it will be ready for release.

Plenty more to follow, hopefully, so keep an eye out.

DARREN EMERSON

Darren Emerson has, more or less, been a part of this evolving international scene since the very beginning and has grown to be one of the world's more influential figures. After his Underworld efforts, glorious DJ sets across the world and collaborating with the likes of Depeche Mode and Bjork, among others, he's certainly earned his stripes.

He's also head honcho for labels Underwater and Detone, and has helped spread the Global Underground vibes around the globe with some classic sets.

When I met Darren backstage at the Wooferland Festival in Amsterdam he actually initially found me and came bouncing over with a big hug. I was really blown away by his friendliness. We'd never met and he basically had virtually no idea who I was. It was only the night before that Darren had actually agreed to be interviewed. I was sitting alone on a picnic bench and Darren just popped his head round the corner. He recognised me, came bounding full of smiles and asked how I was.

What a great start to an interview. I asked him how he knew it was me and he said he'd been looking at my social media. Pretty obvious, really, but it did fill me with encouragement and confidence, so cheers Daz!

Darren is still an active member on the DJ circuit, and long may it continue.

For this interview, Darren touched upon his rise to fame, joining Underworld and being chased by the police.

My mum and dad were both stylistics. They loved their soul and with my love of electronic music, the two seemed to fit together nicely. Farley Jackmaster Funk, Robbert Owens, Afrika Bambatta and Kraftwerk were favourites of mine and I could really connect with the soul that they were incorporating into their music. I even had decks at 14, just because I loved breakdance and I wanted to be the next Grandmaster Flash.

I had an ear for all sorts of music in the early days. I remember the Jacking-Zone on Tuesdays and Thursdays, and DJ Jazzy M's weekly shows on LWR pirate radio in London. That was where I was introduced to the Chicago house sound. Jazzy had a contact in Chicago, Rob Olsen, and he would receive all the tunes and artist updates via him.

Jazzy M got me out and about and then the acid house scene blew up, and with Nicky Holloway already doing Trip at the Astoria the whole scene just went crazy.

I started to appreciate all styles, especially the Balearic sound. I was into alternative music, and started to appreciate guitars too, especially bands like The Wooden Tops and The Cure.

In those days, coming from Essex, we all thought we were cool and looked the part. It is only when, as a 16-year-old, you head to the parties in London, that you realise you're not cool, especially not in white floppy socks.

We were going to places for the first time, like Ibiza for example. It was, to us Essex boys, a really weird initial experience. We'd not been in a bar with transvestites in Essex, but this whole scene we were a part of in Ibiza was great - weird but great. New clubs and nights were popping up back home, a new scene emerging, and it was a scene that I wanted to be a part of.

Since 1988, I've been to Ibiza a lot and especially loved the sounds from DJ Alfredo. I loved the breakdance scene, too, and basically any music that was electronic based. The whole Balearic scene was starting to grow back in the UK, thanks to Paul Oakenfold, Nicky Holloway, Danny Rampling etc. I was going to Future and Spectrum in London, where Paul was always rocking it.

Paul is my hero. I love Paul.

I always enjoyed the warehouse parties back in the early 90s. In Essex, we would go to Twilight and head to Sunrise afterwards, where Carl Cox would be playing. Some gangster vibes perhaps, and I was forced to play for hours on end, but looking back it was a great time.

One particular gig, a huge solid lump of concrete crash-landed on top of the turntables.

I first met Carl Cox when he was doing the sound for a Paul Oakenfold night, long before he became the artist we all recognise today. It was in Rainham, Essex, and it was long before the mayhem took over. I was 16 or 17 at the time. All the DJs that I looked up to were playing at this warehouse party, while Carl was in charge of the sound.

At the time I was a young DJ from Essex and my career was starting to take off. I was playing at the Milk Bar, which Nicky Holloway opened back in 1990, and the Limelight Club with

Johnny Walker, both in London. I also played together with Carl Cox in the back room at Turnmills in London, on Wednesdays, back in 1987.

Fucking great days. I was young, but having a great time!

It was through these gigs that I met the brother-in-law of Rick Smith, and he mentioned Rick had a really cool studio.

I also started a record label called Effective Records, and our first release was Passion by Gat Decor, which featured a remix by me, back in 1992.

In '92 Rick and Karl were interested in the dance music that was beginning to emerge, and they wanted a DJ on board. Their rock band had previously been dropped by their record label and they were interested in the new dance music. I did listen to their music – it was okay – but they wanted something different.

It was a bit of luck really that I got involved, but we spoke and sorted it out. They had a really nice studio, and I wanted to be involved – because *I really liked that studio*. I basically told them all I knew, what worked and what didn't. Rick was explaining his studio to me and we kind of learned from each other. I remember Rick was showing me his new 909, and I just thought 'Wow, this is fucking amazing. I want to be a part of this.'

It was my name that really made Underworld what they were, and still are. I'm not trying to big myself up, but I was involved in the dance scene and was beginning to make a name for myself. I was getting media attention, especially from FACE and also ID magazine, where they made me DJ of the Month, which, in those days, was a big deal.

Paul Oakenfold was working with Happy Mondays, Andrew Weatherall was working with Primal Scream and I thought I could do the same.

Soon after, I was invited by Paul to his Perfecto office and he said he wanted to sign me. He wanted me to be involved with his label and do some remixes, but Rick wasn't too keen. He asked me why I would even consider it, but I really looked up to Paul. Did I mention he was and still is my idol? I would always be open to what he had to say, but decided it wasn't the right thing for me.

It was a busy time. I was in the studio with Rick and Karl, and I thought it was a bit much to be honest. The Effective thing was cool, but I thought 'I'm working with those other two now' and decided I needed to invest more time in that.

Originally, Rick wasn't too keen. He wanted to go off and do other things, but the two of us worked it out and began producing new music together.

It took us a little while, I'd say a couple of years, before it started to work the way we wanted it to. We used different names to begin with, like Fat Gonzalez, Lemon Interupt and Big Mouth, for example, before Underworld – Mk2.

Rick and I got to know each other inside out, but in the beginning Karl was often away. After their original band was dropped, leaving them skint, Karl went to Los Angeles.

It was when Karl came back from LA that the lyrics and vocals took shape. In the studio, Karl would ask how he could sing over the beats. He had his own unique style which would complement the cut-up beats I was creating. Karl kind of reinvented himself

329

in a way. The two of us really started to connect, as he'd been over in Los Angeles, and it was originally just Rick and I working together. Soon the three of us were rocking!

We performed so many shows worldwide, but the Pink Pop Festival stands out as probably our best gig in Holland. Japan was always a great experience, always rocking.

Playing the Pyramid Stage at Glastonbury back in 1999 has to be my most memorable Underworld gig. We were on after Texas, and before the Saturday headliners, Manic Street Preachers. The sun was just starting to set and it was a beautiful scene.

Just before our set I was elsewhere at the festival, playing back-to-back with Carl Cox, which was actually broadcast live on BBC Radio 1. I'm really shy, believe it or not, and don't like talking. So, to be honest, I was more worried about DJing with Carl and talking on the radio than I was performing live on the world famous Pyramid Stage.

As Underworld, we didn't have a set-list, and just before we went on stage, we looked at each other and discussed what song we should start with. It was always different from gig to gig; we never had a plan. We usually just went with what felt right at the moment. One night it could be Rez, the next something else and we just did it.

We were just rocking, full on improvisation, and we did it well!

Sometimes we did shit our pants, but the nerves always made us work harder and we always rocked it. There was the thrill of it, too, as we never had a plan. What's next? We never knew, we just did what felt right at that moment.

I haven't looked back since. I put a lot of hard work in, really grafted hard.

During an Australian tour, I remember an occasion in Melbourne with Huey Morgan and his Fun Lovin' Criminals.

I had decided to stay an extra night in Sydney, while Karl and Rick headed to Melbourne. It all relates back to a girl that Karl was previously involved with, and that a current Fun Lovin' Criminal was now with. Unknown to me at the time, Karl had previously written some lyrics about him, which were subsequently released on a track, and the Criminals weren't having it.

Rick and Karl were in Melbourne at the same time as the Fun Lovin' Criminals and they surrounded Karl and Rick and had a run-in. As I mentioned, I had stayed an extra night in Sydney and so, unfortunately, I missed it.

I arrived in Melbourne the following day, heard what had been going on, and thought it was best for all concerned that we sorted it out. I decided to go to the Criminals' after-party, much to the annoyance of Karl and Rick, who had told me to stay away. Their head of security was on the door and I actually knew him from the old days. He was happy to see me, we spoke and had a catch-up. The whole discrepancy was put to bed.

As a band, we never had the maddest time. Karl had stopped drinking and Rick didn't drink too much. They weren't rock and rollers – that was my job. I was the rocker, since I was in the club scene and they weren't. I was going out and fronting it, basically.

If I hadn't come from that scene, perhaps Underworld Mk2 might never have happened.

331

Our job, as a DJ, is basically sitting on our arse. It really is. With all the travelling, it's just a nightmare, but with some great experiences along the way.

Uruguay was a special moment, in 2000, when I recorded my first Global Underground mix. Being in South America for the first time with my mates, and a few others, was a great time. We would spend days cracking on. I can't remember too much of it – so we know we had a good time!

There have been a few occasions when I've arrived home after a gig, only to realise that I've forgotten, or lost, my records, including special acetates of exclusive Underworld live tracks. I've even jumped back in the car and driven back to the club to find them.

One such occasion was after playing at the Drum Club. We were so close to the club, but the bloody police pulled us over as we were speeding. The club was only around the corner so I decided to make a run for it, so desperate was I to be reunited with my records. The policewoman chased me and stopped me but, eventually, she did actually help me get my record bag back!

Another panic is when you're playing with USB sticks and you realise, when you're about to start playing, that you've got your mates' sticks rather than your own.

It was the Beat-Herder Festival, in Lancashire, England and 24 hours earlier I was playing elsewhere with Danny Howells and Dave Seaman, whose sticks I had mistakenly taken. Beat-Herder was a more techno set and I was stood there with Dave's music!

Luckily enough, I had some back-up music in my bag, which

saved the day and no one was any the wiser – until now.

DJ DIABLO

In 1987 Daniel Englisch, aka Diablo, caught the house bug after tuning into Amsterdam radio station Radio 100. It soon spread around his school, with all the school kids amazed by this new sound. Three years later he bought his first set of turntables and DJ Diablo was on his way.

Diablo is an Amsterdam all-star after working in the legendary Groove Connection record store and promoting parties such as Nightbreed and Underground Heaven. He is also co-owner along with Ziv Avriel of Amsterdam techno label Defuse Records and deep house label Cosmic Disco Records.

Daniel and I have made a few tracks together over the years in his studio, including Supadupadose, Spooky and the 808 State tribute remix of Cubik, which are all available to hear over on my soundcloud page – soundcloud.com/kreed.

I was also fortunate enough to have two tracks released on Daniel's Cosmic Disco label, too, including the Is This Soul EP. We also enjoy playing back-to back, often in Amsterdam's Kashmir lounge.

That was before the irritating worldwide lockdown consumed the world which is, in my opinion, extremely excessive.

For this interview Daniel spoke about his unforgettable trip to DJ in China.

Enjoy...

Back in 1997 I was busy organising the Underground Heaven parties, my own organisation, in Amsterdam, and playing regularly at various clubs and parties in Holland, but especially Amsterdam. I was putting on events at Mazzo and Trance Buddah, and everything was going well.

At the time I was also working at Groove Connection, a record shop in Amsterdam, together with the owner DJ JP.

Times were good, but they never seem to last! Unfortunately, as I had imagined, it wasn't long before all this started to change.

It wasn't long after that when Trance Buddah closed, to later re-emerge as The Bulldog Hotel, and Mazzo was soon to follow. This left an unfortunate gap in the underground nightlife Amsterdam had to offer.

Everything was changing and there was nowhere to organise my Underground Heaven parties. The obvious locations were gone, the gigs started to dry up and so did the work at the record shop, unfortunately. I decided it was time for a change; time to start something new.

One morning soon after, while I was reading the local paper, I noticed an advert asking for DJs, musicians and dancers to go to China and perform at a club for a whole season, anywhere between three to six months and with an extension to one year if necessary.

I had nothing to lose. 'Why not,' I thought, 'I'm going to apply.' The thought of being paid to DJ in China for several months, plus having food and accommodation provided as part of the deal, all sounded too good.

The idea was to introduce a more western type nightlife culture to China, less mainstream but more electronic underground music, with house and techno being most preferred. 'I can do that, it's what I do,' I thought.

I applied but after talking to some DJ and musician friends in Amsterdam I learned they had also applied, plus many others besides.

After hearing this I wasn't feeling quite so confident. Time seemed to move slowly in the weeks that followed. I was checking every day to see if anything had happened. I had started to give up on the whole idea until one day I received a letter saying I had been selected to DJ and, coincidentally, three of my friends would be joining me. One was Freddie Cavalli, the bass player from Herman Brood's band – Herman Brood & His Wild Romance. The second was an American called Matthew Williams, who was an R&B and soul DJ living in Amsterdam and he was also DJing on Dutch national radio. My friend Leoni was selected to be the dancer.

The four of us met in Amsterdam before we left for China. It was nice knowing that we would be sharing this experience together and we tried to prepare ourselves as much as we could before we set off on our adventure into the unknown.

We were heading for Chengdu, the fourth largest city in the People's Republic and the capital of Sichuan province in the south west of the country. We flew to Beijing and then had a six-hour transfer to Chengdu. Tycho, the guy responsible for placing the advertisement in the paper, was already over there and he would be looking after us while we were in Chengdu.

Tycho picked us up and drove us to our home. We were greeted by an older woman, who would basically be our host and cook for the time we were staying there. She didn't have much money – no one did to be honest – but she took so much pride in helping us with basically anything we needed. She was lovely and she really made us feel welcome.

Also present was Tycho's older brother, who was also assigned to drive us around and generally take care of us. After chatting with him it soon became clear that he was a high-ranking officer in the Chinese military, while their parents were both Army generals situated in Tibet.

Tycho, the black sheep of the family, had escaped Tibet with two Dutch nationals many years ago and was smuggled into Holland. He managed to find work, save some money and opened his own Chinese restaurant, plus a Tibetan restaurant with more to follow over the years.

This was how the opportunity to go to Chengdu came about, after he discussed it and made all the arrangements with his older brother.

Upon arrival we were given a contract to sign. All very official, you might think, but it turned out to be only good enough to wipe our arses with! Total lies, every word of it.

Seeing as it was a modern western nightlife scene that they were trying to build, I thought it was best to pack my finest house and techno records, which were previously rocking Amsterdam dance floors. Now I was trying to do the same on the other side of the world in China!

They actually wanted me to bring a mixed bag of sounds, in case they didn't like the boom, boom, boom stuff. I had a load of hip-hop and reggae music available as back-up but as soon as I played some house, then techno, the place went mad. They really loved the techno and the crowd went ballistic. From that night on, the hip-hop and reggae stayed at home.

Matthew, the American Amsterdammer, would MC and do percussion during my set, as well as performing solo. Freddie would also perform a solo set, playing Bass and the piano. Everything seemed to be going well, we were all doing what was expected of us and we were being well received by those in the club.

On the third night I was approached by a man in the club who asked me to go to his table and talk to him. He was from the rival club in Chengdu and he had heard about the artists from Amsterdam who were in town. He made it clear he wanted a bit of the action.

We were actually the first Western DJs and artists to visit China since Michael Jackson had spent seven hours on Chinese soil, only we were performing and MJ wasn't.

This guy told me he could arrange everything and anything for me, and that he wanted me to quit the club and leave the rest of the gang to go and DJ in his club on my own. He was going to make me a star, he said. But much to his disappointment I declined his offer, left and went to DJ.

A few nights later a bunch of well-dressed guys in expensive suits came in. I was playing at the time but spotted these guys at the back of the club when one of them gestured to me to come over. I had a full dance floor so I couldn't just stop and walk away.

I then noticed them pushing Freddie, Matthew and Leoni into a backroom. I immediately stopped playing and ran over and followed my Dutch family into the room, where we had Chinese police badges held to our faces.

We were fucking terrified!

They asked to see our passports. No one else had thought to bring theirs out but I happened to have mine in my bag, although I didn't let on and instead told them I didn't have mine with me either. The last thing I wanted was for the four of us to be split up.

We were all taken to the local police station, where we were, strangely, all interrogated together in the same room except for Leoni, who was escorted elsewhere.

The head of police was a funny character, as were all of them to be honest. He was talking to us loudly in Chinese while smoking his cigarette. He would hold it between his fingers in like a V shape, a bit Star Trek-like. He was taking a drag, blowing smoke in my face and asking me all sorts in Chinese. It was just like something out of a movie, so surreal.

Matthew and Freddie both had about six police officers interrogating them, all shouting in Chinese at the same time. What did they expect to uncover? We didn't understand a bloody word!

As time passed, the police just seemed to be repeating themselves with no actual gains and I thought this was a good sign. I began to feel at ease and believed I had nothing to fear as I hadn't done anything wrong. Or had I?

I gave Matthew a reassuring nod, only for him to respond with a terrified look on his face. Clearly, he was anything but at ease and even gave me the right-hand flick across the neck gesture, which suggested he really believed his time could be up.

My thoughts began to change when they threw a piece of paper down in front of me. There was something written in Chinese and they wanted us all to sign it. "What is it?" we asked, but they just laughed and continued to demand that we sign it. Perhaps it was our death sentence; we really had no idea. In broken English we were then told that we would be thrown in prison if we didn't sign.

What had we gotten ourselves into? What the fuck? We looked at each other and thought we had no choice but to sign the paper. So we did.

Fortunately, we were spared jail, but we had apparently signed away any possibility of performing in China ever again.

And just for good measure, we had been ordered to leave China just after arriving. This all happened in our first week! We had thought we had several months left and we had also signed a type of work contract with the club.

Being from Amsterdam, we didn't give up too lightly. After being told we couldn't perform and that we had to leave, we thought 'Fuck that!' Instead we each performed the closing set separately every night, in the club we were supposedly banned from playing in and in a country where we were clearly not welcome.

Perhaps not the smartest move, as we later learned that our every move was being monitored.

Our hotel was also raided by the local police after prostitutes were spotted. Freddie and Matthew assure me they weren't to blame! Fortunately, this time, we weren't arrested.

I later found out that it was the guy from the rival club that had called the police and told them that there were four illegal spies from Holland in Chengdu acting as musicians and artists. He obviously didn't like being told 'No.'

We had a contact person assigned to us by the Dutch consulate, but he was a Chengdu local and only spoke Chinese. We were not really in a position to trust him – or anyone for that matter. We even started to doubt Tycho, the guy who arranged everything in Holland, and we even questioned the advert in the paper. Was it genuine? Had we fallen for something, which took us all the way to China, only for it all to be one big lie? What was going to happen to us?

My emotions were all over the place. We had arrived in China with so many positive expectations and a real sense of excitement, but this was all falling away rapidly. I had no work in Amsterdam, no gigs, and I wasn't prepared to just give up and return to Holland. None of us were.

A few days passed, the tension seemed to ease and we were a little more relaxed.

Tycho decided it was best for us to have a few days out of town to chill. We thought it was a good idea but we had problems trusting people. He drove through a jungle, up through mountains and we all thought the worst. The paranoia began to set in

341

rapidly. This was it – we were going to be dumped out of sight.

Suddenly, we turned a corner and we were greeted by bars, terraces and restaurants. It was a totally unexpected, but nevertheless well appreciated, shock to the system. Just moments earlier we were all fearing the worst and now, suddenly, we were being bought beers and nice food.

We all started to feel more relaxed, albeit anxiously. There was a trek up a nearby mountain which we thought was a good idea and with Freddie being the senior member he was carried up the mountain on a throne-type chair by two locals. At the top was a Temple and a place to stay. We ended up staying the night and I remember a stunning shrine in the middle, where we all sat and prayed for our families plus a safe end to our Chinese adventure!

That was a great experience, despite our original fears, as we spent the night surrounded by monkeys.

A few days later we drove back to Chengdu with everything appearing to be calm and settled. We were back in the club and the hotel was tranquil, which was what we had wanted from the start. Maybe now we could actually begin to relax and enjoy our adventure.

By this time we had been there for two very eventful weeks and I received a call at the hotel. It was Tycho, our contact guy, who informed me that he was on a train and would later be flying back to Holland without us. "What the fuck?" I yelled! He even had the cheek to ask if I would pick up his laptop and bring it back to Amsterdam for him.

His girlfriend was still in Chengdu and she told us that there was a big family crisis, which had caused him to flee. Seeing as the family consisted of high-ranking military officials we took the decision to leave ASAP!

This left us completely stranded without transport so it was time to get out of there. We all had open return tickets and we were all able to book a flight home the following day, but our movements were being monitored by the local police and we had to shake them off if we could. We dived in a taxi, lied down on the back seats and shouted "Drive!" Again, it felt like we were in a scene from a movie! We made it to the airport in one piece and flew back to Amsterdam. We were safe, we were home. Phew.

A few weeks later I found out that the owner of the club who hired us had died in suspicious circumstances. He was a really nice guy and he was so passionate about the music. It was his passion to introduce western-influenced nightlife to Chengdu, so to hear that he had died was really shocking.

Before we originally left for China, Tycho told us that there wasn't a sound system in the club. They had speakers but no turntables or mixer. It was my job to buy two turntables and a new mixer and take them with me on the plane. Thankfully, I had been given the money in advance to buy what was required. This wasn't my usual preparation for a gig but I had been after a new adventure and I'd certainly got it.

A few years later I noticed that DJ Tiesto was performing in China, not only in Chengdu but at the very same club where we had played and on the actual turntables I bought and had taken over there from Amsterdam!

PAUL JOHNSON

Daft Punk released their debut studio album Homework, which featured the track Teachers, way back in 1997. That track is a tribute to the artists around the world who are recognised as legends and pioneers – and the very first name you hear is that of Paul Johnson.

Paul is a Chicago house legend, a huge inspiration. He is also very comical with a huge, loving heart; even his smile is extremely infectious.

His story is pretty shocking but he has never let it affect him or his attitude to life. Paul explained in detail for the very first time exactly what happened and it's not what you may have read on Wikipedia. I really appreciated the time Paul took to discuss his situation in such detail. It can't be easy but Paul spoke with so much love, positivity and compassion, it was impossible not to be moved by his words.

Paul is still very much an artist in worldwide demand and in 2020 is planning 30 gigs in 30 days over in Dubai. "If I can't smoke for 30 days straight, then damn, it's not worth it, man," said Paul jokingly. He really loves his marijuana.

He has produced, remixed and collaborated with a vast majority of the scene's major players and has always gained billboard recognition worldwide with both his and their productions. His track Get, Get Down has just celebrated its 20-year anniversary. Now that makes me feel old, ha-ha.

I asked Paul if he was running for President, what wouldn't he want the people to know about him? "I'm a goddam alien but I can't tell you where I'm from, otherwise I'll have to kill you!" he chuckled.

For the interview, Paul reflects upon the early days, his personal life and how his career has evolved, plus studio time, gigs and meeting fellow Chicago legends Ron Hardy, DJ Rush and Green Velvet for the first time.

Get down...

I caught the scene back in 1983 when I was 12. At that time it was happening, but I didn't really know 100 per cent much about it. My cousin, Mark, who was 15, had the equipment. He was the only person that I knew who had DJ equipment at that time.

I didn't know how the music was being played, or how to play it, except for seeing Mark do it. It wasn't R&B, it wasn't disco, it was something else and I liked it. My cousin Mark was a big influence for me in the house scene.

Other influences were the Hot Mix 5, who were already on WBMX, a radio station in Chicago. From midnight to 3am they played house music every weekend.

Right after that I learned about Steve Silk Hurley and Farley Jackmaster Funk. Farley was on the radio and Steve Hurley was doing parties around the city. Another two major influences for me, right there.

This is the crazy thing about Chicago; we were already having parties but they were called sets. We would have sets in our basement and apartments in the late 70s and in the early 80s the music started to change, and that's when I noticed it. I didn't really know what DJing was but I had heard the music on the radio. I was breakdancing and I had all this long curly hair down my back. I was literally dressed as a break-dancer all the time and we used to walk around with our vinyl or plastic to other neighbourhoods and battle. That is what I was doing back in 1983 and then the music just hit me!

I saw my first DJ back in 1983, and I stood there at the front staring at him and what he was doing. It was a block party and he was playing Denroy Morgan's I'll Do Anything for You. It was a record I had heard on the radio but he was mixing it. I just thought 'Wow, I like this!'

It had the da-boom, da-boom, da-boom and so I asked my mother if she could let me DJ. It wasn't just about putting the record on; I also started to learn different things about the records. I thought 'Wait a minute. I'm hearing something in this. Forget the dancing, I want to know how they're making this,' and that is when it all started to change. That was when I really started getting into the music and going to record stores to see what they had.

One day back in 1985 my cousin Mark and I walked into a record store singing Frankie Knuckles and Jamie Principle's tune Waiting on My Angel and then a bird shat on me! I was like 'Oh mannnnnnnnnnn'. Crazy that while I'm singing those words a bird shits on me. That was so funny.

When I graduated 8th Grade I asked my parents to buy me DJ equipment. Also, I told them to tell my friends I was on punishment and I couldn't go outside to play. They would come round and ask for me but I was upstairs mixing. All summer I was up there teaching myself to DJ.

The tunes at the time were Inch by Inch by The Strikers, Angel Eyes by Lime and lots of stuff like that. You know what I mean?

A lot of breakbeats, too, but this was 1983. House music was still very minimal and wasn't even a thing then. But in 1984 everybody started making house music.

It was, like, whatever the radio was playing is what I would buy at the record store. I would spend all my allowance on records and spend all day up in the attic mixing.

I had this 15" woofer built into a speaker and every day I would put my speaker out the window so everybody had to hear me spinning all day. My friends were asking to come up but I wouldn't let them, ha-ha.

Then in 1985, bam, here I am…I'm a DJ. "No, you're not a DJ," my friends would say. But I used to battle other DJs. If there were other DJs in my neighbourhood I would go to the battle with only my headphones and that would instantly scare the other DJs. "Where are your records at?" they asked. "No, no, I'm going to beat *you* with *your* records. When you're done I'm next" I replied.

That was how I became famous in just one year. I beat everybody I was playing against. I wasn't listening to anybody; I taught myself how to play and blend. I would sit there for 12 hours blending, doing tricks. My mother hated it, my brother hated it, my grandma hated it, but I would still spend all day DJing.

In 1985 I was ready. When I was battling the other DJs, they were like 'Holy shit, this little dude is something. We have to pay attention to him!' I was now 15 years old and I was already turning into somebody. That's how I became famous so quickly.

Erik Martin was my best friend at the time and his sister Anita owned a company she had started called Avant-Garde Promotions that threw parties for Ron Hardy. At the time, I didn't know about Frankie Knuckles. He was older but I knew Ron because of my friends. They were also going to The Music Box. I think it was probably two years later that I met Frankie and Jamie Principle for the first time.

I met Ron Hardy first. I was only six years old when Frankie came to Chicago back in 1977. My 12 year old mind caught on in 1983 but Frankie was already doing his thing in the 70s.

My sister and cousins were already jamming to Frankie but I didn't know where I was at. I was too young and I didn't care about much. I was playing around, getting dirty and breaking shit. I was just a kid.

In 1986, when I first heard a tape from Frankie, I said: "Oh, okay, I see the difference." Ron Hardy was different; he used drugs, went crazy and he was my type of DJ. I wanted to get high and go crazy too! Frankie wasn't that; he was real precise, he was real professional and so I could hear the difference. I liked Frankie's music, man. I thought it was really cool. He really kept with the disco but Ron Hardy was like me. If you gave him a tape with a track on it he would play it next and that's exactly how I am. I want to hear that shit. Ron always said he would play it next and he did. He's the DJ I model myself on. Ron would always go all over the place with music but it sounded so good.

That is the way I spin now and if you asked me what I played I wouldn't remember. I can remember the first and last record, but in between I'm going through all different folders, thinking what you guys should hear next. There's never a plan.

Ron created that vibe by getting high. Because we were so young, he used to tell us when we were in Music Box not to drink the water or eat the fruit because there was acid in the water and acid on the fruit.

They had it in the water fountain, so everybody who drank it would get high. It was so incredible, man, such an experience. I never drank it and it took me a long time before I did trip. I took it without knowing, so I was freaking out. In Cincinatti in 1986 a girl asked if I wanted a lifesaver, a sweet, and I said: "Yeah." I didn't know she was dropping something on it and put it in my mouth right before I was about to DJ. I looked at the lights and they started melting. "What the fuck is going on?" I said and I could see the speakers coming out at me. I started freaking out, dude; it was fucking hilarious man!

I've been shut down by the police as I was playing, maybe five or six times. As soon as I put a record on the lights came on and it was the police. This has happened many times. Sometimes after my first blend, sometimes 20 minutes into my set, whatever. This has happened many times around the planet too. I'm headlining most of the parties I'm playing at, so I'm usually on last. That's exactly the time when the neighbours are fed up. That's the time for me to turn it up and bang it out. So, yeah, I've been stopped by the police many times.

My most memorable gig, I guess, would have been back in 1999 when my mother, my aunt, my uncle, everybody came. It was in Chicago, at the Harvey Expo centre. They came to party, which is something they never did. They never went to parties. But at this party there were 5,600 people and it was my birthday. Everybody wanted to meet my mother and it was just so
349

incredible.

Back in the 90s we could just throw a party and there would always be about 5,000 people there without question.

Right when all this crazy shit happened back in 2001 it was Osama Bin Laden who changed the whole party scene. It really sucked. Before that we always had 5000 people.

This is the funniest shit in the world – I used to cut 8th period at school, which was the music class! I always used to cut this class and go home and DJ, and so I'd get an F in music all year long.

I would tell my teacher: "I already get it." I don't know how to explain it to you but when I hear something I can instantly play it over, even though I don't know what the instruments are. I instantly know how to find them. I couldn't explain that to my teacher, so all year long I failed music.

It's so funny, but I was the best DJ!

I also cut class the day I got shot. I wanted to go home and listen to this new track from DJ Pierre – Acid Tracks. I had it on cassette and I wanted to go home and play it. When I got home I was DJing in the basement. My best friend Antoine had just joined a gang, and he had the smallest fucking gun you could get, you know what I mean? It was a 25mm, something you could hold in your hand to protect yourself.

He was dancing with it in his crotch and as I was DJing and all I could think about was if that gun went off my mother was going to kill me. So I stopped the music and said: "Antoine, take the clip out of the gun. I don't want you to shoot yourself." "Okay," he said.

Why the fuck did I say that? If I hadn't I wouldn't have been shot. All he did was go to grab the gun and it just went 'POP!' It came right towards me and hit me while I was DJing. I had my head down and I looked up and saw a light. Then it felt like a truck was on top of me. What the fuck was going on?

First thing I said was: "Aaaah, my dick. I can't feel my dick!" I couldn't feel anything at the time but all I was thinking about was my dick. I didn't give a shit about anything else, ha-ha-ha. It was so funny, man! I was shouting: "I don't care about living. I just wanna feel my dick, man." I kept thinking I wasn't gonna be able to fuck no more but the feeling slowly came back in my arms and my chest, and everything. It just never came back in my legs because of where I had been shot.

The spine controls everything. All my feeling was there but further down it gets disrupted. If you break your back down at the bottom you probably won't feel your feet. In the middle, you lose your arms, and you just have your head. Where the bullet shot me, it was the t7 vertebra. So I had all of this feeling above and I couldn't feel my legs.

I couldn't feel my left arm either. It was a shocking experience. So I just lay down out on the floor for a few moments until they tried to pick me up. It was crazy. My brother and my friend didn't know that I had been shot. I said: "I think I've been shot, come and pick me up." They were crying as they tried to help me up but couldn't. When the ambulance got there, that's when I knew I had been shot. I wasn't bleeding out, I was bleeding internally. They didn't know I had been shot until they cut all my clothes off and saw the tiny bullet hole.

It's the weirdest shit ever. When you see somebody get shot on television they say their life flashes before them. I'm telling you, that shit really happens! Holy shit, it's so true. I saw right back to when I came out of my mother and everything since then. In fast, flashing layers right before me. Everything I'd ever done, right there – flash, flash, flash, flash, flash, flash, bam, bam, bam, bam. That's what happens, man, your whole life flashing before you while you are falling. But it wasn't in real time; it was like slow motion as I fell to the floor and as I hit the ground the last thing I heard was the gunshot.

Ain't that crazy? It's the weirdest shit ever.

We were all young. I was 16, my brother was 13 and Antoine was 15. He didn't know he had shot me; he just went to remove the clip and it popped. We didn't know what the fuck had happened.

It sucks because it was all just a fucking accident. I would still be walking if I hadn't cared about my friend shooting himself. I could have just kept my mouth shut. He had just joined a gang and he had an initiation gun, a stupid fucking tiny little gun, just something to carry to protect himself in case a member of another gang came up to him.

But this really fucked him up and he literally went crazy after he shot me. He didn't mean to do that; he was my best friend. He completely lost his mind. It's so sad and I hate it that my best friend lost it and couldn't come back from it.

He tried to come and see me for an entire year after that but he would just sit on my porch and cry. He wouldn't even come in the house. My parents would say Antoine was outside, but he wouldn't come in and just sat there crying. But I understood him; he had just shot his best friend. We used to wrestle together, play together, but this really fucked him up.

I think it was also because of the entire neighbourhood's shock reaction. I had been DJing for two years, I had become famous and they couldn't believe my best friend had shot me.

I never had a prosthetic leg because I never wanted to look all mechanical. I'll just sit in a chair, I'm good. Women didn't mind, ha-ha-ha, and they still don't. They automatically jump up on my lap and they'll knock me out of my chair jumping on me, ha-ha-ha.

One day I was in my chair and my back was feeling tight. I was in my house alone. I had already had one amputation, my left leg, and I knew something didn't feel right, so I decided to do some exercises. I put my leg up and was doing some twists, then I grabbed a stand and twisted my upper body from one side to the other. All I heard was my back go crack.

I broke my entire back.

The fucked-up thing was that it was below where I had feeling, so I couldn't feel it. I heard it, though, crumbling like crackers. It fucked me up and I started screaming. Holy fuck, I'd broken my spine and my right hip, so that was when the second leg had to go.

It wasn't a car accident as it says online. I don't even know where that story came from. I was at home, by myself, chilling and exercising. My stupid ass twisted round and cracked the bottom of my spine. I've looked at Wikipedia and thought 'That's not true and neither is that,' you know. I wanted to change it to what actually happened but then it was changed right back. Wikipedia is just stupid!

My mother and father raised a gladiator because this life has never bothered me. As long as I can wake up and be here, that's all that matters to me. My mind is fresh as hell, so I can just laugh it all off.

I think to myself 'Oh, okay, that's my situation, but what about you? I bet you're probably more fucked up than me.' Ha-ha-ha.

My life has been an incredible accident, just all accidents and shit. But the beautiful part is all the music that came out of it. My mind was never affected, and it just keeps getting crazy. You can't make that shit up.

A lot of good has come out of the shit that happened.

I really appreciate living and how much I love to give these sounds to everybody. Look how it makes you all feel! I really don't know what's on the inside, but I know how I feel when you tell me how you feel. My heart grows so big, you know what I mean? It's the feeling we get from it that keeps me going.

That feeling just spreads around; it's reciprocating.

I first met Green Velvet back in 1993 at Hula Mahones and the Outhere Brothers studio. We met right after he made the album Percolator and we just collaborated after that. He said he was going to start a label and I told him that I would do a record for him, and then bring him more artists.

That's basically what I tell everybody. I'll do a record first then I'll bring all the artists. That's how I've been doing this stuff all my life.

I first met DJ Rush when he was playing at the Powerplant in 1988. He let me borrow one of his drum machines and I just started making tracks right into the machine. I've given them all to Rush and we've just gone back and forth, but if I'm honest I can't tell you which tracks they were.

There are some tracks that Rush did and I released them as mine, while he has released some of mine as his.

We did this a lot. Some tracks I started and Rush finished, and vice-versa. It was so cool, man. We've been on each other for a very long time and I think he's really cool. He was actually the first DJ to start doing tracks on Dutch label Djax Records and flying to another country to perform.

But to us Americans it's always been pronounced as Dee-Jax. Whenever we spoke with Saskia – Miss Djax – she never corrected us. Why put the D there if it's silent? Just take that shit off, ha- ha-ha, and make it Jax. Silent letters in words are just so silly, man.

I'm the biggest procrastinator and you might not think I'm doing a lot of stuff. But the thing is, I turn down two thirds of the stuff, and it's like that with everything I do.

I'll start tracks then just delete them and start on another. I'll take bookings that I actually don't want to do. Yes, I do a lot of that.

I'll take my time, wait until the last minute. If you ask me to remix something and, say, I have three weeks to do it, I'll wait until the very last night before starting on the remix. That way I force myself and it makes the outcome better.

My backstage stories are pretty much X-rated. Women are
355

incredible and when they want to do something they'll fucking do it right away! They don't give a fuck who's watching. This is true all over the planet. I've had girls who don't even speak English who just grab me and leave with me!

Even during my sets it goes down but I can always remain focused. Even when I'm engaging with the ladies I'm still concentrating on my blending. It never throws me off and it comes from me, back in the beginning, concentrating on my spinning 12 hours a day. My brother would often come into my room and throw some dirty socks or something at my head. It wouldn't really bother me and I would just keep on doing what I was doing.

You can always come up on stage while I'm spinning. We can talk, take pictures, sign records, it won't bother me. Girls being drunk and wild are just something that I'm used to. They are always fun and always want to do some funny shit.

It's a nice life.

CARL COX

*If the name doesn't ring a bell, then let me tell you he's The Boss.
Since day one Carl has been continuously entertaining thousands
of people worldwide on a regular basis. Whether it's a sweaty
rave full of a thousand grins bopping to 170 BPM, or to the
smooth sophisticated sounds in the Caribbean sun, Coxy
delivers.*

*I always enjoyed seeing Carl play in the early 90s when he was
usually the highlight of the night. Often at the wonderful
Mindwarp parties in Colchester, Essex, but in those days he was
playing rave and hard, fast German and Belgium techno. I did
see him perform live once, behind a keyboard. It was a live PA
with his I Want You (Forever) track and others at the Colchester
Hippodrome back in 1993.*

*Only once I'd moved to Amsterdam did I see and hear a different
Carl Cox. Still techno, but the tough, fast aggression was
replaced with a much deeper pumping techno, with the
occasional classic thrown in.*

*My favourite Carl Cox moment was on Sunday, July 16th, 1995,
at DJ Per's Time Machine night at the Melkweg when he was
playing the closing set. At the end of his set the crowd applauded
along with the usual cries demanding more. Suddenly, the room
went dark and the lights began shooting around in all directions.
What was going on? Then all the lights stopped directly above
the DJ booth, Carl raised his hand and played Josh Wink's
Higher State of Consciousness. It was the first time I, and
probably everybody else in there, heard that track. What a
monster and we went on for another hour.*

357

There's not really a great deal I could say about Carl Cox that hasn't already been said. Google him and you'll be busy for days. If you do, though, check out his back-to-back set on YouTube with Green Velvet from the Exit festival from 2009. I love it.

One thing, though. His was the one interview that always seemed to elude me. Many requests were made but with me being a bit of a rookie I guess they were a bit unsure about granting me an interview, which was perfectly understandable. He's a megastar and I'm sure he can't say yes to every request. Eventually, with a host of interviews with many of his colleagues completed, much to my surprise and delight I was given the thumbs-up. Oh yes, oh yes.

I was especially keen to ask him about his role as Pablo Hassan in Human Traffic, one of my favourite movies. Carl's scene realistically portrays the length people will go to in order to blag their way into a rave. The movie is excellent and Human Traffic 2 has recently been confirmed by director Justin Kerrigan. Reach for the lasers...

I interviewed Carl over the phone but we were able to meet during a gig in Amsterdam at the wonderful Loveland festival. I was invited to join Carl and his right-hand-man Ian in his dressing room after his set.

What a privilege. What a moment. Cheers, boys!

Carl spoke about his rave days, acting, and an amazing world exclusive acid house story.

Oh yes, oh yes!

Abergavenny is probably the most obscure location I've played at – in a scout hut. I think there must have been about four people there! Can you imagine? I jumped in my car and drove all the way there and I can't actually believe that I'm talking about it in such a way because it was such a nonchalant gig. It took so long to get there, only to find out the promoter wasn't even present. He thought that if he booked me then people would come, but he forgot to actually promote the event. The thing was, it was just one of the worst events ever, because I completely wasted my time going down there.

All the way back in 1990 I did actually play right close to the edge of Cornwall, the most western county in south west England, right down in the foot. The party was in St. Ives. I played elsewhere that weekend in Cornwall and they asked if I wanted to play at this other party. The party was on the beach, we played out towards the water and it was beautiful. A really amazing event and I played for nothing, of course, simply because I was already down there.

It was something that I'd never done before in the UK, to play right down on the southern tip of England. It was fantastic that they had the ability to do that because nobody bothered us at all. We went on until probably 9am the next morning. It was actually really warm too, because normally in Cornwall it's bloody freezing. It was a complete one-off. It really was beautiful right on the water's edge and the people were fantastic. It was like a pop-up party compared to what we do today.

It was amazing, actually, the original days, and I have another amazing story. I used to sell tickets to events with my girlfriend at the time, Maxine Bradshaw, in Brighton on the south coast.

People knew about these events but didn't know how to basically get there or get back, so I used to lay on a coach or mini-buses.

I would sell the tickets, then outside my door I'd get people to come there and collect them, at which point I would tell them to meet me at the bus station at a particular time and then we'd go from there.

So I'd maybe have a coach full of about 50 people or two mini-buses with about 35 or 40 people, which was how I'd get them from A to B.

But the thing is, going from A to B, we didn't know where we were actually going until I had received a message on my pager, because we had no mobile phones at the time. The message had a number for me to call, so we then had to go to a public telephone box and on the other end of the line there would be a brief answer-phone message revealing the mystery venue. On this particular occasion we were told it was near Gravesend and it was around 11pm. I had 50 people plus the coach driver saying: "Where are we going?" I would reply: "I don't know at the moment, just waiting for my pager to go off, and then we can start our magical mystery tour."

At the same time I was also running the sound systems for a lot of the early rave parties, including this one. So I had my guys out ready to set up the sound system and since I had already been paid half the money up front everything was fine. We sent the trucks down to the event but they always had to wait until I knew exactly where it was. So my boys headed off to Gravesend and then, basically, they couldn't get on site because of a hold-up. We arrived and nobody would let us through. Security were saying no but as soon as they let us through it was about midnight and there were police everywhere!

The whole event had been run by the police and we were all victims of an elaborate sting set up to catch us all.

Basically, I was taken away by the police for the weekend along with all the other guys who arranged the drivers and hire cars, plus all the booze and the lights, that sort of stuff. I had to tell everyone else to go home because there was no party and you can imagine my name was mud. I spent the weekend locked up.

The mad thing about all of this was that I thought all the people we dealt with to get this party up and running were friends or people that they knew. But they were all policemen, every single one of them. I cannot believe that I was unwittingly helping the police, which was incredible.

So we all ended up in jail and I met people on the inside there and we got talking. Some ran a bar, others did security, you know, the type of things you need to put on a show, and after that we all became friends.

On the Monday morning we were taken in a van to Gravesend Magistrates Court to face the music, right. We were all standing there in the dock when they said: "Mr Cox, we are here to charge you but, unfortunately, we have insufficient evidence so we are going to let you go.'

Yessssssss, how's about that!

The court had a mountain of paperwork that they wanted to chuck at us but because they couldn't actually make any of it stick they had to let us all go, which was incredible. I was thinking to myself, hang about, is this April Fool's Day? Or am I on Game for a Laugh and Jeremy Beadle's going to pop out and

361

say: "Wahey, we got you there, man!"

But unfortunately, from everything that had happened, all the clubs I worked for in Brighton, nobody wanted to work with me anymore because after the sting I was now associated with being one of the acid house kings of the south coast. Bloody hell, I was like 'Oh my god, now I'm an acid-house king,' but all I did was hire and set up the sound system, sell the tickets and take people to the event.

I can't really remember so much of the early days. But after putting the structures up, the sound system and the monitors, all that kind of stuff, it was always very basic. At the time – and not many people know this – for me to be able to do any of those parties like Mindwarp, Biology, or any of those events, there was only an hour to play my music. So I used to have a shoulder bag full of records and what was in that shoulder bag was what you were going to hear, end of story. Therefore, we would go in and the DJ on before me might have had to play on longer because I was unable to get there any earlier and he would be running out of records, so we had all of that stuff going on. Then I was off elsewhere with the same bag.

Today, a lot of the events you see are like Rolls Royce events, you know. You've got beautiful monitors, great backstage areas and lots of other great stuff going on – back in the day we had nothing! We would just literally run on stage, get our vinyl out and play. Sometimes the needles would jump and break, and we'd be trying to find new needles from somewhere, all that kind of stuff. I remember one time playing a record and all you could hear was this loud roaring feedback, and there were people out looking for tennis balls to help compress the sound. I mean, we were terrible and that was the problem with a lot of the early parties. It was certainly hardcore.

Nobody knows this – until now – but the mad thing was that I did a screen test for Human Traffic. It would have been easier for me to play a cameo as a DJ, and that would have been my bit. They really wanted me to act as somebody else in the movie, even though it was me, Carl Cox. They wanted to see how I could act and so they wanted me to pretend that somebody had just run over my pet dog, a hit and run basically, and how I would feel about that. I was just like 'Well, I would be really upset about it' but they wanted to see how I would really feel. I felt like I wanted to kill somebody. 'That's the passion, that's what we want to see,' they said. 'You've got the job!'

Bloody hell, I didn't realise that it would go so far. But they really pushed me. It was incredible and amazing how, when I was focused so hard on something like that, I was able to make my reaction so believable. Because, guess what, I've never owned a dog, far less had to suffer losing one in that way.

Many years ago when I was seven or eight years old I did have a cat. The doorbell went one day and it was our next door neighbour, holding a Sainsbury's bag and looking anything but happy. He had found our cat but it had been run over and killed. I was screaming 'My cat, my cat' and it was so sad. My mum and dad took the carrier bag from our neighbour and it was buried in the back garden. We never spoke about it again because it was too traumatic and we never had any more pets after that.

That feeling kind of related back to what they wanted for the film, so I thought I would use that for the screen test. That's how it all came about and that's how far I went in the screen test. I have never spoken about that until now.

When it came to the scene of me in the office and what I had to portray as a coked-up club manager, they wanted me to be really mean to a guy trying to get a ticket to get in to be with his girlfriend. Me being mean to anybody is quite difficult because usually I just laugh things off. But they were like 'Ready, Coxy? Here we go, here's your scene. Ready, action, GO!' Every time they said go I just kept giggling and laughing. Everyone around me was laughing and we must have done about 10 or 12 takes. It got to a point where they were saying that nobody was allowed any food until we got it right. Believe me, that next take was perfect. Everybody was so happy, thank God for that.

It was a really dark, moody scene, everyone was skinning-up, and I did not want to be the person who had to walk between that lot. He wasn't supposed to be able to get close to me, he shouldn't even have been there in the first place, and that's why that scene is so intense.

The mad thing was, at the premiere in London it was the first time I'd seen it on the big screen and as soon as everyone saw me they just laughed. They had never seen me act before in any way, shape or form. They almost missed my scene because they were laughing so much.

Also, I had to go back to Pinewood Studios because my voice was quite high in the movie and they wanted it an octave lower. I had to basically over-dub my piece of the movie for the final cut.

It was a magical movie moment for me! I had a great time doing that; it was good. There have been movies since Human Traffic that have come nowhere near close enough to the authenticity of that movie. One of the reasons why is that you can absolutely relate to the people in the movie or identity with scenarios you've been in yourself. That's what makes it so endearing.

We talk a lot about Germany and its techno, and France with Laurent Garnier's Wake Up and the Rex Club in Paris that I used to do on a Wednesday, which was awesome. But Holland is probably the most important country to have such a strong development of dance music from right back in the beginning with its festivals and sound. As a DJ, if you had the support of the Dutch people it was incredible. They were some of the most amazing festivals, even to this day, that I've ever played. I played recently at the Awakenings weekend in Amsterdam and it was just out of this world. It was just phenomenal.

When I did my first-ever big party in Holland, which was the gabba and hardcore parties at 200 BPM, I just couldn't believe how people would dance to this music for hours and hours and hours, but that was only for a certain type of person to enjoy. They also had the biggest and loudest sound systems known to man!

I was asked to play at the first Dance Valley in 1995 but I very nearly turned it down. I thought, they want 5,000 people in a field, in daytime with local Dutch club DJs? But they really wanted me to be there.

There were only two English DJs – me and Billy Nasty – booked to play the Mainstage. To be asked to play in Holland was quite an honour to be honest, to play at a brand new festival in such a way. There were different areas, but the valley with the Mainstage was just awesome. It was an incredible place and to this day I still think it will never be equalled. Just unbelievable!

Their first event was for a few thousand people. Me and Billy were playing near the end but we had it full right to the very last.

The mad thing was that when we finished at 11pm, the time Dutch people usually go out, they started chucking beer and drinks on stage to try to 'persuade' us to carry on. Me and Billy were trying to take cover. This is no way to end a bloody party, I thought. You could clearly see the Dutch were just so passionate and they really wanted more, but unfortunately we couldn't because of the licence. It was like, 'Thank you, good night' and BOSH, a beer in the face!

But they really did stumble upon something that became a national treasure for them. Dance Valley was at one point the biggest dance event in Holland for years and years, and Billy and I were at the complete forefront of it. I think I was one of the only DJs to be asked to play, more or less, at all of the Dance Valley events. I think I must have only missed about four of the first 20.

Nowadays it has just turned a corner. As soon as the Swedish House Mafia did the Mainstage, and maybe Tiesto before that, it started to change. We did try to have an alternative techno stage, which we did for a few years, but it still wasn't good enough for me. They need to be EDM or techno and it would be very difficult to have the two together in some ways based on popularity, because if you're going to have a stage for EDM you're going to have your capacity number, and you're not going to be guaranteed your capacity number for techno. With somewhere like Awakenings, it's predominantly a techno event so, you know, that's it. Everywhere you go you have people who actually want to be there for that type of music, end of story.

That's what is actually happening in Holland, for sure, when you have to split the vibe now between what EDM actually is compared to techno. That's probably one of the reasons why I don't play Dance Valley any more. I don't see what kind of

366

difference I can make, for me being who I am, to the event. We tried to do that at some events but it didn't work so I just walked away from it at the end of the day. I don't play Holland as much because of it, but now with Awakenings it's been absolutely amazing to play in front of a crowd who are there for that specific music. It's very strong what they have there and people absolutely love it. The production and the infrastructure are incredible. Everything that they've done to make sure everybody has the best time possible, it's probably one of the best events running that I've ever been to. It really does stand out from all the other events I do around the world. They really care, which I find to be truly amazing.

They've been going for so long themselves, more than 20 years, and are going stronger now than ever before. To be honest, there was no other techno event apart from that at the time, so I was really happy to be at the forefront of it all.

As you know, I've been doing it for a very long time and I really enjoy that people are still interested in the attention of who I am when I'm playing, like at Awakenings for example. Whether it be a smile, a gesture or a record that they like, or for me just being there is something I always enjoy. I'm at home in front of the turntables performing and that kind of thing.

I'm now doing fewer parties, but because I'm doing less I'm giving more to the party that I'm at. Rather than coming from party number three and doing only an hour and a half, I'll do one party and make sure that one party is the very best it can be, and I make time to be able to do that sort of stuff. It's important as artists that we make the time to do that.

I've got to leave later today for Tomorrowland in Brussels but I'm actually playing tomorrow. To infiltrate the main stage is to play

367

early and I did it last year, 2017, from 12-3pm. By three o'clock there were 30 to 40,000 people in there. So for me it's perfect because I can play whatever I want and, because they absolutely loved it last year, I thought I'd do exactly the same again this year so people are expecting me this time.

Last year people had no idea why I was there at that time and were upset that I was there so early. "You should be here later, you should have your own room, you should be on in the evening," they said. But I like to change things up at the end of the day. I'd like to think that if you're walking into Tomorrowland and I'm playing, it's a testament to Tomorrowland to put on a premier DJ before you've really started.

So here we are, you know, rather than a couple of kids knocking out EDM, you get me. They've never really filled that area before until around six o'clock, but I have people into it by three, so it's a big plus for them. People are coming in and getting warm to the idea of being on the main floor without having to go anywhere else. I'm the only DJ with the balls to go and do that. Most DJs wouldn't do what I'm doing in the sense of warming that place up. I find it really satisfying because I'm introducing myself to a whole new generation of people who would never go to see me on the main stage, so the only way to do it was this way. I absolutely loved it – to me it felt like playing the biggest Space terrace in the world.

Playing in the daytime really changes things. You don't have to rip it up and you don't have to see people, you know, as it's not the main time yet.

It's nice to do the main time. You play the records, it goes off and everyone thinks you're the king. But when you actually have to work, when more people are enjoying the sound and enjoying

368

what you're doing, that's where you get more fulfilment because you make that work for yourself. That's the reason you are who you are.

Also, for me, when I walked away from that it solidified who I am and the reason why I was there. Some people couldn't understand it but others thought 'He's a DJ, why wouldn't he do that?' They think it's brilliant they can see Carl Cox playing after just walking through the door and without having to go and find me later in the pitch black, with everything else going on around me. Some are maybe too knackered from the night before and wait until the next year. But no, absolutely everybody walking through that door will see me first, you know, to begin with and that basically sets the tone for their whole weekend and whatever else is to come.

I'm still a big part of that after doing it all these years. I think I've found my place, or my niche, in Tomorrowland, rather than just being another name trying to make the best of playing late in a room, like I used to try to do. Tomorrowland is quite an endearing place to be to do the beginning, and so I said to them: "Why don't I do that?" They were like: "Well, do you really want to do that?" I said: "Why not, they're going to come in anyway."

I want to be able to play the music that makes sense to me, anyway, and for people who want to experience me at this time and in that room. They were like: "Wow, that's a great idea, how long do you want to play for?" "Three hours," I replied and they said: "Okay, the floor is yours." So that was it. Everybody that came through the gate and saw me playing, they were so happy and joyous and everyone felt like that.

It started at one point with nothing, which you can see online because they recorded it all, and at the end there were 40 to
369

50,000 people. I could have played for another three hours and had 60,000 people, because I would have kept that groove going all the way through until the end. The organisers could see that there was a good rapport and the crowd were experiencing me playing for the first time in the early slot.

The mad thing was that last year I did my thing up to three o'clock and it was going off. I kept it with nice chunky techno at 128 BPM. Everyone was having a great time, people on each other's shoulders. The girls were having a great time, the guys were having a beautiful time, all singing along and then two EDM upstarts came on and that was it. 'Alright, hands in the air, come onnnnnnnn, bing bing bing bing.' You know, I was like 'This ain't good.' This year they've got a couple of DJs on to continue the sound, and build upon the foundations I lay down.

Now that people actually know that I'm playing at that time they will run through that door and enjoy that first three hours of Tomorrowland. It's nice for me to follow up from last year, so people don't think I'm just a one-trick pony.

DAVE SEAMAN

In 1990, together with Steve Anderson, Dave formed Brothers in Rhythm. They were producing for the Pet Shop Boys and Kylie Minogue among others, and also did remix work for the likes of David Bowie, New Order, and Michael Jackson etc. back in the day.

In 1991, Brothers in Rhythm had a number one hit in the US Billboard Hot Dance Club charts with Such A Good Feeling, which also reached number 14 in the UK singles chart.

Dave was boss of independent record labels Stress and Audio Therapy, and together with Steve Parry, Selador Records is now under their control.

Dave continues to tour the world and after famed DJ mixes for world-renowned Global Underground and the Renaissance Master Series, he never fails to disappoint.

For the interview, Dave spoke about his introduction to the music scene via an unforgettable New York trip, a chance meeting with the hand-of-God cheat Diego Maradona, touring the world and getting banned from a certain country.

Enjoy...

I lived through the whole breakdance scene. I was obsessed with dance music and DJing long before it was trendy. It was never considered a career opportunity or anything like that. I was doing mobile discos, weddings, youth clubs and school discos, all that kind of thing.

I used to get the DMC albums because it was the only place you could really get the remixes of the latest songs in those days, and Mixmag, which was a DJ-only newsletter at the time.

Getting my job at Mixmag is a crazy story in itself. I was a member of DMC, the Disco Mix Club, and in 1987 I attended the Dance Music Convention, the awards night, where they held the mixing & scratching DJ championships. It was there I put my name into a grand raffle, sponsored by Camel cigarettes, and it was pulled out of the hat first. At first I honestly thought it was a big wind-up but I won a week in New York at the New Music Seminar, which at the time was the equivalent of the Winter Music Conference in Miami.

I was only 19 years old and it was a dream. I was obsessed with what New York had to offer, especially the nightlife and all those clubs like Danceteria, Mars and The Paradise Garage. I went out for a week and I got to hang out with various bigwigs from the record industry, label chiefs and artists.

On the final day I had been out shopping all afternoon and I was starving, so I went to McDonalds on Times Square, which was where our hotel was. As I walked back into the hotel, everybody was standing in reception, about to go for dinner. A little bit gutted I'd just eaten, I asked: "Where are you going later?" and they replied: "Nells"."Okay, I'll meet you there" I said, without a second thought. What I didn't know then was that Nells was one of the most exclusive places to go and the hardest place to get into in New York at the time. Plus, I was only 19, not even old enough to go to a club or drink alcohol.

What they didn't know, though, was that I'd just met the door guy from Nells in the queue at McDonald's and that he had invited me to the club. Talk about fate.

So I went to Nells and spent a couple of hours drinking thanks to my new-found friend's hospitality. It got to about 2am and there was still no sign of any of the people I'd planned to meet up with.

I thought it was best to go back to the hotel as it was our last night but when I walked outside I found everyone still stood outside on the pavement because they couldn't get in!

I turned to Michael, the doorman and my new best friend, and in my drunken state I was feeling pretty confident. I told him they were my friends from England and I got them all into the club!

This was what helped me get my job at Mixmag. The DMC owners, Tony and Christine Prince, asked jokingly: "Who the fuck is this kid?" I had just got them into the most exclusive club in New York yet I wasn't even old enough to get in myself. They were so impressed that they offered me a job!

I started working at DMC, doing Mixmag, in 1987, right during the eye of the great storm. Mixmag was a DJ-only newsletter at the time but the scene soon grew to such an extent that we launched it to the public in the summer of 1989.

My first time travelling abroad to DJ was an eye-opening experience. I was still young and quite naive. My first trip was to Brazil but then I flew to Australia, where I was offered a tour through my Mixmag contacts.

I had three gigs to play but it was still early doors in terms of the scene's development. There wasn't much in the way of wages but
373

they had agreed to pay for me and my best friend for two weeks away, all expenses paid. In exchange I played the three gigs – that was the deal.

I was told to arrange a tourist visa because I wouldn't be earning any money so I didn't need to get a work permit. That seemed to make sense to me; there was some logic in that.

A rival promoter then tipped off the local customs that I didn't have the right permit and the morning after the first gig, when I was feeling a little worse for wear, two customs officers came to my hotel and escorted me off to immigration. They wanted to deport me there and then but after the promoter pleaded with them that he would go bankrupt if I had to leave the country immediately, they let me stay to do one more of the two remaining gigs planned.

I thought I had got away with it but, when we did finally leave the country, customs gave me a big black stamp in my passport. I wrote to the Australian High Commission trying to explain everything but I was actually banned from entering Australia for three years. It wasn't a good start to my touring and it's still something that occasionally causes me problems to this day.

Global Underground spread around the world and it's really amazing how many people in different countries around the world grew up with those albums. They couldn't access the records very easily but it was a lot more straightforward to get copies of the compilation CDs.

I've played in all sorts of crazy places thanks to the worldwide popularity of my Global Underground series of DJ mixes. I remember being in a car with two complete strangers driving through the middle of the desert in Jordan and we were driving into the middle of nowhere. I had no service on my phone and for all I knew we could have been heading into Al-Qaeda territory. This wasn't long after 9-11 in New York!

When I went to Cape Town for a Global Underground gig, there was a bomb scare in the middle of the night. It was actually my birthday and I remember we all had to evacuate the building. I honestly thought it was a joke. While we were all standing in the car park everyone starting singing Happy Birthday to me. It was a moment to remember, for sure. An announcement was then made that it was a false alarm so everyone rushed back into the club and the night really kicked off from that moment on.

Sometimes, when you get these interruptions, it can really make the night. It's these communal experiences that can somehow give an extra boost to the party.

For people like Darren Emerson, Danny Tenaglia, Sasha, John Digweed, Nick Warren, myself and that whole era of DJs, the success of Global Underground really was a massive contributing factor in having our names promoted around the world.

I've played at Murmansk, the most northerly city in the Arctic Circle, right through to the jungle of deepest, darkest Central America. I've literally played in every corner of the globe. It's such a privilege to make a living doing something I love while simultaneously getting to travel the world.

I've played in Amsterdam many times before, both club nights and a lot of the big raves back in the day. I played at the Paradiso quite a bit also and I did a lot for Earth and Time Machine at the Melkweg with DJ Per and DJ Remy.

Never in my wildest dreams did I ever think, since wanting to be
375

a DJ when I was just eight years old, that I would have been able to do what I've done. In those days wanting to be a DJ wasn't a career option; we were just happy if we managed to get a gig in the local nightclub. That was it – that was the ultimate goal!

Once, while playing in Uruguay, I had a funny experience. Back in 2001 I was DJing and the crowd started cheering, going absolutely crazy. I thought they were really enjoying the track I was playing but as I looked up they all turned around and left the dance floor. I wondered what was going on, until I was told Diego Maradona had just walked in and was standing at the back of the dance floor.

He later came into the DJ booth, where I offered him a high-five before withdrawing my hand and telling him he was a bit too good at the old high-five!

I've met a few more celebrities in the booth whilst playing. Oliver Stone, the American director and screenwriter, came into the booth while I was playing at the Shadow Lounge in Miami. No kidding, he was so drunk I had to ask security to remove him. Bruce Willis hung out in the DJ booth in New York one time, plus Bono and Helena Christiansen, the supermodel, came to a Renaissance gig in Sydney, Australia, where U2 were on tour at the time.

I've spent a lot of time in the studio writing and producing, and I've been lucky enough to work with the big artists such as Kylie Minogue, Pet Shop Boys and Take That.

Working with Take That was a crazy time. They were the biggest band in the country when we worked together. As Brothers in Rhythm, together with Steve Anderson, we produced the tracks Never Forget, Sure and a few others at Gary Barlow's house, where he had his own studio. We were trying to concentrate and do some work but these coaches full of teenage girls kept pulling up outside. It was funny but very distracting and we spent most of our time watching the commotion outside.

That's another thing about the DJ lifestyle that we're so lucky to get a little taste of – what it's like to live the good life without having to deal with a lot of the trappings of fame.

We very rarely get recognised outside of clubs, which are our working environment, so you really don't mind having photos taken and chatting with fans. In fact, I positively encourage that. I can see it would be tiring if you couldn't go to the supermarket without constantly getting approached like major stars are and I suppose it goes with the territory.

Another great thing about the job is that we never stop learning and that's the exciting thing about it; it's constantly evolving. The minute you think you've got it all sorted is when you drop the ball. There's a quest and a thirst for that next big thing – everybody is always searching for it – and that's the excitement of the scene.

Having said that, however, at the moment the scene does appear to be going round in circles and we are kind of repackaging things for a new generation. But it's the nature of fashion, I suppose, where old trends are modernised and become trendy again, like how MA1 flight jackets and Dr Martens have enjoyed a recent resurgence. It's exactly the same with the music.

I just feel very lucky and grateful to still be doing this after all this time, especially as DJing these days is such a completely different game. It's so much more about marketing and branding, and it's so competitive. There are probably 100 times more professional DJs now as there were in the 90s, and there are not as many clubs and places to play. You do the math.

So for me, having been able to travel the world and do this for 35 years – after starting out doing school discos – is an incredible thing. I was very lucky to be in the right place at the right time, to be there right in the eye of the storm in 1987 when Coldcut, Bomb the Bass, Marrs, S-Express et al showed you didn't need to be a classical trained musician, or any kind of trained musician for that matter, to get involved with the scene. You didn't need to have lots of money for expensive studios; music was being created in bedrooms.

The DJs knew what music would work, technology provided the tools to make it work and the whole dance scene just blew up.

DANSOR

Born and raised in the Hungarian capital of Budapest, Anett Kulscar moved to her adopted country, the Netherlands, in 1997. Dansor has gone on to be a successful international DJ and producer, as well as a record label owner, and she also runs her own increasingly popular club night - Multiversum.

Dansor has recently been signed to American artist agency Conflux Connect, and has big plans to conquer the States. It was helped largely by the fact that Annet proved her worth, passion and commitment by flying, at her own expense, to Miami to meet artist manager Jori Lowery. It proved a smart move, because agency owner Jori was obviously impressed with her commitment and signed her up. It looks like 2020 will be a great year for this extremely talented, hardworking and intelligent artist cum business woman.

My most memorable Dansor experience? Easy. It was when we played together at the Contact party in Amsterdam at OT301, on March 24th, 2017. What was special was the fact we were playing alongside rave legend and Altern-8 founding member Mark Archer, one of my original old school heroes.

I have been fortunate to share the decks with Dansor several times in the Amsterdam scene, and she certainly is a talent.

For this interview, Dansor reflects upon her early days, studying, Ibiza and the challenge of breaking America.

Enjoy...

My original artist name was Ms. Syche, pronounced 'Sy-key'.
The problem was that nobody could say it or read it properly – so
I decided to change it.

In those days I was playing in the psy-trance scene in Budapest,
before moving to the Netherlands in 1997. Around the year 2000
I was playing progressive house and breakbeat, which helped to
kick-start my DJ career in Amsterdam.

I studied Media Technology at the Hogeschool van Utrecht, and I
was curious if I could control music by movement with the help
of sensors, so that became my graduation project. I didn't want to
be an artist standing behind a laptop. My friend, Stijn Kuijpers,
helped and encouraged me, and together we managed to create a
device that I would wear on stage when performing. I also made
a patch and a reactor, and it worked. I could control sound
through movement.

This project needed a name, and because I was using sensors and
dance, the name Dansor was born. I wanted something simple
and I continued to use the name when I performed, and it wasn't
long before I decided to use it as my new artist name.

Soon after, Haarlem DJ and promoter Alexander Koning asked
me to perform my Dansor project at his birthday party. There I
was on stage, doing my performance, and suddenly all the sounds
suddenly stopped. The room fell silent. I had even created a
happy birthday loop for Alexander which I was going to use, but
I wasn't able to.

I was still moving my arms, which usually created the sound, but
something went wrong and, annoyingly, there was no sound.

There was a problem with the wiring and I needed to solder it, but I was on stage and this wasn't possible. I still had to finish my performance via my laptop, which was really not the idea. When I finished, I just walked off the stage. That was really embarrassing.

To avoid this happening again, I changed the set-up. I adapted it with Bluetooth technology, and even managed to hack the Wii handheld controls. It helped me a lot that I was studying media technology, and I would use these to trigger the sounds during movement when I was performing live. I did sometimes experience problems with this, because of mobile phones interfering with my mobile connections.

Living in Haarlem, I was lucky enough to play regularly at the Stalker. It was 2000, I think, and I was playing a more progressive house style, alongside UK DJs Danny Howells and Anthony Pappa, among others. I really loved those days, especially the drummer, Proper Beating, who would play the drums during DJ sets.

I was a regular at Trancentral, the record store in Haarlem run by Alexander Koning. One day, he asked me if I knew a Hungarian girl called Szilvia, who at the time was the girlfriend of Rotterdam DJ Misjah, the founder of Dutch techno label X-Trax Records. I didn't know her, but he recommended we should get together. Alexander said I should call her, but I was thinking 'Just because she's from Hungary, it doesn't mean that I know her.'

Anyway, I did call her. We spoke, which was a little uncomfortable, and we still didn't realise that we knew each other. Not long after, my friends Mario and Jeff organised a party in a club in Amsterdam's Red Light District. He invited Szilvia, along with DJ Estroe and me, to play.

At the party, I was introduced to Szilvia, and I immediately recognised her. I did actually know her from high school back in Budapest! What a small world.

Our friendship grew and she suggested that we start to organise our own regular night together. I agreed and we decided to think about what to call it, and we both agreed on Budapest Delight. We ended up doing this for about 10 years.

Previously, I organised parties called Woman Waves, together with DJ Alison Marks from England. She was a regular booking at the Stalker and I was starting to play more regularly, so they decided to put us on the line-up together. It was then that I thought we should call it something. It was pretty simple. She was a woman, me too – so Woman Waves was created. I did more parties elsewhere under that name with DJ Isis, another female DJ from Amsterdam.

At one particular party, in 2000, at Patronaat in Haarlem, I had the idea to include a fashion show.

I had previously met a girl from Austria, who was studying at the Rietveld Academy, a fashion and design school in Amsterdam. She was designing and making her own clothes, so I thought it would be good to bring the two together and have a fashion show at my party. I needed models, so I asked my neighbour to help and she then asked her friends. The models were arranged and they really were amazing. They weren't really wearing clothes, but instead underwear, which was the designer's collection. At first I wasn't sure if they would agree to wear it. But they said they would, as long as they could smoke cigarettes at the same time as they were modelling. We agreed and they really were amazing.

I also had Oddo 7 performing. He's an aroma DJ, heating up and creating different aromas live and blowing them around the club, often alongside the DJ. This particular night was his first gig ever. DJ Isis was playing and she was so impressed with Oddo that she signed him to her artist agency at the time, MAGMA. He's now performing all over the world.

I wanted to record a music video for my Theory of Love track, which features on my album of the same name. I had been searching for at least a year for a suitable director, but there always seemed to be an obstacle in the way. One had family problems and the other was experiencing relationship difficulties. I actually thought that would be the perfect situation, because the video was about the theory of love. Unfortunately, he didn't agree.

Eventually, a friend asked me if I had seen a specific music video which had been directed by a Hungarian woman. She said she would be the perfect choice for what I wanted to do. When I checked it out I immediately thought 'Wow, this is really cool,' and I knew instantly that I wanted to work with her. I got in touch with her via Facebook and we started to get to know each other. I congratulated her on the video, as it was her first attempt. She won some music video awards in Hungary, too, which was actually the reason my friend told me about her.

We met each other in August 2015 when we spoke about the scene and ideas for the video etc. I had sent her the track previously, because I only wanted her to be involved if she liked the music. I wanted her to recognise the feeling and put it into an image.

I booked a flight to Budapest, along with the singer Ayden Vice, who had asked me previously if he could be in the video. He was the singer, so I thought he should be in it. I asked the director if she could write him into the video. I thought it was a nice idea to have the singer actually singing in the clip.

We filmed at five different locations in just two days and everything was planned perfectly, or so we thought.

Unfortunately, after initially meeting the cast, we realised there were still two gay guys missing. This was still an issue in Hungary and we were having some problems finding two who wanted to be involved. If I had been shooting the video in the Netherlands, it would have been so much easier. People were reacting on Facebook, saying they wanted to be involved, but then they would immediately cancel. This was happening every day.

Gay people didn't want to be seen as gay in Hungary, especially in a music video. We ended up putting an advert on a gay website, hoping we would find the two gay guys we needed.

On the first day of filming, we had to start at 5am. The evening before I had to arrange all the food for the crew of 15, and I had already rented the video cameras.

Day two and there were 30 people on set, and they also needed feeding. Everything was my responsibility and at my expense, plus the right nutritional food was needed. It was a very stressful experience, although everyone was super professional, despite the tension. The guys using the cameras had short movie and music video experience, which included working alongside several major artists, which was a big help.

Eventually, two men responded to our advert. It was about 8pm
384

on the final day of shooting and we still had to shoot the clip with them, but we did manage it.

It was the last day of filming and I had simply had enough. It was so stressful so I left the set and went back to the hotel. The crew finished the shooting and soon after, they called me. They said that some girls had to leave straight away or they would miss the last train home. They were not from Budapest, but about 60 kilometres away. I was then informed that they also had to take exams on the Monday and needed to do school work. I immediately thought 'How old are they?'

I discovered they were only 17 and at that age in Hungary you needed permission from your parents if you were asked to work. It meant that after ringing their parents to confirm they would consent we then had to drive the 60 kilometres to their homes and get their mothers to sign the necessary paperwork giving us permission.

There's one clip in the video, at the end, where you see the two guys hugging. This was supposed to be a kiss but we dropped that idea. We thought we might have some problems doing that in Hungary. But the scene looked great, so hugging was probably the better option in any case.

The funniest moment was when we were filming scenes in a forest. There were 15 people on set, all with make-up and yellow wigs on. Suddenly, lots of hikers appeared and started walking close to the set.

They looked at us strangely and I couldn't stop laughing.

In 2019, a woman added me on Facebook, but I didn't know who she was. We started chatting on Messenger and it turned out that
385

she was an agent in America that had only started her business about a year earlier. She was looking for new talent and had found me online. I told her a bit about myself and she asked me to send her a press kit, which I did and she got back to me to say how much she liked it. She mentioned that the Art-Basel Festival would soon be taking place in Miami and asked if I would like to be part of it.

After more texts, our friendship grew, and we would discuss ideas within the industry. It soon became clear to me that we were on the same page and we had the same thoughts and feelings. She was of the view that I should make the trip to Miami and I discussed it with my friend, Simone, who helps me organise my Multiverse events.

Simone and I both decided we would go and had to book flights. I was paying my own way and I looked upon it as an investment. The agent wanted to meet me, so I decided I would demonstrate my commitment by purchasing my own ticket. It was a long 20-hour flight via Houston and when we arrived we met up with the agent, who had arranged accommodation where we all stayed, together with some of her friends.

She was working alongside another promoter from New York City, from Lovemedicine, and it was there that I was added to the line-up and was able to play.

We went for three days and it proved beneficial, although it was also expensive and exhausting. I looked at it as an investment, plus I met some wonderful people. It was a very worthwhile experience, because Jori is now preparing a contract for me and also arranging an artist visa on my behalf for when I tour there. This can take a while to arrange, but I'm happy she wants to do everything properly and official.

It was also nice to know that she was connected and could arrange guest lists for us anywhere. That was good to know and I trusted her more because she did know influential people. It was nice getting to know her better, and who she was, because it was our first time meeting each other.

I'm already longer in the scene than most of the female DJs who are around today, but I'm getting there through talent and hard work – and not because I'm female. I'm not into all the dance moves when I'm playing but my boyfriend, Remko, says I should laugh and interact more with the crowd. When I'm really happy and feeling the energy I will jump, but that's mostly it. When I stupidly jump a few times I always think 'What am I doing?' Ha-ha.

Mostly, I'm too focused and not even looking at the people. So, for me, it's just about hard work and keeping my head down. That's how it goes for me.

I'm certainly gaining more recognition now and I just keep doing what I'm doing, and at the same time I find I'm getting to know more and more influential people.

Booking international artists for my Multiversum events has also helped my career, as I was booked for the 2019 Feel Festival in Germany by an artist I had previously booked.

I started Multiversum back in 2018 and not only is it my brainchild, I also finance it myself. Amsterdam Dance Event (ADE) in 2019 was our biggest by far. I booked Bookashade, Dominik Eulberg and Christian Lovera, and it was held at Ruigoord in the church. We have had six events to date and it is going really well.

I am in Ibiza for the IMS – International Music Summit – every year and it is very much like ADE. It's nice, because I'm always celebrating my birthday there and I'm promoting my stuff at the same time. There's not only Multiversum, there is my record label Comport and also me as Dansor, which means I can promote everything. I love meeting new people as well as seeing those I already know. In 2019 it was very emotional. The father of Avicii spoke and I was there in the room. It was very heavy and very sad too, of course. There were also talks from medical professionals, psychologists and artists. It was a very heavy atmosphere; intense but very touching. The whole theme was mental health, which is becoming very important nowadays in the scene.

During the IMS of 2017 I played at the legendary Cafe Del Mar, which was great. It's always nice to play at a famous place or location and it was at the new site, which was different to the old one. The terrace was much bigger and with several different areas. I was playing in an area that was more chilled and relaxed, with people enjoying the sunset while sipping their cocktails. I was trying to play my slowest tracks, at the slowest BPM possible, but the organiser came to me and said my set was too hard. He said I should be playing in a club and I simply replied: "Yes, I know."

It was a nice experience, together with my friends, but I wouldn't like to go back for a second time, simply because it was too slow for me. I play harder! Ha-ha.

Also in 2019 we were at a rooftop party, where I was introduced to French artist Megablast. Fortunately, one of his friends spoke Hungarian, much to my surprise, and actually lived in the Netherlands as well. Megablast has a studio in Ibiza and I was

388

invited to go there. Of course I said yes, but on the day I went Megablast had to play in Austria, so I was in the studio with his sound engineer Igor, who is also responsible for the mastering of Megablast's tracks.

I was invited to play at Vertigo, in San Jose, Costa Rica, through an IMS connection. I went with Remko, so we planned it as a holiday, but while my wage helped towards the cost of the holiday, unfortunately it wasn't quite enough to cover everything.

It was an interesting experience, albeit a bit hectic. We arrived in San Jose and an hour later I was playing in the club. This is how I imagine a regular touring artist would do it, before flying somewhere else straight afterwards. If that was me I'm not sure I would be able to remember which time zone I was in!

I can totally understand the mental health crisis within the scene, especially when artists aren't sleeping and only travelling.

You have to have a certain mindset and it is important that you plan a few breaks in between the travelling, just so you can maintain the lifestyle. I don't think just anyone can do it, flying from one side of the world to the other to play. Artists are touring now one continent at a time, which helps because they are not travelling back and forth. Also, I don't think the money is worth it in the end. Your health, especially mental health, is far more important. That is how I think about it.

When I DJ, I often leave my USB stick in the CD player, so I always need a friend to remind me, or at least recover it for me if I have left the venue. The worst part of that scenario is that my keys are attached to the USB. No stick, no keys. That is the reason I attached my keys, to prevent me from forgetting it. But I still forgot it when I played at the Sziget Festival in Hungary.

My biggest disappointment was when I played at the Paradiso in Amsterdam, for the TWSTD DJ contest, in the early noughties. I was expecting to play in the main room, but instead we played in the empty basement. I had made it to the DJ contest final, but playing in an empty basement was the reward.

I was asked to play at Fox & Badge in London, England, at The Steel Yard, whose parties always have an adult theme – including some fetish nights. It's not a super posh party, just great DJs. Another DJ from the Netherlands, Miss Melera, was also playing there. I was unaware of this when I was booked, but it's funny because I know her from Haarlem, my home town in the Netherlands.

I took public transport to the party because they were too busy building up and decorating the venue. I didn't know where to go but I found it on Google maps, and which station to use.

I was on the London Underground but there was some maintenance work going on and the station I had to use was closed. I just thought 'Fuck, where do I go now?' It was my first time playing in London. I had been very careful to plot my route and now I was forced to completely change it. Fortunately, I was being helped with directions by a fellow passenger but I still managed to get completely lost!

I have a friend in London called Molique, who is a singer. He had previously been in Amsterdam to record vocals for a track I was working on, but that track had never been released. He asked if we could perform the track at the Fox & Badge party. We had never previously performed the track live, so we needed to do a soundcheck before opening. Molique was already at the party waiting for me, and he was calling me to ask where I was. I told him I was on the tube, but I was lost. "I don't know when I will get there, could be a long time," I warned him. In the end, there was no time to do a soundcheck, so he just started rehearsing by singing to other records the first DJ was playing. I finally arrived, and when I played I started with our track and Molique was able to perform with the song's introduction.

There were lots of performances going on at the party, including naked women having hot wax poured over them. The costumes were amazing, and they had been busy preparing them for months. I was watching the people arrive at the party, and was amazed at how great they looked.

Oh my God, that was a very special and a very memorable experience!

DJ JP

I used to be a regular at Groove Connection, the record shop owned by John Peter Strijker – DJ JP. I remember once asking JP over the counter for a bunch of new records to listen to. Much to my amazement, he said I could just walk around and select from the crates myself. Now, he wasn't being lazy, he was allowing me to enter the inner-circle for local DJs, meaning I could simply select my own records. I thought I'd made it, rubbing shoulders with Amsterdam's DJ and dance floor elite.

It wasn't just a record shop; it could be an all-day hangout if you wanted it to be. Cannabis filled the air, you could buy clothing and the turntables spun all day. I miss the weekends and the record shopping vibes; it was always much more than simply listening to records. You would meet promoters, international artists, fellow local artists etc. It was a great start to any weekend and you always knew where the best parties – legal or illegal – were taking place.

JP plays under a few guises. DJ JP is his hard house moniker, whereas Lone Strijker is his underground house and techno title.

With an obvious hand in how Amsterdam and its nightlife have moulded over the decades, JP is still very much an international artist in demand. With history now spanning three decades, he shows no sign of letting up and continues to grow in popularity.

JP talked about his early involvement with Dance Valley and in particular the 2000 edition. If you are unaware of that year's events, let me just say that I have never witnessed such desperation and, in some cases, an increase in violence in the face of such desperation.

Along with many others, no doubt, I still have a very vivid memory of that day. Orbital were closing the Mainstage after a stomping two-hour techno set from Carl Cox. They started really slow and it kind of killed the Mainstage vibe for me. We decided to leave at that point and head back to the Amsterdam city centre, where we hit a few bars.

Dance Valley still had an hour or so to go by the time we departed and just as we made it to the coach heading for Sloterdijk railway station, where we intended to take a train to Amsterdam Centraal, the heavens opened. Not just a bit of rain, but instead the most severe storm I've ever witnessed. The last train had already left to Amsterdam Centraal – due to the weather all the coaches were either massively delayed or not running at all – so everyone had to walk from Sloterdijk to Amsterdam Centraal, which was probably about 45 minutes to an hour.

We eventually made it into the city and took shelter in a bar, but we were truly shocked along with everybody else at how the day was ending. Mates were calling me, but they were still stranded and wanted to know where I was. We were so relieved, but there were still tens of thousands of people on the festival site with nowhere to go.

Buses had stopped and people couldn't get back to their cars. Large groups of people leaving the site were shuffling down main roads under sheets of black plastic they had torn off the fencing surrounding the site. Hundreds of bikes were destroyed by the weather, again leaving people no way of returning home. Coaches deployed to ferry party-goers back to Sloterdijk and elsewhere decided they weren't going to operate in the storm,
393

and the drivers simply turned back or parked up where they could. Thousands of people who were depending on the coaches were instead completely stranded. A large group tried to hijack a bus and when the driver refused to budge they decided to set it alight. It was not an act anyone could condone, but an indication of how sheer frustration and anger had overcome some people.

It had been a glorious summer's day and no one was suitably attired for a monsoon. It was huge news, hogging the headlines on Dutch television and leaving the organisers to answer to government officials.

JP describes his experiences of that day, alongside other early Dance Valley memories, as well as his early days, various gigs, touring South Africa, and Groove Connection tales etc.

Enjoy...

Before becoming a DJ I was into new-wave music and funk – but no disco. I hated disco!

I used to be a drummer in a band when I was at school and we were called Weird Monkeys. I was only 13 at the time. We were a cover band, with some of our own music too and we played at our school parties.

We used to rehearse at the Sleep-Inn, which is now called Hotel Arena. There were session chambers in the basement and for 25 guilders a time we could practice there, which we did on a weekly basis. We were also able to stash our equipment there.

Occasionally, we could perform on the stage for the young tourist audience. Through playing at the Sleep-Inn, we were also able to play at the open-air stage in Vondel Park during the summertime. We were 14 to 15 years old at the time and we thought it was great being able to perform on such a big stage. It was brilliant – until the neighbours complained about the music being too loud.

Queensday was always nice too, because we used to be able to take our equipment outside on the street and just start playing, anywhere we wanted but often outside a bar.

It was Amsterdam DJs Dimitri and Marcello who got me on to the dance floor. Back in 1990 I had bought two mixed cassettes of DJ Dimitri and I learned a lot from listening to them. My friends and I were regulars at Club It, while we would occasionally visit The Roxy, but the door security there was often quite difficult.

I had been going to It for two years and even had my own membership pass, which original owner Manfred Langer had given to me. According to Manfred, we were all gay-minded. In the beginning there would be four of us, but our group just grew and grew until there were about 15 to 20 of us every Thursday and Sunday.

One of my best friends lived across from the club and we would always hang out there. We went the first night it opened and entry was not restricted to non-gay people.

For the first two years I never had any notion of becoming a DJ. I was having so much fun on the dance floor – until one night I was kicked out of Club It.

It was back in 1991 when a bouncer came up to me and said that I had to leave. I asked if he was joking, and if I could buy him a drink. "No, I am serious, you have to leave," he said. "Okay, but can you tell me why?" I replied. He said there had been complaints made against me. I asked if I could tell my friends I was leaving but he wouldn't allow it. I had to follow the bouncer and give my ticket to the girls in the cloakroom in order to collect my jacket. They knew me and asked what was going on. Just as I was handed my jacket the bouncer grabbed me around my neck, put me in a headlock, dragged me out by my hair and pushed me on to the street before quickly closing the door behind me.

Seeing as I couldn't go to Club It any more, I started going to Mazzo. The sound system in Mazzo was on a limiter and wasn't a full sound, but the sound in Club It was awesome. Mazzo DJs weren't as skilled as Dimitri or Marcello, either. I missed the sound system from Club It, where I could really hear the music properly. Unfortunately, that wasn't the case at Mazzo, although it did eventually become our new regular weekly haunt and that's where I performed some of my most memorable DJ sets.

Back in those days, the staff working behind the bar at clubs weren't really into the music, but at Mazzo everybody loved dance music. DJ Cellie was a glass collector in the beginning, before switching to become a resident DJ and booker.

Seeing as I could no longer hear my music properly on the dance floor, I decided I needed to start DJing myself and all my friends said I should go for it.

At the time, 1992, I was working in a pool bar called The Pool Dog, which is now coffeeshop Resin. The owner was older but also enjoyed clubbing and loved his house music. The bar was being renovated and when the work was completed more space became available. There was more room under the stairs and I could imagine a set of turntables and a mixer standing there. I asked the owner if we could put some turntables in and he agreed it was a great idea.

He gave me money to go and buy them. There was a special offer at the time in a shop on Haarlemerstraat so I went there with a bundle of cash and purchased the decks, which were so heavy that I could only carry one at the time through the busy streets. I made the required two trips and then I headed for the record shop.

Soon after that I opened my own record shop – Groove Connection. I had access to a lot of vinyl and I would use the records in my sets before selling them the next day. This taught me to look after the records and their sleeves.

I used to drive to England every week and fill the car with new records and imports from the English distributors. I would leave on a Thursday night because Friday was the day the distributors received their new records. By Friday evening I would be driving back to Amsterdam and I would spend Saturday morning stacking the shelves ready to sell them.

When I started, the house scene was really big in America, Belgium, the United Kingdom and Ibiza. But that was it; business wasn't booming anywhere else in the world and so when I started travelling to play and everywhere I went it was something new and exciting for the people. Also, because the music had no lyrics, it was really crossing boundaries. The crowd reaction would be the same as back home and it was pretty amazing.

After a long flight, often alone, I make it to the party and step into the booth. Because everything looks the same – the mixer, the decks, the crowd, the lights, etc. – it is easy to forget where I am. It can often feel like I am at home in Mazzo, or anywhere else in Amsterdam, and it's only when I look up and see they are all strangers that I remember where I really am.

It's really inspiring to play in different countries. The first time I played outside of the Netherlands was at the end 1992. I went to Cape Town, South Africa, for three months. There was a group of DJs and two organisers. Apartheid was just ending at the time but the old regime was still in place, which was a weird feeling. In those days, South Africa was really tense and the white people were really afraid for their future. All of their houses and gardens were surrounded by fences, and people would build layer upon layer to raise a wall, with broken glass on top, in order to keep people out. When we arrived full of love and happiness from Amsterdam, ready to party, we just wanted to share the music with all the people.

We had hoped to reach out to more of a mix of people but, sadly, it seemed only the white people could afford to attend the events.

I went with Dennis Luts, who later worked for Dance Valley, and fellow Amsterdam DJs Ambient Daan and Mick, from The Richter. The whole point of the trip was to promote our own events, but the local promoters weren't very good. We even managed to organise three gigs in the first two weeks we were there, but it didn't give us enough time to promote, look around and get a genuine feel for the city to ensure we reached the right audience.

We did, however, play for other organisers at their Christmas and New Year parties, from which we each made a little bit of money. Luckily for me, I took enough money to last the time I was there, but Mick and Daan didn't and were broke after just two weeks.

Soon afterwards, a new club called Playground opened on Long Street and we became weekly resident DJs. It was previously a rock club and we played down in the basement, which had become the new house room. There weren't any DJ monitors but that actually taught me so much as a DJ, helping my concentration and making me work even harder. The music was new and it was our job to bring this new sound to people who had never heard it before. We had to convince them with quality house music and pay attention to their reaction on the dance floor. There was also no closing time and the management ruled that as long as there were people on the dance floor we should not stop playing. Initially, that was great, but we were playing sets of more than nine hours, which was crazy.

The experience did teach me a lot, though. When I came home I played in Mazzo and it was so nice because everybody was there for the music and wanted to hear the very latest records. Plus, we had DJ monitors and a quality mixer after the tools to do the job in South Africa had been of such poor quality. It was very refreshing to come back home to play with proper equipment again, which actually made it easier for me to play.

To coincide with our return to Amsterdam, coffeeshop 222 opened – the very first house music coffeeshop in the city. I already knew owner Ricardo from the days we used to go to Club It. He had never danced before, but the ecstasy opened him up and he wanted to organise his own parties. He soon became the Dance Valley organiser and main man.

It was through Mazzo that we met DJ Paul Jay. At the time, Paul's girlfriend was best friends with Ricardo's girlfriend, so that was our connection. Paul was already booking artists for Mazzo, so that became his responsibility, and the rest of the friends
399

would arrange the decoration and flyers. Basically, anything that was needed we did it.

This group grew and grew, and everybody knew each other. It was something very special, just for fun, but everybody helped where they could in order to have a good party.

The first parties were called Evlo and soon afterwards Paul Jay started a new night at the Melkweg called Electric Circus. Several dates were already booked in but the first two events were not successful. Paul lost money and couldn't afford to do it any longer, which was when Ricardo stepped in, although Paul remained involved because he was already on board and was booking artists for our events. We took over the remaining dates and HQ – High Quality – was born. Our first event was on Queensday, April 30th, 1995.

Jason, from Radical Rehousing in the UK, was a 222 regular. He was organising parties in England, but wanted to do parties in Amsterdam as well, and after hearing me play in the shop he asked if I wanted to join him. He hired the venue formerly known as Okshoofd, which later changed its name to Herenhuys.

Because house music was growing, the Herenhuys decided to do more nights and ended up giving me every Friday for the next year. I could invite other DJs as it was my own night, which really helped me build a network. I had a night at which other DJs and organisers could come and check me out. That helped me out a lot because I got to know more and more people from the Amsterdam nightlife, especially as I had only started mixing the previous year.

In 1993 the Radical Rehousing boys also did a night at the Paradiso in Amsterdam, with Way Out West performing live and me DJing. After the live act had finished their equipment was moved down into the basement. During my set I noticed some guys walking through the main room with synthesisers under their arms and walking straight out of the Paradiso through the side door. I didn't realise at the time what was going on, but I soon found that they were actually stealing all of the equipment from downstairs and walking straight out of the club, right past me. I just thought they were roadies. Way Out West's new album was still programmed into the synthesisers, so they actually lost the entire new album too.

After hearing me play Maz, who works at the Paradiso, asked if I also wanted to become their new resident DJ, a role I was already in at The Stalker in Haarlem. The Paradiso gig actually became my most memorable gig because it gave me a new residency in Amsterdam alongside the one in Haarlem.

I was playing Friday at the Paradiso and Saturday at The Stalker, plus gigs in Mazzo, of course, with its small dance floor but always with a committed crowd.

There was an amateurish side to doing things back then. ID&T's Mystery Land featured other styles of music along with hardcore music. Dance Valley was just simply a house music festival, which was how it was marketed.

The first edition in July 1995 was an exciting time and about 5,000 people attended. Preparations began weeks before, with the building of the tents etc. The guys from the office had bicycles to get around the site and at the end of the day everybody was so tired from all the biking. There weren't enough walkie-talkies to go around either, so Ricardo had to shout at everybody to have any chance of being heard.

On the day I was playing I could see people running up to the fence, climbing over and immediately running onto the crowded dance floor. The following year we put up a double fence to prevent this, plus there was also a river separating the Mainstage from the crowd. I heard a story from people working backstage that they saw two guys take their clothes off outside and began wading through the water, holding their dry clothes above them. The security saw this but actually let them enjoy the party for a bit before taking them backstage and kicking them out. Just to have enjoyed that moment was probably enough for them.

The day after we had the clean-up operation and the local Scout group was brought in to clean the entire festival site. One thing, the night before when the crowds had left, we walked around all the empty tents and stages with searchlights to look for all the drugs and money people had dropped. We found so much stuff and bundles of cash!

The following year, 1996, people knew where the site was and a few weeks before the festival they would go there. It was a public space and they would dig holes on the site to bury their booze and other stuff.

Dance Valley grew exponentially and doubled every year. It went from 4,000 to 8,000 in the second year, to 16,000 in the third, 32,000 the fourth etc. There was some extra land owned by a farmer, who agreed to rent it to us. It's the responsibility of the council to prepare the land we used for the festival, along with an external company. There were also a lot of bushes that had to be removed and we managed to pay some extra money to have them all removed. The council also works with the police and the fire department, usually with the aid of a giant map, so everybody knows where everything and everyone is.

Everything has to be official and organised to the best standard possible.

In 2000 we had a difficult festival due to an unexpected tropical rain storm. I was on site, but in my tent, where I always slept before and after the festival. I awoke from all the noise from the severe weather and decided I needed to go back to my home in Amsterdam. I jumped in my car and drove off the site but it was raining like crazy! Just as I approached the road near the ferry crossing for Zaandam, I could see that party people from the festival had erected a shelter next to the road. People were wrapped in foil sheets because of hypothermia, while others had ripped the black plastic sheets from the temporary fencing and were huddled under it as they hobbled down the road. That was actually nice to see because people were clearly helping each other. But there was a terrible mess everywhere and I wasn't completely sure what was going on. I also saw a burnt-out bus and I shouted: "What the fuck?" Honestly, it looked like a war zone and it was a scary experience. It felt like there had been a nuclear war while I had been asleep and there was an obvious bad vibe among everyone involved in the organisation.

The following year they were not allowed to have as many people attend, with a strict limit imposed of 40,000.

They eventually did organise a Dance Valley weekender, too, on the Friday and Saturday. Unfortunately, the week leading up to the first edition, it rained every day so the campsite was completely flooded. Of course, this also affected the outdoor stages.

Nowadays, Dance Valley is not so much about unity, like in the old days. Today it seems to have become extremely corporate. There is way too much EDM and I'm no longer really a fan of the

403

festival.

A few years ago I did organise the HQ area and it had been some time since I had done that. The following day the newspapers reported that the HQ stage was the only stage that had a different sound, because the other stages all sounded similar, and it felt nice to read that.

Often at Dance Valley you would have a musical build-up throughout the day, especially the Mainstage. Nowadays it's just bang, bang, bang from the first minute to the last, and I think that is really boring.

As I was no longer involved with Dance Valley, together with ex-DJ Danny D we started our own festival. We have organised two outdoor festivals so far at the Stadspodium in Amsterdam. Originally, Dance Valley said we couldn't use the name HQ, despite our offer to pay them a percentage from each event, so I decided to call the event DJ JP & Tom Harding Presents.

Since 2019 Danny and I thought 'Fuck it, let's just use the name HQ again.' And that is what we did – because we're old school. We didn't own the name but we went ahead and used it. It's no longer under copyright and there haven't been any complaints from anyone.

Despite parting ways with Dance Valley, it is still my most memorable location to DJ, plus the sound and production levels were immense.

Carl Cox and Billy Nasty also mentioned that the English parties in the mid-90s had low production levels and seemed like they were being run by amateurs. They were impressed by the professionalism of Dance Valley, especially the sound and production.

Billy was the closing DJ at the first festival in 1995, but Carl had stayed after his set and there was a huge party backstage afterwards. Incidentally, Carl was the only person to have a mobile phone and we were all, like, 'Wooooooah, he's got a mobile phone. Wow!'

It helped when we asked him to order pizzas for everyone – and he did!

The cigarettes were quickly finished and because the organisers had the 222 coffeeshop there was loads of weed going around. Because we had run out of cigarettes, we were just rolling pure joints. Never had I heard anyone cough so intensely as Carl, who had tears in his eyes. He just kept saying: "This is nice. It's really nice, man." Ha-ha-ha.

We had a lot of fun backstage. What was especially nice was that the following year Carl was playing again and he remembered my name from the previous year, and there was always a big hug whenever we met. For an artist held in such high regard he was very down to earth and open-minded, very friendly and honest too. His mixing in the vinyl days was something else; it really was unbelievable. One year, I was watching him from the side of the Mainstage and thinking 'This is a nice record.' But then he would play a new record and I found myself thinking 'This record is even better.' That continued to be the case throughout his entire set because his mixing was so amazing.

Carl was also the first DJ to grab the microphone during his set and MC himself.

In 1996 or 1997 I played in Prague with DJ Bicker, who is also from Amsterdam. Bicker was playing regularly in Prague and could invite another DJ, so I went with him one weekend. The party was in an old communist building, in the middle of a residential area, and the promoter only spoke broken English. He just kept saying: "Follow me, follow me," but we had no idea where we were going.

We entered through a small door but could hear nothing. There were thick concrete pillars everywhere and we walked down a dark corridor before going through another door, at which point we could hear something. It was a small bass kick in the distance, slowly getting louder, and when we walked through a third door it was BOOM, BOOM, BOOM, BOOM....we were on the dance floor. Wow, it was incredible. The building was so well insulated, but it felt strange to have entered a building and at first be greeted with total silence.

We had brought hash and weed with us, and were smoking in our dressing room before we were told to immediately evacuate. There was a bomb scare and the club had to be emptied, but we had to leave our stuff in the dressing room. When the police arrived they searched the entire building for the bomb but, rather fortunately, never found our weed, otherwise it would have been a very different story.

It turned out to be a hoax. The call was made by a rival promoter who didn't want the party to go ahead and so he ruined it for everyone. Unfortunately, at the time of the hoax call, it was still very quiet inside and the promoters didn't make enough money to pay us.

They assured us both that they would eventually transfer our fee but, annoyingly, they never did.

DJ LEVIATHAN

Michel Klaassen, aka Leviathan and Tellurian, is an originator of the Dutch hardcore scene.

In 1985, Michel started his production career after producing for hip-hop crew D-P – Digital Power.

It was through his love for the early house music scene that he eventually progressed to the harder sound and became a prominent member of the Dutch, and eventually international, hardcore scene. Through DJ or live sets, he soon proved his worth and the gigs began to follow.

Deciding to invest his earnings in studio equipment was a bold move that proved very fruitful for his eventual career.

Michel has produced for many hardcore artists, while also developing a love for a variety of styles. In 1993 he started producing for Amsterdam hardcore label Mokum Records. It was then that his reputation began to grow and Dutch company ID&T became interested. He worked on the label side of the Thunderdome project, among others.

In 1996 he started his own label, Cenobite Records, which is still in operation today.

Michel spoke about a legendary live show, Los Angeles, warehouse parties and playing in Dubai.

I remember an old warehouse party back in the late 90s in Amsterdam which had two stages, one on top of the other. The top stage was for DJs and the lower for the live acts, I'd never seen a set-up like this before and now I know why. Unfortunately, every DJ had sound issues. The needle of the decks would skip across the record due to the people on the lower stage, where the vibrations were shaking the top stage and decks above. I was actually tip-toeing across the stage because I didn't want to be the one that made the record jump and I only wish more people had done the same.

At one point during the night I looked up at the booth and spotted that the DJ was clearly rather tipsy. Seconds later, I also noticed that he had disappeared. The music was still playing, the crowd were still dancing but there was no sign of the DJ. I won't mention his name to avoid any embarrassment, but he knows who he is!

Anyway, it turned out that at one point during his set he wanted to take a little rest and focus his eyes, so he leaned against what he thought was a wall. It turned out to be nothing more than a curtain and he fell from the top stage, behind the decks, and slammed on his ass in the backstage area many metres below – total knockout! The crowd were oblivious to this and once he came round he asked what had happened. And then, to be fair, he climbed back up, brushed himself down and finished his set like a true professional, ha-ha-ha!

Another time, back in 2008, we were on a flight heading off to play in Los Angeles. We had a stop-off and connecting flight in Chicago and the DJ I was travelling with was too drunk and obnoxious for my liking. There we were on the plane, about to take off from Amsterdam, and I'm thinking 'Fuck, man, I've got another eight hours of this crap.'

We made it to Chicago and were in the queue for customs when he was stopped by some officials who asked him: "What is your profession?" A simple enough question but, unfortunately, his English wasn't so good and he struggled to understand properly, so he just replied, innocently: "I work with weed."

Actually, he wasn't joking or trying to be clever. He worked as a cleaner for the council in a local park. He cleared all the weeds and maintained the grass, too!

The guy was covered head-to-toe in tattoos, flying in from Amsterdam, and the customs officials must have thought they'd caught a couple of smugglers.

The customs people said: "Weed?" and he just nodded. All completely innocent and after some questioning they let both of us through to travel onwards to Los Angeles.

We made it to LA and later that evening we were taken to the party. He was first to play – followed by me – and just as I was starting he announced he had to leave and return to Amsterdam because he had to be back at work on the Monday morning. Luckily, I had an extra day free after the party to enjoy some of LA and have a look around the city.

It turned out he had somehow managed to miss his connecting flight and was sat at the airport in Washington for several hours waiting to be put on another flight. Meanwhile, I was busy enjoying what LA had to offer.

Our return flights were via Washington and although I left a day after him, to my amazement I arrived in Amsterdam just one
409

hour after him!

People still talk about one of my live shows from over 20 years ago – where a leg was chopped off with a chainsaw.

It was Hellraiser, a hardcore party in Amsterdam, and the theme for this particular edition was horror. I met with the organisers and discussed what we could do as a live show, and we came up with the idea to chop a leg off live on stage.

It was actually very complicated to arrange. It took something like two months to finalise everything and on top of that we had to do rehearsals.

I knew someone who had only one leg and he was happy to be involved. A fake leg was made and he put it on as if it was real and we came up with the stage act, featuring dancers, him and Hellraiser – the pin-head character from the movie. In those days you couldn't buy a Hellraiser costume so we had one made by a bunch of students from a local film school. It looked great, complete with the face of nails, and they also made the fake leg, as well as tons of blood.

We had two dancers covered in flesh-looking paint designs and they had to grab the unsuspecting two-legged victim from the crowd before we strapped him to a chair on the stage.

The pin-head Hellraiser monster then returned with a chainsaw and started to chop his leg off. Blood was squirting everywhere, people were turning white and the place was in total shock. That was how it looked to the crowd but, obviously, this guy was switched on stage for the one-legged guy under the disguise of the smoke machine.

Suddenly, without warning, two paramedics appeared on stage and started to treat the victim while pin-head's walking around the stage with the chopped leg held high, showering everyone in blood. The paramedics took him, screaming, off the stage on a stretcher and through the shocked crowd into a room somewhere.

That was one mad, mad, gig that is still talked about today!

I remember playing at a party called Pyramid in Switzerland with Technohead, an English DJ. He only wanted to DJ, rather than do a live set, so they put him on the flyer as Technohead – DJ Slut instead of DJ slot! The party itself was in an old factory but it was surrounded by police, despite having a licence. Too many locals had complained about the noise and the police stopped it at 3am instead of 7am. The place was full of ravers and they didn't want to leave. They all just sat on the floor refusing to budge, with others trying to start a beat by banging on tables etc. In the end it was pointless because there were far too many police officers. Everybody left.

It's funny, because that night was also the first time as a DJ that I witnessed two people shagging in front of the stage.

I met a French guy called Denis Ravizza at another techno party in Switzerland about 20 years ago. He was doing a live act with two of his brothers and another person, and they were called 4-IQ.

I was watching them set up their gear before a soundcheck and he showed me his wireless controller. Being a producer myself, I was always keen to check out other artists and their set-up. This really blew me away – I had never seen anything like it before.

During their performance he would hand his controller into the crowd and the crowd could then add their own sounds and effects into the live show. In 94-95 this was unheard of. It was really amazing – the crowd were part of the live act!

Not long after, he was performing in Amsterdam and I managed to arrange a record deal for him with a Dutch label and we became really good mates.

Eventually, he moved to Dubai with his wife, where they created and started the Esmod French Fashion Institute, which was a franchise of worldwide institutes. We lost contact but several years later we met up and he invited me to play at Esmod, to DJ at the students' graduation party. I was playing a bit of everything, chilled and then heavier, and Denis kept asking me to play hardcore techno for the end of the night. I'm pretty sure I was the first DJ to play hardcore music in Dubai. They really enjoyed my set and the locals were dancing until the end. I've been fortunate enough to return three or four times since.

One particular gig in 2013 was at The One and Only Hotel on Palm Island in Dubai. The furthest left leaf, right on the tip, that's where the resort was located. It just happened to be the night Dubai was trying to create a Guinness World Record for a firework display.

At midnight I was told to keep on playing music and not to stop. Because of this, I missed the firework display – the biggest in the world! And the dance floor was empty – everybody was down on the Palm beach watching the fucking fireworks.

Little did I know, but there was a huge screen behind me with a live broadcast of the world record firework attempt.

If only I'd turned around.

GENE FARRIS

Not surprisingly, since it is the birthplace of the genre, Chicago is very rich in house music history and Gene has fully earned his right to be rated alongside the very best.

In 1998 Gene created record label Farris Wheel Recordings. Fellow Chicago legends Paul Johnson and Stacy Kidd have featured on this highly-respected label, as well as many releases from the main man himself.

With bookings worldwide on a regular basis, this family man is showing no signs of slowing down, despite the sadness that ensues when having to leave his young sons and go perform on the other side of the world. If you follow Gene on social media you'll see that he is a sensitive soul and always shares adorable family posts after returning from overseas. Big love!

I got to know Gene when he was living in Amsterdam and we would often spend too many hours propping up the bar in the Grey Area coffeeshop, a weed haven for many a Chicago DJ!

Gene spoke about how he first became a DJ, touring, Amsterdam, meeting old friend Green Velvet for the first time and the nightmare flights DJs must endure.

Enjoy...

I was really lucky growing up. Everybody, well perhaps not *everybody*, but most of those I looked up to were already busy

DJing in their basements. I had dreams of being a DJ and I wanted it but to headline a neighbourhood party in someone's basement was enough for me.

When I started I was only 10 years old. Sadly, just two weeks before my 10th birthday, my dad passed away and I still miss him every single day.

He died in May and my birthday is in June. In August that year, 1982, I played at my first party. It was in my neighbourhood for all the friends. The guys in my neighbourhood took me under their wing and that's how I started my hobby as a DJ.

After learning how to mix and to be able to DJ as a hobby it was time to *become* a DJ.

When I was 14, maybe 15, I entered a DJ competition going on in the neighbourhood and I won. From 16 I was hanging up the posters for The Powerhouse, which featured both Ron Carroll and Ron Hardy. I kind of became Ron Carroll's groupie, although he was a friend of mine. Also, his older brother actually worked with my mother.

Ron knew I was a good DJ, albeit a little young. One day he let me open up at The Powerhouse for him and the rest is kind of history from there. I continued to open for Ron Carroll and Ron Hardy, and then Boo Williams, and eventually DJ Rush.

Back then, Rush's style was disco which, along with funk and soul, were the genres I was playing when I started. That was kind of the Chicago way.

We would be playing the disco sounds, plus tracks which we made, along with Lil Louis and Armando tracks etc. – that was the Chicago way of partying back in the 80s. Some people still do it like that.

So that was Rush's original style, that was the way he would play in those days. Together with me, we kind of developed a new style, a way of performing our own tracks, which we had produced, live in our DJ sets.

Back then we would be using reel-to-reel tapes and cassettes.

I liked to play my tracks during my sets and there are some that still haven't even been released to this day. Back then, when I was 17 or18 years old, I didn't even dream of playing my songs out to crowds.

I developed as a DJ, playing to local crowds that had been listening to me – and dancing to my songs – for years. I never even dreamt of having my songs signed and then released by a label. Most of us were just happy with our own music and being available to play it among ourselves, but it was actually being liked by the whole of Chicago!

So, you know, the vision I had of being a record producer didn't happen until many years later when my first record was released.

At the time I was only 21 years old but it had still taken a long time for things to become fruitful.

I've been friends with Ron Trent since our school days. He had friends at my school and I had friends at his school, which is how we became friends.

I was 21 and I had some tracks and there was one particular track I had made which, when I was playing out, people would always ask me to play. I was starting to get a lot of street-rep and people were enjoying what I was doing.

When I had just turned 22 I really wanted to have my tracks signed, so I went along to see Ron Trent.

Ron had a label, Prescription Records, which he was running at the time with Chez Damier. It was more deep house and is probably, to this day, still *the* best deep house label. The stuff I was doing was more tech house, or techno you know, some banging tracks.

Ron thought the tracks were dope but said he couldn't put them out on his label. He said he would take me over to the office, where there was someone who was in charge of all the distribution and he said I should meet. In fact, this guy was in charge of pressing the vinyl, distribution and everything else.

His name was Curtis, better known as Green Velvet, and he was busy with the harder techno sound. He was busy putting out the harder stuff elsewhere and after Ron Trent introduced us we went on to do a lot of tracks with each other. Curtis is still one of my best mates today.

We've been recording a lot with each other recently and there have been tons of funny moments when we are in the studio together. I'm just trying to think of one that he won't be mad me telling you, ha-ha-ha.

Years ago, I had my first gig outside of America at The Ministry of Sound in London. That is where I popped my cherry in Europe!

It was a Relief/Cajual tour, together with Green Velvet, Gemini,

Glenn Underground, Boo Williams, Sneak, me and some others. It was a great line-up for my first-ever gig outside of the USA.

I played my set and received a great reception. I was really stoked and don't forget, at the time, I was still only 22 years old. Curtis came over and told me how he had enjoyed my set and then told me to go backstage to the green room to get a drink.

So, being from the south-side of Chicago and still only young, I was shocked, happily shocked, by all the alcohol. There were boxes of Grolsch and it tasted amazing. It was probably the best beer I had ever tasted and before I knew it I had finished a box of 24 bottles.

I passed out in The Ministry of Sound and Curtis had to get help from the security guys to help me back to the hotel. I had managed to make a complete ass of myself.

There is one thing, though, that I have learned in this industry and that's not to fight the beast. The good thing is that it didn't hinder my career!

Perhaps Curtis's tracks, Flash or La La Land, were inspired by my actions that day. It probably also has something to do with why I don't drink today.

One of the funniest things about meeting Curtis and this whole story is that on the day, the exact same day I was at Prescription Records, DJ Sneak was in there trying to get Ron to sign his tracks. That's how Sneak and I met for the first time.

It was the day that the whole Gene Farris productions era began too. Curtis loved my tracks and so I released my first EP in 1994 – The Farris-Wheel EP. Later, when I began my own label in

417

1998, I used that same title as my record label name.

It was crazy how things came together, you know, and life certainly takes you in different directions.

The Boom Boom Room was nice and I shared a residency there with DJ Diz, a good friend of mine. We were bringing in a lot of talent and being able to have a residency in a decent club, promoting quality nights, and in my hometown too, was definitely pivotal in my local career in Chicago.

The same Boom Boom Room isn't really happening any more but the good thing is that my number of fans probably doubled due to the old days and they still follow me today. To me that is a beautiful thing and the Boom Boom Room will always share a special place in my heart. I had all my friends there partying, including the local drag queens, and I had mates working the bar. They are still some of the best friends I have today.

While living in Amsterdam there was one particular gig that was very influential on my DJ career and they let me organise my own stage and book the artists I wanted.

It was Extrema Outdoor back in July 2003. I managed to get Sneak, Mark Farina, Benny Rodrigues and Derrick Carter to come and play. It was great to be able to get my good friends from Europe and Chicago involved and playing, especially on my own stage.

Another big Amsterdam moment, again involving an Extrema gig, was when I played with Roger Sanchez. It was the first time I had played with him and for a little while we decided to do a tag set, back-to-back, which was really cool.

Roger is now a really good friend of mine and I'm working on some remixes for him right now, actually. It's great how things just go full-circle.

I also had a residency at Jimmy Woo while I was living in Amsterdam. There were some great nights there, it was a great experience and I have nothing but love for Amsterdam. It is truly my second home.

I had some great times with my good friend Brian S, a local Amsterdam DJ. We played together at Club NL, also in Amsterdam, and numerous festivals throughout Holland. Victor Coral is another local DJ with whom I had a great time.

Dimitri is also a good friend of mine and we played some great parties together. Oh man, I have nothing but love and amazing memories from the Chemistry parties. Eelco, Marcello, Brian, Victor, Dimitri, all those guys, they're like my family – my Amsterdam family – and the Grey Area coffeeshop, that's my Amsterdam home!

My most memorable gig of all time was when I played in Scotland for a Soma party at The Arches in Glasgow. It was in the late 90s and I was playing with Basement Jaxx, Sneak and Green Velvet.

Wow, those Soma boys really know how to throw a party. The crowd was really up for it and, due to the heat, there was water dripping from the ceiling. It was a truly memorable night.

Another memorable gig was in Paris, at what I believe was a Magic Garden party with Daft Punk. That, too, was back in the 90s. I remember it being an absolutely huge party. The venue was a garden but the area I was performing in was indoors.

I have the pleasure of knowing Thomas and Guy, and the Daft Punk boys are great, I really love playing with them. They actually gave me a shout-out on the Homework album, too, on the Teachers track.

Thomas's girlfriend at the time was a photographer and she worked on the cover of my Religion album, released on Soma.

Thomas and Guy had a great relationship with the Soma boys and it was through their connection that I got to meet them. I remember a time when I stayed at Thomas's home in Paris and we did a photo shoot together. It was a really long time ago but still great memories.

I love touring and playing in other countries but the travelling can be crazy. However, I'll never say I will never do it again, because I'm just so crazy for it all. My last tour was simply amazing. I was playing in Australia and the gigs were amazing, too. The hospitality was the best I'd ever had, but I had the journey from hell to get there.

It was August 2016 and I had to fly from Chicago to Los Angeles, which was four hours. In Los Angeles I had a two-hour layover then I had to fly 18 hours to Sydney. That was already 22 hours in the air, with a further two hours waiting in Los Angeles, so a total of 24 hours by the time I arrived in Sydney.

I had to go through customs and everything, which meant a further two or three hours before my flight to Perth, which added another six hours airtime. It was a total of 33 hours of travel before I got to my bed!

My Australian tour began on the west coast, starting in Perth. It was then on to Melbourne, Adelaide and Sydney before I worked my way back to the east coast of Australia, to fly back to Los Angeles and eventually home to Chicago.

So, 33 hours of travel before I could get to my bed for some sleep and play my first gig in Perth. It was murder and I had never experienced anything like it until then.

I had travelled to Australia before but normally my tour would start in Sydney, which meant I would be okay. Starting the tour in Perth and then working my way back was just madness.

I loved Australia, the gigs were some of the best I've ever played and the hospitality was great, as were the Aussie people.

With all the travelling it was just a bit too manic, but would I do it again?

Fuck yeah!

MISS DJAX

*Saskia Slegers, aka Miss Djax, is the Acid Queen, a title she has
earned after stomping, old-school acid sets and as the founder of
internationally acclaimed record label Djax Records. The label
has featured some major names from the techno world, including
DJ Rush, Felix da Housecat, Claude Young and Luke Slater.*

*Djax Records has recently celebrated 30 years in the business, a
fantastic achievement considering so many labels have shut
down in that time and a real testament to Saskia and the Djax
family, who know quality music when they hear it.*

*Miss Djax has also been fortunate to receive several best-label
awards and is regarded as one of the finest female DJs ever. An
Eindhoven local, in the south of the Netherlands, Saskia
continues to push her sound worldwide with appearances at the
world's biggest techno events.*

*For this interview, Saskia spoke about her early days as a DJ,
being a label boss and her most memorable gig.*

My first experience of music was when I was a young child and
used to buy seven-inch singles. I was also listening to albums
from my mother and father. I especially remember The Beatles
but also a lot of classical music. I already knew then, at an early
age, that I wanted to be a DJ, maybe work in a record store or on
the radio – anything that involved music.

I started DJing between 1978 and 1979, and in those days there was no house scene. I loved discovering new music and sharing it with the people.

I was playing in a local club, Vox Club in Eindhoven, and there was absolutely no house music played at all. The DJ was just a walking jukebox and that's all I ever wanted to be. I would go on my bike every Saturday night to the club and I would play from 10pm to 2am, or through to 4am, and earn my 40 guilders.

For me, it was my dream to play records to people and to play new dance music. At the time it was disco then new wave and hip-hop etc. I loved playing for the kids and I'm still doing it, the only difference being that I don't play new music. I play the records I played in the 90s and for a lot of people it is new music, especially the young generation that don't know the music from the 90s. Plus, of course, there's still the old generation that come to my gigs.

Back in the day, I went from disco and funk to new wave – very dark new wave like Joy Division. From then on it was electro and new beat, then on to hip-hop, with a lot of rap also coming from the States.

The acid house scene then finally took off. Well, it exploded to be honest. The scene evolved and I was becoming inspired by the harder sound of acid techno. It felt like a normal development, actually.

At the time – late 70s, early 80s – nobody would have expected DJs to go on to have the careers they have had. Why would somebody ask me to go to Spain or America to play? 'They are not going to send me on a plane all that way. They have their own DJs,' I would think.

Nobody knew that this could actually happen. It wasn't even that I was dreaming about it because in my mind it didn't even exist.

The only thing I wanted to do was be involved with music. I was a DJ and I also formed a new-wave band called B-System, in which I played the bass guitar. I worked in a record store, too, as I had previously predicted I would and, of course, there was my label which I ran, Djax Records and later Djax-Up-Beats.

I had all the things in place for what I had always wanted to become.

In the early 90s, techno was much more than it is now. There were not so many labels and not many categories. The techno and rave scene was much more open-minded back then, whereas nowadays you have 150 styles of music.

I'm very loyal to my style and records, which are all acid-techno. I still love that sound. Sometimes, over the years, I didn't always feel like that, but it's my sound and I just keep on doing it. I have a following that likes it and I'm not changing! I haven't bought any new music for years. I don't follow it because I love what I have from the 90s. It's only old music and it's gone with me everywhere, and I have often had to buy new copies of some old records, as the originals had completely worn out. For me, it's good that I don't have to listen to all the new stuff that is coming out. I don't like digital releases, either. It's only about the sounds and the records from the 90s as far as I'm concerned.

I really love re-living the 90s and with parties like Wooferland it is possible

When you're playing on the underground scene, and you are at the top, you influence different people. Some of my music has been taken and used in a commercial way, meaning they have benefited commercially from something which was initially underground. This happens, unfortunately.

Regarding my label, Djax-Up-Beats, if there's a track that I like I will release it. I don't care where the producer is coming from, but it must have that specific Djax sound, which is personal and just my own taste. It has to be rough and raw sounding, too.

I've had a lot of reviews over the years from professional people within the scene that gave me a lot of credit, too, for being responsible for a certain techno sound. It's cool to be recognised but everything is from the heart. It was my passion and nothing was planned for success.

I released a lot of different styles. The first release on Djax Records was a hardcore hip-hop production from 24K, back in 1989. I also released breakbeat records, too. Everything was rough and underground, just the way I like it.

My most memorable DJ experience has to be Love Parade. I had my own truck from 1995 to 1998. During the 1996 and 1998 editions I was fortunate enough to be truck number one, leading the parade with a huge rocket on board with 20,000 watts of acid techno power. I also considered myself fortunate to play at the Victory Column and that was probably the most beautiful experience for me, playing for one million people.

Nowadays, I don't have as much passion for running a label as I used to have. It's too digital for me and too much internet. I do still run the label but I'm not releasing anywhere near as much these days. I'm busy with my own releases and also with Dutch techno artist Oliver Kucera. He's one to watch out for – I like him a lot.

MELON

Jeroen Hofer, aka Melon, is the Netherlands house specialist. I have known him since the mid 90s.

He was 17, and in those days we were both Mazzo regulars. There was a whole bunch of us who would religiously attend the Mazzo several nights a week. Jeroen was living near Alkmaar at the time with his parents, and was always partying in Amsterdam. DJ Angelo at the Mazzo on Thursdays was always a great night, and Jeroen always had to take the first train home in the morning as it was Friday, and he had to go to school! It wasn't long until he moved to Amsterdam, and his career began to take shape.

Jeroen was already DJing, not at the level he has since risen to, but he was beginning to earn a reputation as a quality and reliable DJ.

With an interest in drum machines at the ripe old age of 8, you know this fella was already on the road to a life in music.

Jeroen and I would often DJ together in the late 90s and beyond in Amsterdam, often at The Greenhouse Effect, Vaaghuyzen and Twstd. But this emerging DJ and newly named DJ Melon soon began to spread his wings and was internationally in-demand. Decades later, and he still is!

His record collection spans more than 35 years, and is a guaranteed base to delivering quality DJ sets around the globe.

Melon has a few different guises when producing music, with names such as Nitzi and Je Davu often gracing the sets of the world's leading house DJs.

For this interview, Melon spoke about several airport adventures, public nudity, Amsterdam gigs and an unforgettable Moscow debut.

Enjoy...

I've always been interested in music, ever since the day I was born. My parents would go to a lot of concerts, even when my mum was pregnant, which I suppose was the first time I came into contact with music. We didn't really watch television as kids. Instead we would paint, draw and listen to music. I didn't have a traditional musical upbringing either; no Beatles or Rolling Stones, but instead more Motown and soul, especially Aretha Franklin. My dad was really into his jazz and African music, while my mum loved her soul.

Back in 2007, during my divorce, I was playing in Munich, where I had a Ratio – the name of my record label – residency. The night before was messy and I hadn't slept at all. I can't really remember completely what had happened, but it was at the time I was going through a split and I was kind of homeless and staying with a friend. It was a tough time and I just wanted to party.

I was playing a lot, earning good money, but the problem was that I liked to treat myself to nice things and when I was touring I would often buy my then wife lingerie.

On this particular day, before flying to Munich, I went shopping for some underwear – for myself – and I found a designer store selling what I wanted. I felt the material on this certain pair and it was nice; I mean REALLY NICE! They were pink in colour and had the word Rebel printed on the arse. I had to have them so I bought them and immediately put them on.

Remember, I hadn't slept from the previous night, and after shopping I headed straight to the airport and flew to Munich.

Munich Airport has a reputation for being very strict and I was immediately removed from the line after arriving. They took me to one side and asked if I had any drugs on me, and it was at this point I remembered I had a couple of grams of hash in my record bag. I told them that I did and even showed them where it was. They weighed it and it turned out to be 4.5 grams, I was then taken to a small room where I was ordered to undress.

I was stood there in my pink designer briefs with Rebel printed on my ass. I was laughing so hard, I couldn't stop. But they didn't see the funny side and continued to search me – with a flashlight – before they realised I had nothing more on me. They slapped me with a fine of 800 euros, which I had to pay immediately. It was lucky that I only had 4.5 grams of hash because anybody with five grams or more is sent to jail.

The promoter was waiting for me in Arrivals and I was being held in the police station. I was being asked all sorts of questions about myself, whether I was married or not etc. I explained that I was currently going through a divorce and one of the officers seemed to take pity on me. He was also going through a divorce and said to his colleague that they should let me go. They were speaking in German, but being Swiss I could understand everything they were saying. I didn't tell them this, though, and

428

continued to speak in English. Silently, I was thinking it was going well and they then said I only had to pay 200 euros, which they put straight in their pockets.

I paid the money and I was let go. I then met the promoter at Arrivals, told him what had happened and he too couldn't stop laughing!

London Heathrow is another crazy story. Somehow I always managed to have an issue in the UK. I was playing in London at T Bar, not the old one but instead at the new one in Aldgate. I was playing together with Steffi and Jennifer Cardini downstairs in the basement.

After the party we went back to our Travelodge, a small basic hotel, and we all went to our rooms. Now, when I'm in a hotel I always sleep naked. I do it for a reason, because sometimes I can't arrange a late check-out. Someone always seems to come to my room around 10am and I like to get out of bed yelling "What the fuck!" which makes them run away.

On that particular day they didn't come back until 2pm so I had my late check-out! Ha-ha.

Although, at one point I heard somebody knocking on the door, or at least that's what I thought I heard. I wasn't sure, so I opened the door, had a look around and bam, the door closed behind me. I was like 'Fuuuuuccccccckkkkkk!' I was naked, standing in a hotel corridor. I had to go to the reception, but it gets worse. This Travelodge had two separate buildings and, yes, I had to go out of one building, walk across an alleyway and into the other one.

But I needed my room key to swipe and enter the outside door!

I was just stood there, naked in an alleyway, but I have to say that I did see the funny side and it was fun. But the fun soon stopped because I had to walk around to the front of the building and then walk in the front entrance. I was stood at reception, hands around my bits telling them: "You don't want to know, but I'm locked out of my room, please help me." They did, and I made it back to my room.

The next day we flew home. I don't know what it is, maybe all the partying, but the time difference always seems to fuck me up. I headed for Heathrow's Terminal 4 and it was extremely busy. I had forgotten about the one-hour time difference and I was already an hour late. I went to the check-in gate but despite the fact that I only had hand luggage they refused to check me in. There was still 45 minutes until departure time but they really weren't letting me on. "What the fuck?" I said. Because I used the F-word, security were onto me and I immediately had my hands pushed up against my back. They told me I wasn't allowed to curse in the airport and in the end I had to book another flight for later that day.

In 2017 I had a similar experience. I was playing with Gui Barrato in London at a Halloween party and was flying home with a friend two days later. We had different flights but we would be back in Amsterdam around the same time. I had my recording gear with me and the microphone had lots of wires. The customs had to check everything and they told me I would be too late for the plane. Again, I had to book another flight home.

My friend was already back in Amsterdam and waiting for me in a cafe. I eventually made it back and went to his place for a drink. Around 6am I left; I'd had enough. I made it home and stumbled up the stairs to my floor. I was trying to get my key in the door, but the key wouldn't fit. I looked up at the door and there was a written note from the police. The note said that there had been a leak in the building, which meant they had to break into my apartment. It added that there were new door keys waiting for me at the local police station.

This was the last thing I wanted to have to deal with!

"NO, NOT NOW!" I screamed. I was completely trashed, ready for bed but I wasn't able to enter my house and had to head for the police station to get the keys. When I finally made it in, I noticed immediately that my place had been completely trashed. Everything had been moved, the cupboards emptied and the walls were ruined.

I called the police and asked if they were actually allowed to enter a house and do that. They said that in an emergency situation like that the police can gain entry with a plumber and just do their job. They don't have to clean anything and must leave as soon as possible. Even though I wasn't responsible, I was stuck with all the mess.

I actually still have the police note pinned up in my room!

It was a crazy period and I was touring like hell, and there was another long crazy weekend around the corner. It started in Ibiza on the Thursday. I was playing for the Kompakt agency in the Red Box room, upstairs in Space, while fellow Amsterdam DJ Steve Rachmad played downstairs. The next day, Friday, I had to fly to Dusseldorf for a party over there. On Saturday I flew back to Holland to play at the Lowlands Festival, where I was playing in the Bravo tent. The previous year, I played a five-hour set back-to-back with Ricardo Villalobos in the India tent. I actually pretty much played the entire set alone because he was late. This time, I was playing alone between the Scissor Sisters and Josh Wink, and I remember it very well. It was one of the biggest crowds I had ever played for, I think there were probably between 10 and 15,000 people, like the mainstage crowd at Awakenings for example.

I was standing there on the massive stage in this tiny DJ booth and had my artist name, Melon, displayed on all the screens around me. It was a truly memorable gig. On the Sunday I flew to Georgia, because I was playing in Batumi on Monday.

There wasn't a direct flight so I flew first to Istanbul, where I had an overlay of six hours. I wanted to see Istanbul for a bit, so I started to walk and immediately there were loads of taxi drivers giving me their best offers to see the town. I said it was too much so they then began to reduce their prices. I think I got it down to 25 euros in the end. I saw a little bit of what Istanbul had to offer before returning to the airport. It was already dark by the time my flight left for Trebzon, which was the airport closest to the Georgian border.

It was a very small airport, which literally only had one runway for landing and taking off. Next to it they had an army tent where the luggage was stored and all the passengers had to search for their own suitcases. I got hold of mine and then I walked to the exit and saw a little guy standing all alone with a Melon sign. He couldn't speak much English, so he just gestured for me to follow him to an old, nasty, yellow pee-coloured Mercedes. He was going to be my chauffeur for the next few hours and drive me to Batumi. I sat on the back seat and it immediately curled around me because it was just so fucking old.

He started driving and we just followed the coast line. He was driving like a maniac and I wondered where we were. I couldn't

432

talk to him and I kept thinking, 'If something happens no one will know where I am.' It was just one of those situations.

As we approached the Turkish border it was already after midnight. They asked me for my passport, asked us to get out of the car and walk over to customs. We had to walk down this lane, which was next to a prison, and I could see the prisoners in their windows with their arms through the bars, all screaming at me. It was a bizarre situation.

At the customs, they searched my taxi driver and then his car. They were all looking at me asking what I was doing there and why I was so late, after midnight on a Sunday, with a case of records and a Swiss passport. They searched my records and found nothing. Behind me, a guy was being busted for bringing booze into the country.

One thing I have learned with travelling and customs is to keep on smiling, because as soon as you make trouble you're fucked. So I kept smiling, made a couple of jokes and then we were on our way. After driving through no-man's land, we ended up at this kind of strip, full of clubs. There were Ferraris and Lamborghinis, and it looked as if we were in Cannes or Ibiza, rather than Batumi. I was playing at Prozac, a club on the beach, together with American DJ Gene Farris.

There are literally no drugs in Georgia so everybody gets really drunk. You become accustomed to playing in clubs where there's a certain vibe, but in Batumi they just get more and more drunk. Before long, they were completely out of control and there were a lot of fights. It felt really weird because it's such a different energy to what I'm used to.

Anyway, the club closed at five, so I left and had some street
433

food somewhere before I went to the hotel. The next day, the promoter picked me up and took me for breakfast, where I ate caviar and eggs. It was Ossetra, yellow caviar, and it's the best around apparently. It was actually way too salty for me to eat for breakfast, but we were already drinking; which made it easier.

I was booked on an early flight out of Batumi that would have meant me leaving straight away. But I wanted to stay, particularly as it was the last gig of the weekend, and see some of where I had ended up and I rescheduled. Usually, everything I see is always in the dark and then it's time to leave again.

My rearranged flight was leaving from the Georgian capital, Tbilisi, at 5am on Wednesday. On Tuesday evening, I had dinner and afterwards the cab came to take me to the airport, which was still a long drive away through the mountains.

We started driving and at one point I really didn't feel comfortable any more. I couldn't talk to the driver easily because I hadn't slept that much in the previous few days.

I also had a fear of flying at the time, but I overcame my fear some time later but that's another story!

The driver was behaving like a maniac speeding through the mountains. I remember all these trucks driving through the mountains as well but they were going really slow. A couple of times, he almost ran into the back of a truck. He soon figured out why they were driving much slower than him.

He then started to drive like a maniac again and I saw his head shake. He was clearly falling asleep and I started talking to him in order to keep him awake. 'Okay, okay,' he replied.

We were coming towards a corner when he started to doze off again and there was a truck heading towards us. He didn't see it and so I shouted at him. His response was to turn the steering wheel, which almost caused us to drive off a cliff. At that point I said to him: "Enough, enough. Stop the car and get some sleep." He parked the car in the middle of nowhere, miles from Tbilisi, and in the pitch black. There were some trucks parked up behind us and although their drivers were sleeping, I just had a feeling that it was all a bit uncomfortable. I mean, if they were going to kill me then no one is going to find me. It was really crazy. I tried to call the promoter from Batumi to explain what was going on but somehow, annoyingly, I couldn't connect with him but I could connect with my wife. I explained what was happening and everything was fine.

Anyway, I was sat in the car with the driver asleep next to me when, suddenly, the car was surrounded by a pack of wolves howling at the top of their voices. All I could think of was, 'What the fuck?' We were in the middle of the mountains with wolves around the fucking car.

We still had quite a while to go until we reached the airport, so I just sat back and decided to chill. After about 45 minutes I woke the driver. The wolves were gone, but there was still a truck behind us and the driver said we should leave quickly as he didn't feel comfortable. My driver took off, again driving like a maniac. We had almost left the mountains when the car stopped and what do you know? We had run out of petrol and I started to get really annoyed.

There were some villages in the distance, where there were obvious signs of life, but we were unable to drive any further. It was the middle of the night and we had to get out of the car, grab the jerry can and ring some doorbells to try to find some petrol.

We managed to find some and we put it in the car. By now, I was able to connect with the promoter and he just said: "Give me the fucking driver!"

He started screaming at the driver, who then began to get angry at me, but I couldn't understand him! The promoter then actually called the airport to make sure the plane didn't leave, telling them I would only be 20, 30 or 40 minutes late. We got there just in time to see my plane taking off and I was told the next available flight would be in two or three days because all the other flights to Amsterdam were fully booked.

I rang the promoter again and after I explained the situation to him he couldn't apologise enough. "My family live in Tblisi and they will take care of you for the next few days," he said. They organised a hotel and everything was paid for. The cab driver, who at this point wasn't amused as by then it was six or seven in the morning, drove me into Tblisi. I remember the streets were wide and there was army stuff displayed everywhere.

But the story doesn't end there. Driving into the town and about a kilometre before the hotel, we got a flat tyre. He didn't stop, though, and carried on driving on the metal rim of the wheel, with sparks flying everywhere. He pulled up in front of the hotel, and I checked in.

I remember seeing an elevator that had no door, which I found really scary. There was this big gap in the wall that you could look down. I made it up to my room and straight away called my wife. She said: "You're supposed to be home, I haven't seen you in ages!" But all I could say was: "Sorry darling, but it's going to be a few more days."

Tblisi was really nice. I stayed for two more days and the family really took care of me. The food was awesome and so was the wine. I learned that Georgia is actually one of the best places for wine.

So that's how I spent my time and, of course, I decided to buy a couple of bottles of good local wine which I sealed.

I was flying with Austrian Airlines, via Vienna, and I was flying from Tblisi to Vienna. I had my bottles of wine and, of course, they took it away from me, despite the fact it was sealed. Stupidly, I started to argue and started screaming, which almost got me arrested. The wine was thrown away and after another four or five-hour overlay I finally went back to Amsterdam and I was home.

I returned home on a Thursday and immediately it was the weekend again! A couple of weeks later I was playing for the first time in Moscow, Russia. I had to send my passport off and arrange my visa before flying, which took about a week.

On the Thursday before leaving for Moscow I was playing at the Sugar Factory in Amsterdam for Vreemd, which means strange in English. I had cocaine on me, about two grams, but I soon lost one gram somewhere in the club. Everybody got on their knees, using the flashlight on their phone, and searched for the missing G.

It wasn't obvious at all what we were doing! Anyway, it wasn't found. I spent the next day chilling before flying to Russia for my Moscow debut.

A good friend of mine was accompanying me and we both had to fill in customs papers just before we landed. I stood up from my seat and went to grab my jacket, while a very camp air steward kept talking to me. I was telling him about my work as a DJ, blah, blah, blah, and as I pulled my passport out of my jacket pocket, boom, the missing gram of cocaine that I thought I'd lost fell on the floor right in front of everyone. The steward hadn't actually noticed because it happened so quickly and he just carried on talking to me. I had to stand on it, knowing this was a potentially serious situation. My mate was sat in the chair behind me and while pulling on my leg he kept saying: "Give it to me!" Finally, the steward walked away and I was able to grab it and give it to my mate, who immediately went to the toilet and destroyed the evidence - up his nose. He had no idea what to do and thought the safest option was to just do it all.

We left the plane, headed to customs and made it through without any problems – despite my maniac travelling companion, ha-ha-ha. The promoter was waiting for us and offered us more drugs, which we declined, and we were driven into the city and dropped off at our hotel near Red Square.

Later that night, I was playing at a sushi bar which transformed into a club at night time. To pass the time at the hotel, my mate and I drank through two mini bars before we were picked up.

The promoter had arranged hookers for us, which we absolutely did not ask for. They were sat in the club waiting for us and I felt really terrible.

Afterwards, we were taken to an after-party in a castle by Anastasia, a girl I had met in the club earlier, before they eventually drove us back to the hotel, where the party continued.

The time came to leave for the airport and before checking out we had to pay our mini-bar bill. They would only take roubles and we only had euros. My mate took out his euros and began to tempt the hotel manager by waving a 50 euro note in his face. First one, not enough, and then two, still not enough. Eventually he took 150 euros and it was sorted.

We made it to the airport, where we were met with a five-hour delay. We were both still really wasted from the previous 24 hours, so we did the sensible thing and drank some more.

We made it on to the plane and discovered we were the only passengers. We immediately ordered more alcohol.

We touched down at Schiphol, where we were met by a mate who drove us back into Amsterdam. We weren't finished – we were still in party mood – and we went to the Vaaghuyzen, a DJ bar in Amsterdam, where I played a six-hour set until the early hours of Monday morning!

VISION IMPOSSIBLE

Ruben Langedijk is an expert in motion graphics and video graphic design compositing, and is an extremely valuable member of this world-dominating team of computer buffs.

Often locked away during the daylight hours working on and perfecting new material, Ruben and his Vision Impossible colleagues travel the world and light up the night skies with their superb sought-after graphics, mapping and video displays. With the biggest events worldwide – indoor and outdoor – calling for Ruben and the crew, they are in constant demand. Their work can be found online and YouTube features many videos of their world famous craft.

Vision Impossible exclusively create and customise all their images themselves and they never rely on existing video material. To achieve this, they use the latest technologies in computer animation.

He's also a very enthusiastic VJ – Video Jockey – and is often pushing the equipment to the limit. With Ruben's skills in graphics, Vision Impossible were able to expand their activities from video to print.

Ruben is a DJ and producer, too, and uses the Rubzman moniker when performing. He has tracks released on Amsterdam label Cosmic Disco and Berlin's Code2 label, and is a regular member of the Amsterdam DJ circuit.

In our interview, Ruben opens up about his progression within the scene with Vision Impossible, his DJ career and memorable gigs etc.

Enjoy...

I've always been fascinated with computers and technology since the age of 16, and when I first started experimenting and producing music back in the day it was on a Commodore 64. Within the computer there were pre-made bleeps and you can hear the same original sounds in early house music, and in games like Tetras, for example. Because of this, house music overwhelmed me and took me over. I was living in a little village called Heiloo, near Alkmaar, and the only way I could hear house music was through the radio.

I was surviving on mix-tapes, then came the chance to use samples in the computer. It was very limited with a four-track sequencer but I could put my own samples in there and make music. When the software improved I could use a 16-track sequencer and then up to 32.

Robert Morcos, a friend of mine who was a computer programmer, wrote his own software. We made numerous songs and with his software we were able to create our own sounds. We really went crazy with it but, unfortunately, nothing was actually good enough to release. We were experimenting and we didn't have the quality at the time that you could hear in established artists' music.

To be honest, in order to improve we really needed a bigger and more advanced studio, and we also wanted more hardware and synthesisers in order to improve our music.

I eventually went with Reason, a music computer programme, which provided the potential to make a record. It was still a bit limited, though, and you could hear that the music was made with Reason, due to it being a closed system. Nowadays, it's open and you can use your own sounds. I then switched to Ableton Live, which I used for a number years until quite recently. Now I use Bitwig, which apparently isn't as popular as I believe it should be. It's similar to Ableton Live but is super-fast and intuitive, and has some smart stuff that other software lacks.

Vision Impossible started in 1999 but before that we were Vision Control along with another guy, Joshua. I was still at school at the time when my friend Martijn started Vision Impossible with a friend of ours from school.

At that time I would tag along but there were some occasions when I also did a bit of VJing alongside him. Once I had completed school, and then had a year of freelance graphic design work behind me, I was asked to join the team.

Previously, we had all registered individually as one-man companies. But that stopped, we became one company and we signed the contract. From that moment on we were then officially known as Vision Impossible.

Martijn really was the initiator and he was the first one of us who went to Amsterdam from our village, Heiloo. That was when he became involved with visuals and the scene. He also studied animation at school, when was when I became inspired and got involved with the whole visual and animation scene.

The after-hour parties were where we first began working. We soon had regular gigs where we could work on our ideas and concept, which helped us when we were ready for bigger bookings.

In 2003-2004 we had the idea to create an audio visual set to accompany a DJ because, back then, there wasn't anything like that available. So, together with some friends, we created a visual story, accompanied by an audio story. It was synchronised and featured a logical step from one song to the other. This would increase throughout the set, from a more relaxed introduction to a peak level later in the set. In those types of shows it was impossible to improvise, especially in 2003.

In the meantime, we were still developing our idea and concept.

We had a try-out in Amsterdam, at We Cut Heads, which you won't be surprised to learn was a barber shop by day. Many DJs still playing in Amsterdam today, like Brian S, were also playing there.

We were eventually booked as DJs and an audio-visual company for an open-air event in Malaysia. We had originally met the organiser online and she then visited us in Amsterdam. She really liked the concept, but at the time we were still developing everything, and it took a whole year of meetings and chats back and forth before things came together.

Upon arrival in Malaysia, there was a huge coach reserved for us. We felt like VIPs because it was truly amazing. It wasn't an old cramped mini-bus but instead a luxurious coach that we virtually had all to ourselves. There were just three of us, together with a guide and a driver, on the huge vehicle.

The festival, called Revelations, was in Kuala Lumpur and we made sure we arrived a day early so we could check our equipment. We were using Traktor, a digital DJ programme; in
443

fact it was the very first Traktor version and at that time it was really rare for it to be used by DJs. To DJ with a laptop was perhaps seen as a bit weird by others and we certainly had several people question what we were doing. "Why are you using a laptop to DJ?" was a common question. We would respond: "We can do it with a soundcard," but that just seemed to add to the confusion.

Anyway, if we were nervous to begin with, the nerves were really kicking in. I saw DJ Johan Gielen backstage and he was actually praying that his set would be good. He had played hundreds of shows but he looked a bit nervous, so what were we going to be like, full of nerves, on our very first gig? There were 10,000 people in front of us, while Martijn and I were equipped with only a laptop as we were ready to DJ. We had three screens behind us on, to which we projected our visuals and animations, but we didn't have that much experience as DJs, especially with different mixers.

We were worried about our set and really hoped the crowd would like it. It was a bit of a trance event, especially with Johan and Marco V playing, and our set was between theirs. We were nobodies, they were big names; how would we do?

The filter effect button switch remained on from the start for the entire first minute of the set and apart from the fact that I wasn't that experienced, I also totally lacked confidence. "What the fuck is this shit?" I shouted to Martijn. I kept seeing this flashing light on the mixer and as the sound kept playing through the filter I then had the idea to press the button.

It stopped, let's play! Looking back, it was a hilarious moment and I am so happy that I actually managed to figure it out.

444

Despite our problems, it went really well. The crowd went wild, and we had both our visuals and animations on the screens. We also had a lot of samples that we used, like a police siren and air horns, for example. As the crowd heard the sound, the video image would be of the same thing, so they were seeing and hearing the same thing at the same time. We also included some Malaysian themes and created a character that was in sync with the music. During a break in the music, the character would interact with the crowd.

After our set we continued to VJ for the rest of the party, which we had already agreed to do prior to the event.

Afterwards, we were being asked for photos and people also wanted our autographs. For us it was like 'Wooooooooa' because we had never before experienced that type of response to our work. We had become used to always being backstage, mixing with the event crew and never seen by the public, but here we were at the front of the crowd. We felt like superstars, performing in Malaysia and signing autographs, plus the following day we did a couple of interviews for local newspapers.

We were staying in this really fancy posh resort, in a private residence overlooking the sea. All of it was just for us. We could hardly believe our luck and with a fee to pocket as well we really felt as if we had found the mother lode!

On the back of our success in Kuala Lumpur we were booked for a show in Prague called Transmission. There were about 2,000 people there in the early days, but since then it has grown in popularity and crowds of 15,000 are now commonplace. We were involved from the start all those years ago and we had really started to grow as a brand. We had created a logo and there are now hundreds of people who have that logo as a tattoo. That really fills me with pride and I've even seen our logo shaved into somebody's head!

Vision Impossible has worked for UDC – United Dance Company – as well as Art of Dance, Q-Dance, ID&T and many more. A lot of our work is customised to the particular event and we always make sure that we don't use the same design for another event. If we used a certain design when working for ID&T, we wouldn't use it again for UDC, for example. Organisers pay for exclusive content so we have to keep it that way. Obviously, there are images that we create and can't exclusively use for a certain event, but instead use regularly, like flames and fire for example.

We've been fortunate enough to do repeat shows in Las Vegas, at the Electronic Daisy Carnival. Our client was Jora Entertainment, a Dutch company responsible for the stage design, the concept and the script. They work for Insomnia Events, who are the main organisers of EDC, the Electronic Daisy Carnival. Jora Entertainment hired us for the event and we customised animations relating to the script that Jora had created. They are more in-depth than perhaps other clients and we work closely to create precisely what they want.

We had been booked the previous year for the same festival, which helped us a lot with experience for the following year's production. We are always determined to make a party better than the previous one, and on that occasion I think we succeeded.

Last year was quite overwhelming. When you are there for the first time, or at a new place, you can feel quite nervous, but it is exciting nonetheless. At the end of the day, though, it's still work.

For that particular show we were preparing about two months in advance. Alongside seven other people, I must have worked a total of 2,000 hours to prepare for it.

We had a drawing of the stage design, which was later upgraded to a more technical drawing, including all the screens etc. We had to sign a non-disclosure agreement because if any designs had been leaked it would have come back to us. The aim is always to make it a huge surprise for all the people attending and a lot of money is involved, so it is essential it remains top-secret. Also, when the crew arrive on the festival site they must sign another non-disclosure agreement so they are forbidden from taking videos or pictures of the event and posting them online. For us, it is all very normal, just part of the job. Why would we want to publish a picture of the construction that looks dull without the lights and all the extras? Plus, why spoil the whole surprise? We definitely don't want to do that.

With other events it is sometimes necessary to change details at the last minute. If certain things like screens, for example, are not available it means that late adjustments are required, which can be stressful.

It is always the case with the larger events that they have a day and night rehearsal, along with sound checks by artist management. Some artists have their own VJ – Video Jockey – who travels on tour with them, and their own lighting guy too. Those guys always do a rehearsal, without the DJ, prior to the event to test their own equipment.

Regarding my DJing, I have had a couple of releases under my Rubzman artist name. When I was together with my ex-girlfriend, Audrey, she inspired me to progress with my music and productions, so DJ Rubzman began to grow.

447

I remember a holiday with Audrey in Malta. We had been lounging by the pool for a few days and wanted to see something different. We looked around and decided to do a boat trip, on a catamaran, and this particular party featured some DJs. We thought that sounded cool so we decided to book it. Audrey suggested we take some of our own music, because you never know when a DJ is going to cancel so we took along some CDs.

There must have been about 50 people on board but there didn't appear to be a DJ or, if there was, he only had one song and another without any mixing. Annoyingly, they even played the same song a few times in a row.

We thought that we could perhaps improve the situation, so I searched for the boat's captain. "What's with the DJ?" I asked. "He missed the pick-up," he replied. "We are DJs," I instantly added. The only problem was that we had forgotten our headphones but we still offered our services and ended up playing back to back, although without beat mixing because of the missing headphones, but it was still an improvement on the original situation.

The boat was sailing towards an island, where we were going to have a barbecue with the whole group and we were allowed to disembark first because we were the DJs, ha-ha.

Everyone enjoyed themselves but it was soon time to climb aboard and head back to shore. Unfortunately, the weather was so bad that the boat was being chucked everywhere by the really high waves that were bashing into it.

Amazingly, we somehow managed to continue to DJ, but it was a real struggle. It was taking ages to eject a CD, with one hand holding on to the side of the boat so as not to fall overboard. We didn't know the equipment very well either – it was an unknown brand – so it naturally took a little longer to navigate around it.

The boat continued to rock from side to side. "What the fuck are we doing?" I was yelling. I started to feel really sick and almost collapsed before throwing up in a garbage bin next to the decks. Audrey continued to play but the next thing I knew was the captain grabbing my arm and telling me: "Now you must go and DJ."

It was still another half an hour before we were due back but thankfully the waves decreased and I was able to play the rest of the way home. At the time, we didn't really enjoy it, but when I talk about it now I think it was a really memorable gig, although not one I'd like to repeat!

Another crazy gig was when I had a broken arm and I had to play at the Paradiso with my laptop. I had forgotten my USB cable, no one had a spare and my only option was to borrow a bike and head home and back in time for my set. The DJ continued, allowing me to race through the city with only one good arm, make it home and grab my cable before turning round for another one-handed cycle back to the Paradiso.

I started to play, not realising my trip home and back had taken me so long that I only had 10 minutes left of my set!

VALENTINO KANZYANI

Valentino is a Slovenian DJ, producer and promoter. He joined forces with fellow superstar Slovenian DJ, Umek, and they went on to DJ together across the world. They also formed the record label Recycled Loops.

I was booked to play for Interparty, the organisation from DJ Veztax, at Fort Bourguignon, in Pula, Croatia back in July 2002.

I flew from Amsterdam to Ljubljana, before a four-hour road trip to Pula. Something, though, didn't feel right, I felt very anxious. I was on my way to Croatia to DJ; why wasn't I excited?

Upon landing it became clear that my small suitcase, full of clothes, was missing. Another 10 minutes later and it became clear my record box was missing. It was in Zurich, while my clothes were in Copenhagen.

There was only one flight a day in and out of Ljubljana Airport in those days, so my options were extremely limited. Veztax loaned me some clothes and we drove to see Valentino at his record shop, where he let me raid his record box and borrow what I needed.

Thanks to Valentino, I was able to play my set later that evening.

The fun didn't stop there, however, because the car broke down on the motorway. We had to wait for what seemed several hours for a repair truck to locate us and we only made it to the party with minutes to spare.

Basically, my artist name is a remix of my real name. I was originally Valentine and then it was changed to Tine. I decided to change it to Valentino, because I liked it, and my surname changed from Kocjancic to Kanzyani, which is how it's pronounced in Italian.

I grew up around music. My father was a famous musician in Slovenia who was responsible for a lot of music and produced a lot of tracks. He came from nothing, but went on to form the number one band, Kameleoni, in Yugoslavia, as it was at the time. He was only probably 17 at the time, and he performed all over the country.

Unfortunately, the old communist regime was unimpressed. My father had more followers than the regime and more people attended their concerts, which the regime didn't like. The band was split up and every member was sent to the army, but each to a different area so they couldn't connect with each other. This probably lasted for about nine years and it hit my father really hard.

He had a troubled childhood and would often fight with his family. One day he disappeared with some friends on their bikes. After almost two months, he returned. He had lost so much weight, his parents didn't recognise him. From that moment he started to play guitar and, almost immediately, this changed his life.

BOOM! Kameleoni was formed and it just grew and grew, and

had a huge following in all the major cities. They were like The Beatles, of that time, in our country.

Then the regime stepped in.

Unfortunately, my father and I didn't always get along. As a child, I would often hear him rehearsing, singing and making tracks. I always wanted to be involved but he would always tell me to go away. I wanted to be a drummer, so I would play in the kitchen instead with my sticks smashing the pans and he hated that.

He left us when I was only eight years old and ran off with a topless model! It was a tough time for my mother, of course, but it was a kind of relief for us at the same time, since my father had been through some tough situations and he wasn't right. He needed to go because he was causing problems at home.

It wasn't until I was about 30 that things changed. His friends would tell him I was becoming more famous than him. He didn't like this and one day he approached me. I was really happy that he did; he's my father and we should be connected.

In 2007, when I was living in Ibiza, I brought him to the island for a holiday with me. It was then that he had an MDMA cocktail for the first time, at an after-party. He was complaining about it, really not happy. "What the fuck is this?" he was screaming. He thought he was having a cocktail, an alcoholic cocktail, but not with drugs. A day or so later, one of his friends arrived in Ibiza. When he arrived at my house, he was asking my father how he was. My father replied, in a quiet voice: "I tried drugs." "Oh yeah?" said his friend. "How was it?" "Unbelievable!" said my father with a big smile. I couldn't believe it because just one day earlier he hated it.

Later that day we went to the opening of Cocoon, and my father and his mate were taking more MDMA cocktails. We arrived and my father, really high at this point, said: "Wow, nice, an open-air party." "No, this is the queue," I told him.

Unfortunately, he didn't want to change his life and he was diagnosed with cancer, even losing an eye. He started to smoke and drink heavily, and he was sleeping on friends' sofas. I saw him before a chemotherapy session and told him that he had to change things, like eating properly instead of fried sausages all the time. He was doing everything he shouldn't do as a cancer patient. But he wouldn't listen and we tried to get alternative medicine for him, including cannabis. He did try the cannabis oil, but it was already too late.

The good thing is my father and I repaired our relationship before he died. He was very proud of what I had achieved, as I was of him.

What's nice is the fact that he gave me his home before he died; the home I grew up in, where I used to hear him rehearse in his studio and hear him sing. It is where I now live and the really special thing is that I use the very room in which he rehearsed to now produce my own music.

I was thinking recently about how long I've been a DJ, and I've actually been playing for more than 25 years now. In the beginning, I would often go on my little motorbike across to Italy to buy records, as my parents were living near the border. At the time I was young and didn't have a lot of money. The people working in the record shop didn't really like me as I could never buy many records, usually only two or three at a time, instead of the 100 records or more that others would buy. People were coming from Zagreb and other cities, buying everything they
453

could and re-selling it in Zagreb.

I started to DJ when I was 15 and my first gig was at a place called Tivoli in 1991, just as the Yugoslavian war was beginning. It was a place where I could practice my mixing and learn to DJ. Once the war had begun to stop, I went back to Tivoli and I was their resident DJ. I used to play two 45-minute sets – usually between all the Rod Stewart music! This is where I actually started to have a crowd. I would turn up with a suitcase full of techno records and they would all be waiting for me to play. They wouldn't go home until I had finished my sets. Wow, my dreams were coming true, ha-ha.

I remember one party on a Wednesday night in a club called Klub K4, in Ljubljana, back in the early 90s. The party was called Raveland and the organiser was a member of the first electronic band from Yugoslavia. The party was full, with a crazy light show and all, and this was really important. There wasn't a lot around with electronic music and it really inspired me, and gave me the energy to play.

It was the same club where I eventually met Umek.

Ambasada Gavioli had originally approached me in 1994, when I met one of the owners at the seaside. I thought he was crazy, as if he had just escaped from an asylum. He was telling me about this special club they wanted to do, and the special music they wanted. And they wanted me to do it! I have to thank them, because they approached me when my name was becoming more known around the country, and maybe without them I wouldn't be here now.

They took me to their office and showed me the plans, and I thought: "What the fuck? This is from another time." They wanted 2,000 people inside, with moving DJ booth and palm trees, and they were serious. I thought 'Okay, let's do it' and I started to work with them. There were four owners and four completely different minds. The main guy had a massive ego; he was an ex-bodybuilding champion from Italy and drove a Ferrari. He didn't like it when I told him what to do; it was hardcore.

At one meeting, I was told that my time as an artist had passed and I wouldn't make it as a DJ. 'What the fuck? I'm 23!' I thought. A year later I left the club, but by then I had played all over the world.

At 21, I was actually managing the club, and booking international artists like Richie Hawtin, Laurent Garnier and Jeff Mills for their first time in Slovenia, for example, and I was also managing other local artists.

Umek and I were the first to be DJ residents at clubs in Slovenia, which had a major impact on the whole scene throughout the country, especially as we could, occasionally, book the biggest names.

I remember when we booked Richie Hawtin for my birthday at Gavioli and he asked for four sub-woofer monitors for the DJ booth. I told him he wouldn't need them as it would be too much. He understood, because at that time the monitors in the booth were loud enough for a small club.

In the beginning nobody was coming to Gavioli. The major problem with the club occurred on the very first day it opened, in December 1995. They were charging an entrance fee but not telling anybody who the DJs were. They were also selling drink tokens, which had never been seen before in Slovenia. It was done to prevent bar staff stealing drinks, but it was foreign to us all. After arriving in the club, people were given a small piece of paper which warned them that there was a minimum consumption charge of so many Slovenian tolars, our old currency, which is about 5 euros today. The sound system was not working properly, the music was awful and it seemed everything was fucked up. Some of the people wanted to go outside, back to their cars, chill outside or whatever, but they were being charged for the privilege. The club wasn't located on a high street, but instead a huge isolated building, with a huge car park, miles from anywhere. It was normal for people to chill outside at those types of venues, but not at Gavioli and as a result the club was stigmatised forever.

This made it very difficult for me to promote the place. People were reacting whenever I gave them a flyer. "It's the Devil," they would say. It took a lot of convincing to get people to believe, especially Umek, who really had to be persuaded to come and join me. At first, Gavioli didn't want Umek to play there, but he was the number one DJ and I wanted him to be involved. Eventually, we started to create something together.

I used to go to the airport and pick up the DJ that I had booked, and I would always think how great it would be if someone drove to the airport to pick me up for a gig. My dream was soon to become reality.

Soon after, Umek and I felt it was the right time to start a record label. That was the beginning of the end. The owners didn't want it and therefore we had no alternative but to continue to grow elsewhere.

Eventually, Umek and I left because the owners couldn't understand my artistic side. I wanted to produce music and play at other clubs, and for me it was a dream. But it wasn't
456

everybody that shared my dream!

It all happened automatically so my dream was now reality.

The original owners decided to rent Gavioli and that's when I went back there to play and organise my own nights again.

In 1996 I started to play in other countries nearby for the first time, like Croatia and Austria. I wasn't producing any major music in those days, just working with a computer, so no releases or labels. My first release on Intec, the label from Carl Cox, and the first release together with Umek, was my major breakthrough and I started to travel like crazy.

It's funny, because a year previously, when I was leaving Gavioli, the owners were telling me I was making a big mistake. They actually took my records and refused to give them back to me. It was a very chaotic situation; they were not nice people, not there for the music, and I really had a lot of problems with them. They wanted instant success after investing a lot of money into the club. I wanted to build something, like a new concept with international artists, but they didn't understand. They didn't like the music Umek and I played, so we actually formed our own label, Recycled Loops, and released our own music – the music they tried to stop us playing.

This was a real turning point for me – not so much Umek as he was already releasing music on labels – but Recycled Loops and my DJ name were now known worldwide.

When I started producing in 1996, it was a major hassle to buy the equipment in Slovenia. Then I had to learn how to connect it all, to have the right place to put the equipment and how to generate sound from it. Nowadays, I learn everything I need from
457

the internet.

Technology-wise, it's really great that kids can express themselves with just a computer these days, instead of a drum machine, keyboard, sampler etc.

I remember being asked to play at a party in Kranj, back in 1997, but when I arrived their equipment consisted of only one turntable and a mixer. Some people really didn't understand what was going on. It was a party organised by professional hockey players from Slovenia and they had no idea. There was an in-house CD system but DJs weren't playing CDs in 1997 and I only had records. Funnily enough, I managed to play and the people were happy. I would play a record, take it off, talk about it or something else and then play another. I think I managed a two-hour set and not long afterwards I was booked for Australia. It was funny how all these crazy things were happening to me.

Love Parade in 1999 was when I was introduced to Carl Cox by Talida Wegener, the manager of Sven Vath and Carl's European manager at the time. But Carl didn't want to shake my hand.

Not long before our meeting Sven had played with me at Gavioli for the first time and at the time I was trying to book Carl. Booking Sven was hard enough but first I had to book other Cocoon artists, including Toni Rios, in order to book Sven for his Slovenian debut. Eventually, Sven was booked and he knew all about me and my efforts to get him to Slovenia, which was when I started to earn points within the scene. People were starting to recognise the Slovenian scene, for which Umek and I were responsible.

Back to Love Parade and I was stood by the main stage, together with Talida, and she wanted to introduce me to Carl. At the time

I had coloured spiky hair, I was a proper raver, and Talida told Carl who I was and that I wanted to book him for Slovenia. He had a towel wrapped round his neck and looked at me and said: "Slovenia? I don't think so." He refused my hand, too, and it's a moment I'll never forget.

In 2001 I fell in love with his new Intec record label, especially because of the first release, Intec 001, from Christian Smith and John Selway entitled the Metropolitan EP.

At the time it was something really new. Not like the tribal techno of the time, more tech-house, and I thought it was really fresh. I really wanted to release a track on his label and I don't mind admitting I was desperate. It wasn't long before I released Fever, as part of the International EP Volume 2 on Intec 007.

In 2002, Umek and I were booked again for Australia as part of our Recycled Loops tour. Just before one of our gigs started, a promoter came up to me and told me he couldn't wait to hear my music. Carl Cox had been playing there previously and had mentioned me to them and told them how good my music was.

Remember, in 1999 at Love Parade he didn't know who I was!

The message here is to always believe and keep smiling. When I look back at things that have happened, I'm amazed, and I have learned to just enjoy my experiences, as you never know what will happen next time.

Other gigs on that tour included a memorable night in Perth. The equipment was so bad; the needles kept jumping, really bad turntables, shit monitors and Umek had definitely had enough, so he was off. I was up next and after flying all the way to Australia I was really excited to play, despite the awful turntables. I was

459

just about to start, full of excitement and energy, when the monitor speaker fell and crashed on top of the turntable. It was completely smashed. Set over.

I remember a funny time with Umek when we went to Bogota in Colombia, to play for the first time. It was at a time when the country was still experiencing drug problems. The venue was great and about 2,000 people came along. The gig was great, too, so we were really happy. The following day we were with the promoter and he told he was happy nothing happened. "Nothing happened?" I said. "Yes, because the local mayor's son and the American ambassador's son were both at the party and we thought we would be hit with a bomb or something," he replied.

I'm still travelling a lot but occasionally I get the feeling that the music is always the same, like in 2003-2005. There were times when Surgeon, Ben Sims, Umek, Richie Hawtin and I were all on the same line-up and playing exactly the same music. This is why different genres of techno started to appear, like the minimal stuff, and I didn't particularly like the transition between techno and minimal.

I was inspired by Ricardo Villalobos and Luciano, among others, and their new, fresh take on techno. I was living in Ibiza at the time and I fell in love with this new sound they were playing. This transition took me back to the days when I was playing sets of different house and techno. In 2006 I began to change my style, not an easy thing to do for a techno artist. Initially, my fans didn't understand my move, although many did. In my opinion, if you don't feel something, it's better you don't do it.

It was a difficult transition for me as I wasn't getting gigs and living in Ibiza was expensive. These were hardcore times. We even had a contact with an ex-criminal who was stealing food for

460

us from the supermarket. I was still being asked to play, but they only wanted to hear the old music I was known for. My manager didn't want to work with me anymore, so she refused to take bookings. It was tough, but eventually I found peace with it all and started to produce new music again. I was being booked again, often in Romania, and my career was again on the up.

Many people think it's a dream job and it is, but it can take a lot of sacrifices. I'm really grateful for everything and for all the opportunities I have been given. I'm still inspired by new music and new artists, and hearing great DJs at a party. I might be 20 years older, but I'm still inspired by the scene.

One of my favourite moments being an artist was when I heard Richie Hawtin playing one of my records. In those days, my English was very bad but when Jeff Mills came up to me and said he enjoyed my music it just felt like my dreams were coming true. Carl Cox inviting me to Barcelona for the first time to play at his Intec party was another dream come true. These are moments I will never forget, especially as they didn't want to know me in the beginning. I had to learn Spanish, too. I was being booked a lot for Spain but nobody spoke Slovenian and my English was bad. It's these moments that made me who I am as an artist. I look back at these times and feel really lucky to have been there.

I don't like places that don't respect the smaller names. I remember in the beginning, I was playing at a party with Carl Cox, and he would have a crew around him and everybody dancing. Then I would play after him and everybody would leave. What the fuck?

Umek and I also had the same manager as DJ Rush. Often we were booked to play the same parties, but we would play after him.

We never played this hard and heavy techno sound. He would play at 160 BPM and we would take over. He did slow it down as he finished, to maybe 145 BPM, but it was still so fast for us. Playing those types of sets would make you stronger and work harder, to try to create something. We would play at about 130-132 BPM, but it was still a massive transition from 160 down to 132 BPM, perhaps comparable today to a techno DJ being followed by a deep house DJ.

I remember a time in Spain when there were about 3,000 people in the club. They were there for Rush and we were on after him. I could sense that the people were really after something big. At the time, I was playing with three turntables, and I could really create a lot with a third turntable. For me, the music was not so interesting, so it was really special that I could travel around doing my own thing with the same records other DJs were playing. I always rocked it and left people asking: "What the fuck just happened?"

When I look back, in those days it was something special to play with three turntables. We were maybe the first DJs, along with Marco Nastic from Eastern Europe, to play with three and really do it well. Carl Cox had the British crowd, Marco Carola the Italian crowd and Sven Vath would have his German crowd, but we would turn up from little Slovenia and rock the shit out of the place!

It was a nice feeling.

GERT van VEEN / QUAZAR

*The UK has Trevor Fung, Paul Oakenfold, Carl Cox etc.
Germany has Sven Vath, Westbam, and Dr Motte. The US has
the late, but legendary, Frankie Knuckles, Larry Levan etc. But
the Netherlands has Gert van Veen, plus a few others, and Gert
is still very much a prominent part of the ever-evolving European
techno scene.*

*Still packing a room, filling a festival tent or field, Gert and
Quazar are still on the top of their game.*

*Gert himself, as well as being an excellent producer, has become
a specialised writer within the Dutch music scene, both as a
journalist and author. He has written books about the Dutch
music and party scene, and is also the brains behind Welcome to
the Future, a very popular Amsterdam movement still going
strong today.*

*He put Amsterdam firmly on the international techno map with
the release of the critically acclaimed 12" Seven Stars back in
1990 and continued to stamp Amsterdam's importance on the
scene with releases on record labels Bush, Superstition and Go
Bang!*

*Gert is also the only Dutch artist to have been awarded a
Lifetime Achievement Award twice. And rightly so!*

*For this interview Gert spoke about his role as a promoter, artist
and recalled some funny tales from his colourful career.*

I've been a part of this scene from day one, since 1988.

My original aim was to become a professional musician but that didn't work out. I was offered a job at the Dutch newspaper, de Volkskrant, and after accepting it I did my best to become a good writer.

I was a writer at de Volkskrant for 15 years, from 1985 until 2000, and they were very strict. I learned so much working there but they were not easy to please. They would question every sentence. "Why is this important?" they would ask, before adding "What does this have to do with that?"

I studied Musicology at the University of Utrecht and that's why I was offered the job at de Volkskrant as a music journalist. The music director at the newspaper always chose people from musicology if he was looking for someone to write about classical music. His idea was to teach someone who already knew about writing music because he believed that you can't teach a journalist about music. He would always go to the school to ask for possible writers.

In 1985 he needed somebody for pop music. At the time everybody there was into classical music but there was one person who wasn't. That was me.

But house music then started and I immediately knew that this was what I wanted to be involved with. Suddenly, I was very busy with music and so I had to work less at the newspaper.

I went to the first house parties in the Netherlands and together with DJ Eddy De Clercq we recorded the first proper house track produced in Amsterdam back in 1989, as A-men. The track was called Pay the Piper. Soon after we released a record under the name House of Venus on Go Bang!, which was a new label at the time. It was called Dish and Tell, and it was our first international hit record too.

In 1990 I was in *the* record shop of New York – Dance Tracks. They had a Top 30 list on the counter, the 30 best-sellers, and our track was in the Top 10. I was standing there glowing with pride and although I didn't tell anyone who I was I really was very proud. For me, New York was an influential city, like Chicago, and for them to appreciate my music felt great. The USA was a big inspiration for me, way more than the UK was.

I've been playing in bands since the 80s. My history is kind of the same as Underworld and that's how we got to know each other really well. They also started in the 80s as a band.

Back in 1990, there was an illegal party in Amsterdam, in an area now known as Java Island. At the time it was full of empty warehouses. Because the party was illegal they told everyone who attended that it was a birthday party for the organiser. The party was on an island, so if any police turned up we would be able to see them in the distance, at least one kilometre away. Of course, the police came and that's when we turned the volume down low and started to play a Michael Jackson record. We wanted to show the police that we were not having a rave, but instead a birthday party. It was so funny and when the police left Michael Jackson was quickly removed and the volume was turned up again.

In those old days I was partying 24/7.

Another funny story was back in 1994, before the first Dance Valley in 1995. The organisers had already thrown a party at the
465

same location and it was called EVLO, if I remember correctly. It was an after-party and they had arranged transport to take people from Amsterdam to the location at Spaarnwoude.

Everybody had been partying all night, it was 6am on a Sunday morning and I was sober. But everyone else was completely off their heads. The funny thing was that the driver was playing a mix-tape. The person who had recorded it must have walked away when it was recording because one record had a jump in it, which meant it kept jumping and looping continuously on the same bit. Everybody was so wasted that they didn't notice, except for me because I was sober.

The next year, Quazar played the first Dance Valley on the Mainstage.

There were reporters there from Amsterdam news network AT5, the TV station, and they wanted to interview me after my set. But as I walked off stage Ricardo, the organiser, handed me a joint. He owned a coffeeshop called 222, so I should have known that his joints would have a serious amount in them.

I was stood backstage smoking the joint when AT5 walked over and began to interview me when I was still smoking. Normally I would have passed it after a few puffs but instead I smoked it all. The interview went really well and I had even managed to remain focused. But after the interview I went to see my friends and the rest of the band, and then I collapsed and fell to the floor. I had to be dragged away because I was so stoned I couldn't walk any more.

When I have to be focused, like when I'm playing or being interviewed, nothing happens. I'm concentrating on what I have to do. When that has gone, I'm gone!

466

I had to be taken home to the Rozengracht, where I lived at the time. I was on the fourth floor so they had to drag me up four flights of stairs. I really couldn't move.

A couple of years later Quazar played again at Dance Valley, but this time in one of the tents. I had an artist wristband on and on that day it was particularly hot. I was sweating a lot and kept wiping my face with the hand the wristband was on. I kept doing it and my face started to bleed. I totally didn't notice at the time, but as I walked off stage there was blood everywhere. Nobody could understand what had happened. Annoyingly, it didn't stop bleeding because I had used ecstasy and it had thinned my blood.

I started organising parties at the end of 1993 in the Paradiso. They were called Welcome to the Future.

The reason I started organising parties was because Quazar had played Paradiso four times in the previous three years and every time it was a sell-out. I decided to invite other live acts and DJs to come and play at our own party. We had a whole load of people, like dancers, DJs, lighting guys and laser effect people.

That's why I started Welcome to the Future, because I enjoyed that fact that I was able to invite friends who were involved in the scene like I was.

The very first party was Speedy J and Orlando Voorn live. We had Underworld on the second party in April 1994. Twenty years later, Underworld played in the Paradiso and singer Karl Hyde thanked me because that gig in 1994, in the Paradiso, was their big break in the Netherlands.

I have recorded several tracks together with Karl, where he did the vocals.

I was very close to the Mazzo scene and their resident DJ, Angelo, played many times for us too.

I wrote a piece for the de Volkskrant about the unfortunate police raid that happened in Mazzo at the end of 1996 and the police brutality that took place. I was really against it.

De Volkskrant, being a left-wing newspaper, gave me space to say what I wanted. My whole piece was about the fact that drugs are a part of nightlife anyway and always have been, so I didn't see raiding a club as a solution.

Mazzo did re-open after a three-month closure but, sadly, it never recovered. That raid took the soul out of the club.

Quazar played at Mazzo on the re-opening night and, of course, I supported them all the way. Unfortunately, that night wasn't what it was before the raid. They had some good years after that but it was never as it was before.

Holland, by the way, is a progressive country and they offer help and advice through various institutions, which I think is very helpful.

Because of the way the USA was handling their war on drugs it forced the Dutch government to be stricter and less helpful. Despite that, drug use in the Netherlands is not as high as in other countries – even though smoking weed is allowed here. If the rules are not that strict then it doesn't mean the end of the world, not at all. In fact, it means the opposite and it won't be used as much. That's very strange but that's the way it is.

We are still the number one exporter of ecstasy, though, and Amsterdam is not a city full of gangsters.

So, if America points their finger at the Netherlands saying we're not strict enough, all you have to do is look at the figures and you can see we are not the problem, compared to other countries.

The only good thing to come out of Mazzo in those years was the fact that the minimal techno scene started there, which was to become very important around 2005. Bart Skils started there, Melon too and also Aron Friedman.

The minimal scene grew and we were doing 24 Hour Party People at Studio 80. Artists like San Proper, Aron Friedman and Boris Werner were real party animals, really serious party animals.

During my time managing Studio 80 every artist that played there not only always wanted to party but also expected me to be there. They would finish their sets at 5am and it was then time for them to start partying. They were full of adrenaline and everything, and anyway it takes hours to wind down. They would do a line of coke and then the party would continue in a closed Studio 80 until Sunday afternoon. There were some very strange moments. We were inside a dark club and then suddenly outside on the Amstel in daylight surrounded by tourists and trying to find our way home. There's a good reason I always have sunglasses on me.

In 2003 ID&T celebrated their 10-year anniversary and they wanted to publish a picture book, which would have been really beautiful. I was asked if I could write some text to go with the pictures.

469

I started to interview all the guys, wrote down their stories and it became more and more apparent that it was a great story to tell about some guys from Landsmeer and north Amsterdam who built this multi-million dollar company.

Their stories are really very funny.

They were just really good at making money from organising parties. In fact, they were different class compared to the other 90s generation. ID&T were very focused and it did help that they were there when the whole gabba scene started. They were very much into partying themselves. That scene became so big, which helped them sell many records through their record label, from which they made millions. This helped with financing future events. They were really an example to everybody else and that's one of the reasons the scene in Amsterdam, and Holland, is what it is now.

They eventually sold themselves to SFX, an American investor, who eventually went bust. They are now owned by some American banks and they are trying to sell again. The ID&T boys still run the organisation but they no longer own it.

For organising events the Dutch are number one. Musically, it's probably number six, despite the number of Dutch DJs in the EDM scene. I think the UK and the USA are way ahead. There's some good music, though, from the Netherlands but not compared to the UK, USA and Germany. The only thing we are really good at is the business side of things.

Quazar has been going for more than 25 years but there have been a lot of line-up changes in that time. Sometimes I work with specific people for some time and then I don't. I'm the rat through the whole Quazar history. I started it, so why not? I really love to do it, still!

In 2007 we had three gigs booked in one day. The first was at the Welcome to the Future festival, then the after-party at Club 11 and finally Sunday morning at the beach in Scheveningen. We were already high from the first gig and we were totally into it. We had a great gig in Club 11 and later that year we were even invited to play at the Panorama Bar in Berlin.

Quazar also played at the Love Parade back in 1995. After the parade there were parties organised all over the city – in trucks, buildings, anywhere.

Our gig was on the Industriestrasse in Berlin. We drove from Amsterdam with our equipment. We had a map of Berlin and we arrived safely. It was very strange, though, and clearly not a place to party. We totally couldn't understand how we weren't in the right place because it was the address we had been given. A police car approached us and asked what we were doing there. We explained we were performing and we had found it on our map, but we knew something was wrong.

The policeman told us that before the wall was taken down there was an Industriestrasse in both the west and the east. We were already quite late and so we had a police escort with the flashing lights to lead us to the Industriestrasse in the east. We made it just in time!

The set went really well and it was a great gig, but five minutes before the end the guy from the organisation walked on stage and asked me to play for an extra five minutes, because the next DJ was late as he was stuck in traffic. Every five minutes the same guy would walk on stage and ask me to play for another five minutes, and this happened again and again.

471

I had already played everything I had and had performed my set twice. I did improvise a lot, so it did sound different the second time, but eventually after more than an hour the DJ finally arrived.

In 2015 at the Welcome to the Future festival, just before we were due to open at 12 noon, I received the news that the festival had been cancelled. There were many people still standing and waiting in the queue to get in.

It was always something that I felt could happen. I organise the festival together with ID&T, who take care of everything to do with licences. I'm in the creative part of things and I'm very happy that they do that.

They were informed the previous night that there could be a problem with the weather and that the festival might not be able to take place. There was a very specific storm cell that would end up directly above the festival site and, unfortunately, it did.

I was actually quite happy that the storm was as bad as had been predicted. Trees were blowing through tents and people really could have died. Of course, nobody wanted that to happen so it was a good decision to cancel. But, of course, it was awful in every possible way.

We were not allowed to stay on the site, so I and some DJ friends who were booked to play went to my house and played there instead. They were playing in my garden and in the studio. To go from Area 1, my lounge, to Area 2, my studio, you had to walk through my garden but the storm was really intense.

If you are ready to go and play at a festival and then suddenly you can't, it's an awful feeling. You have to release that energy somehow and we had two areas for the DJs in my house.

I did have people who had to call artists and management to say the festival had been cancelled. It was a financial disaster, of course, because 20,000 people had to be refunded. All the artists had been paid in advance, and rightly so. One thing DJ agencies have learned is that if you don't pay up front the artist is not going to come. But the money we paid to the DJs, we never got back. Luckily, we had insurance because the ID&T part of the festival was sold to SFX and they demanded that they were insured.

We had 30 international DJs booked and there were parties all over Amsterdam that day and night. If you are ready to party and it's cancelled, *you will still find a party!*

I own my apartment together with somebody else and I own the apartments upstairs too. The first and second floors are social housing which means that their rent is really low. It's so low that it actually costs me money but I would never increase the rent just for profit. These tenants are in their 80s.

A woman living on the top floor, the fourth, decided to sub-let her apartment to another woman who had a husband and two children. They were making so much noise that the woman living below could no longer stay in her house because it was so loud. We actually measured the amount of noise and it was something like 80 decibels, which would make it impossible for somebody to live there. I had to tell them several times that this way of living wasn't possible. There were some fights and they tried to blackmail me. They said they would go to the police and tell them about a grow-room in my garden.

They thought that I grew cannabis plants in there but in fact it is my studio, not a grow-room. But they still called the police, who came to my house to investigate. "I suppose you know why we are here," said the officer when I opened the door. "No," I replied.

They immediately walked to my garden, straight to the shed, and saw that there wasn't a plantation. They were really disappointed but then spotted five plants, which I was growing legally in my garden, and decided to chop them down. I was yelling at them: "THIS IS NOT ALLOWED."

I was taken completely off guard that time but I will never allow that to happen to me again.

MR C

Richard West, aka Mr C, is an MC, DJ, promoter and actor, who resides these days in Los Angeles, USA.

If you don't know Mr C, he's the frontman from chart-topping indie/rock/dance crossover band The Shamen, who shot to fame in the 90s, as well as an international DJ who continues to perform all over the world. Richard is also head-honcho for Superfreq, his record label and international club night. Freq is short for frequency.

Back in 1992, The Shamen were asked to perform a live PA at half-time during an English Premier League football match. It was all part of the newly formed Premier League and its match day entertainment for Monday Night Football. Ironically, Richard is a hardcore Chelsea fan, and was performing at the home of fierce London rivals Arsenal. On the pitch, in front of thousands of gooners, The Shamen performed chart-topping Ebenezer Goode. Needless to say, Richard was abused from the stands by the Highbury faithful for his Chelsea allegiance but he loved every minute of it!

In reply to an article many years later, Richard tweeted "So funny. Gooners shouting at me "You Chelsea cunt" & me giving back the 2 finger salute leaving the pitch, and having our dancing girls in Spurs colours worked really well. Ha ha ha ha haaaaaa."
After apparently coining the phrase 'tech-house', Richard defined a new genre, which fused the techno and house sound, and tech-house was born.

London, in particular, was the emerging tech capital, with the likes of Mr C, Eddie Richards, Terry Francis and Nathan Coles all championing the tech-house sound.

Richard, together with Layo Paskin, was also behind The End, a club in London's West End with a huge reputation worldwide and which, sadly, had to close its doors back in 2009.

Richard spoke about the old days, war zones, and the gun-wielding mafia, among others.

Enjoy...

Mad moments? Right, let's go back to the start – the Summer of Love in 1988.

I was playing at the RIP parties at Clink Street in London, which was really the birth of rave culture. Not the music – that came from America – but the vibe and the culture created in London and that was really the home of it.

Anyway, these parties were on every weekend, Friday night through to Sunday afternoon.

This particular party took place end of spring, early summer and was absolutely rammed, with people climbing the drainpipes trying to get in anywhere – and anyhow – they could.

Unfortunately, on this occasion the police turned up and shut the party down. However, in doing so they created one of the funniest things I have ever seen.

The police arrived and there must have been 400 people forced onto the street, just shuffling about, with the police trying desperately to disperse everyone. With nobody moving and the police becoming increasingly frustrated, they decided to turn their sirens on, thinking it would force the crowd to move on. Funnily enough, and clearly unknown to the boys in blue, a police siren was the hook-line in Todd Terry's Royal House – Can You Feel It, which was a massive tune at the time, and the crowd's response, rather than dispersing, was to start dancing around the police cars. They were loving it and everybody was going crazy, while the stunned police didn't have a clue what to do!

It was one of the most hilarious things I've ever seen, the police tactics backfiring spectacularly and actually starting a street party. Funny story, funny night.

In 1989 I played at Nick Holloway's Trip night at the London Astoria.

Now, I've always played what I consider as underground music but on this particular night the crowd were used to more obvious type music, which I didn't play.

Basically, for the first 15 minutes of my set they were not sure what to make of it. They were clearly a bit confused because they didn't know the music. The second 15 minutes they started getting into the groove and by the third 15 minutes people were literally dancing on the chairs and tables. It was going off!

Shortly after that I was asked to stop playing and move away from the decks. Shocked, I asked why and they told me it was because some people were complaining they didn't know any of the music and it all sounded like one record to them. I took it as some sort of compliment, because my music *was* underground and my mixing really *was* seamless!

Funnily enough, the DJ who followed me played four tunes that I had also played, because he saw it going off when I had played them earlier. So that was a strange night, not what you'd expect.

I was DJing with Layo & Bushwacka and Pure Science in Johannesburg, South Africa, a few years back. We were booked to play at this rave in the old railway station, as part of The End Soundsystem. We did the gig, everything went well, but the following day it all turned crazy when we were taken to an all-day rave party taking place in what I can only describe as a big pub.

By the time we arrived the police had shut it down, but fortunately the organisers were still there and they invited us to the kitchen for a joint and a chat. With the joint burning away, all seemed well, until these big mafia-type geezers started to charge in. "What the fuck do you think you're fucking doing?" they screamed at us. Stunned and shocked, we didn't know what to do, but fortunately someone explained that we were DJs from England and the mood turned in our favour.

It turned out that the building we were in was owned by the local mafia and we had just met the foot soldiers.

Unknown to us at the time, the mafia chief's main henchman was shot and injured that morning and his boys were not happy. There was a lot of bad energy around and they didn't take kindly to a bunch of English strangers smoking dope on their patch. Guns were on show, tempers flying – it was a very scary moment to say the least.

478

Peter, the local promoter and our all-round go-to man in Johannesburg, stepped in and helped us out. The mafia boys took a shine to us and their main man, known as Pistol Pete, started to dish out the cocaine – initially offering it and eventually insisting we take it.

Now, I don't do that stuff but he insisted we all did it and we were there for hours. He was friendly, but in a very threatening kind of way and he mentioned it was lucky that Peter, our promoter, was there with us. Otherwise, he added, he would have counted to 10 and killed everybody in sight. But if you had your shit together by three you would be okay. He wasn't joking!

So, the moment finally came when he ran out of coke. I took this as the opportunity for us to leave, say our goodbyes and get the hell out of there. We all had flights to catch anyway. To our surprise he offered – well, once again he more or less insisted – to where we needed to go. Not wanting to disappoint him, or for that matter annoy him, we all jumped in his BMW and off we went. In the passenger seat was his prostitute girlfriend, while Layo, Bushwacka, Pure Science and I were in the back.

During the journey Pistol Pete was on the phone to another dealer ordering more drugs and insisting: "It must be better than the shit we had the other night, otherwise I'll fucking kill you. I have some good friends with me and they deserve the good shit, okay?"

I looked round at the boys and nobody said a word.

Sheer shock horror! We eventually arrived at this dealer's place and he sent his girlfriend in to get the stuff.

Now, we're in the back not knowing where we are, and
479

everybody has a gun in South Africa. It's like the Wild West and I was thinking we could come under attack at any moment from a rival gang, the car being sprayed with bullets, who knows? Not knowing what was happening, I decided to get out of the car and tried to find a toilet, just to escape the unknown.

His girlfriend returned, I jumped back in and he drove us back to our hotel, and we thought we could finally call an end to all the bullshit.

Relieved to be back in our comfort zone, and all in one piece, we headed to our rooms before leaving for the airport.

Unfortunately, some asshole had robbed the safe in my room, leaving my passport and only taking my money, nothing else. I never found out what happened but it was an annoying end to a crazy day!

I was at Glastonbury in 1989 and met up with the Hypnosis guys who were organising a party in the Glastonbury car park. Crazy people!

I used to work with Linden C, an amazing DJ and a really lovely guy with whom I'm still good friends with to this day, and he ran the Hypnosis parties.

The party was packed. The east London crew were everywhere and there was also someone who I can only describe as a complete nutter. But this nutter was wielding a massive knife and he was going absolutely crazy. He must have been on so much acid, he really was wasted.

He was swinging this knife around. It was so fucking dangerous and he was really starting to freak people out. The main

Hypnosis boys got together and decided to try to get the knife from him. Eventually they managed to overpower him, pinned him down and grabbed the knife. Good, trouble over – or so we all thought.

Suddenly, a small army of Glastonbury security men started charging towards us. We thought they were coming to help but they had been sent by the police to get rid of us all, by any means necessary, and it truly was bizarre.

Everybody was robbed blind! Not what you expect at a festival like Glastonbury, but they took money, drugs and alcohol. Anything anyone had, they took it.

Party over.

On the back of my success with The Shamen and, of course, being an international DJ, I was asked to play in Zagreb, Croatia, during the war with Serbia in the 90s. I was the first artist from the scene to go and play in this war zone. We were only 30 kilometres away from the front line and that was extremely hairy to say the least.

Before the gig there was a press conference and I was asked: "Why are you here?" by a journalist in a room filled with more than 150 other journalists. I simply replied: "I'm here to help people that have been suffering a lot recently celebrate life and forget about their problems for one night. That's why I'm here." I then asked the journalists a question: "Why are YOU here? There are people down the road killing each other, shouldn't you really be covering that?" The whole room fell silent. The press conference was over and I left for the gig.

Great night, great people. I'll never forget that night.
481

DJ CELLIE

Before I moved to Amsterdam, many moons ago in April 1995, I was a raver enjoying all-nighters around the south of England – Fantazia, Dreamscape, Universe and, of course, local heavyweight Mindwarp. The music was fast and uplifting. After relocating to the Dam, I discovered Mazzo and the delights of Saturday residents Cellie and Carlijn.

The music was slower, deeper and with a hypnotic blend. I was suddenly surrounded by techno heads and this beautiful new sound I was being exposed to week by week. The night was called Sex, Love et Motion. At the time, it was a club night based in Paris, London and Amsterdam. Paris didn't seem to last that long, if I remember correctly, but London was banging each week at The Soundshaft, with resident DJs Keith Fielder, Russ Cox and Paul Tibbs. The Amsterdam and London nights would often book each other's residents. The best club night I've ever had the honour to attend and enjoy.

I soon became a Mazzo regular and often attended the club on any night it was open. Sometimes just for a drink on the way home from work, it was always a great place to frequent.

One Saturday night, Cellie had Jay Haze booked to play. Jay was unable to make it that night, and much to my surprise, Cellie asked me to DJ in his place. I had never felt so nervous, plus it was probably my first-ever club gig as a DJ in Amsterdam. I did have the poster but I can no longer find it, so I can't say when it was exactly but it would have been around 1998, I think.

482

Cellie's girlfriend at the time, Nienke, was best friends with my girlfriend at the time, Roberta, and we would always party together on a Saturday at Mazzo, often with an after-party thrown in. Great times, really great times!

It was great to interview Cellie and hear about Mazzo's history straight from the horse's mouth, as it was a very prominent part in my – and many others' – youth. Cellie spoke about the early days, specific gigs, an unexpected road trip and much more.

I had been interested in music since I was 11 or 12 years old and I was especially interested in playing music to others. I don't know why, but I just wanted to. When I heard a good track I just wanted to play it. That's how I became interested in radio, my first love.

I was raised in Nieuw Vennep and I hated it. If I wanted to hear and buy the music I was hearing on the radio I had to go to Amsterdam. I was going to Attalos Records, among others, and it was there that I would buy the new tunes and, in the process, spend all of my pocket money. But I just thought how awesome it was!

There was also a shop called USA Imports, which had all the latest 12-inch and seven-inch records from America. I would sometimes buy the seven-inch versions because I didn't have very much to spend. It was the 12-inch records that we really loved but for 5 guilders we could buy the next best thing, the seven-inch version. The tunes that I really, really loved I bought on 12-inch and those I considered only okay I would buy the seven-inch versions. Looking back, it was stupid to buy the latter because the sound quality was so bad, but I wanted to buy as much as possible so that's why I bought them.

I then started playing at my high school parties. It was the 80s and there was the new-wave stuff, but I was also interested in punk and, on the other hand, I was really into disco – but the more underground sound of disco. That's why I started listening to the Amsterdam pirate radio stations like Radio Decibel and WAPS, and others. They were great stations and it was a real eye-opener for me as I discovered music that I had never heard before. It was the music you wouldn't hear on the commercial stations.

I was listening to DJs René de Leeuw, Peter Duijkerslot, Adam Curry, Jeroen van Inkel, Barry Pitch and many more. They would DJ on Leidseplein at the Schakel and elsewhere, like the BIOS, the Flora Palace, which later became B-Bop, and eventually Club It, which featured DJ Jean and Marcelo. They were already gay-minded types of clubs but it was just a club. Along with another club – Zorba the Buddha – they were the first clubs I went to. I was 15 at the time, not even old enough to go out, but my dad drove me and my mates to Amsterdam.

At the Flora Palace they would play dub versions of 80s disco tracks and, basically, for me, when I think of it, that was the start of house music. It was repetitive, little or no vocals and it was with a beat and dance orientated. The Floral Palace was in the old Disney theatre, which used to be a cinema.

I remember going to school with my ghetto blaster and playing Indeep – Last Night a DJ Saved My Life to my mates. I had heard it first on the radio and recorded it, long before any of them had heard it. They were like 'Wow, what's this?' It was an awesome track because it stood out. It was deep, so different to other music at the time.

I wanted to start DJing at the local club in Nieuw Vennep, De Kopermolen, where all my friends where going. I wrote a letter to Han, the club owner, because at the time I had heard that he didn't like the DJ he had playing. He called me, asked me to bring my records and said I could play on Friday.

I was so excited because that was *the* place to go in Nieuw Vennep. That night, my first-ever night DJing in a club, he told me to play all night. I was so nervous. I had prepared a list at home but I soon realised that it didn't work like that. You have to create a set on the spot. I was playing my underground disco records, which my mates loved, but because it was a farmer town I also had to play Top 40 hits, as well as Dutch folk singers like André Hazes and Lee Towers. I was really young, probably 15, and I was DJing in my local club. I wasn't really familiar with that folk music but I had to play it because I wanted to please the crowd.

In those days the club bought and supplied the records in the DJ booth and you would use theirs, plus your own if you had them. I had a tape deck and could change the speed, and I had two turntables as well. I was able to perfect my mixing, alongside my mate who would also play. Around midnight, when the dance floor was full, I would mix as many records as possible in, say, half an hour. I would play dub versions of Yazoo – Don't Go, for example, and lots of other 12-inch records. My friend would help me with the vinyl by handing it to me and I would immediately mix it in. It was a lot of fun and it worked out really well.

Han told me he liked it and he immediately fired the other DJ. He was a really nice guy who had been the DJ for years, but it was becoming a bit boring, fortunately for me of course. I would play
485

every Friday and Saturday alone, in the beginning, from 9pm until 3am. I was still at school and I began to suffer from the late nights. Soon after, another DJ – Pedro – joined me and it helped break up the night. We would play back-to-back, which meant we kept changing the music so as to not be too boring.

Han, who liked to keep his money, had the idea that when one of us was not DJing, we would walk around the club collecting empty glasses. We had to convince him we were not there to collect dirty glasses, although that is precisely what we had to do in the very beginning. Pedro and I discussed it and we informed Han that we would not be collecting any more glasses. He said it was okay so we stayed behind the decks.

The locals really loved their André Hazes and despite having a packed dance floor I had to play it. It immediately emptied the dance floor. Han was really happy and he looked over at me from the bar with a huge grin because they had all headed there to order drinks. I learned a lot playing there. Of course, the DJ wants a full dance floor, but the owner wants some money coming in as well to keep the place in good financial health.

I played there for about two years. It was Han that gave me my first opportunity and, incidentally, I saw him not so long ago when the club had a reunion. It was really great to see him again.

In 1984, maybe '85, when I was 17-18, I spotted an advertisement in De Telegraf, a Dutch tabloid newspaper. They were looking for "a superstar DJ", to play at a club called Island Disco in Hagen, Germany. 'That's me,' I thought. I replied to the advert and called the number. I was told I would be booked for the whole weekend, with a hotel, and that I had to DJ on Friday and Saturday as a trial. There were also more DJs coming for a trial. They also had their own collection of records available for
486

the DJs, but I took my own records too.

I didn't tell my parents I was going to Germany. In fact, I didn't tell anyone, except for my best mates.

We went by train and I had two huge crates full of records with me. It was a great place and was packed all weekend.

Eventually, I was playing Thursday, Friday, Saturday and Sunday. On Sundays, I would also play at Gala Tutu, a new-wave type of place which was quite dark and played underground music.

It was 1986-87 and somebody gave me a pill. It wasn't called ecstasy, it was known as the love pill. It interested me, I took it and that was my first experience with drugs. I was not interested in that stuff at that time. Cocaine was everywhere, but I was only interested in the music.

There were a lot of American army bases in Germany, like in Paderborn. At a nearby club, I would play hip-hop for the soldiers every Wednesday. That was a lot of fun. I was even provided with a budget, so I would go record shopping in Amsterdam with 500 deutschmarks every month. That was a lot of money back then, so I could buy a lot of new records. Of course, they were not mine but were added to the collection of the club, and because I was also buying with my own money the collection from which I could choose was huge.

I played in Hagen for about two years in total after relocating there and when I left Orlando Voorn started playing there, as DJ Fix.

Eventually, I had to leave because I was drafted into the army. I
487

had to go back to Holland but at the time I was beginning to feel that it was already enough and I wanted to leave. The club in Hagen had two owners, one was really nice and the other a crook, so I wasn't really enjoying it much anymore.

During my time with the army, around 1988-89, I moved to Amsterdam. I was living with my best mate on the Bloemengracht, which was behind Mazzo.

I used to go to Mazzo as a customer and go dancing, I absolutely loved that place. I was also working as a waiter at Gauchos, despite my busy schedule with the army.

My parents tried to discourage me from continuing with my DJing after completing my draft. They were very negative about it told me my life would go down the drain. "Can you imagine being 40 years old and still DJing?" they would ask, before adding "Imagine how embarrassing that would be."

I was really torn, because it was my passion to DJ. I started a job at Duphar, a large pharmaceutical company in Holland, I also tried working in IT – Information Technology – but it wasn't for me. There was an old guy working in the corner of the office, who looked so unhappy, and I knew it wasn't for me because I feared I might end up like him.

Soon after, I started working at Mazzo as a barman. I loved it, especially the progression of the new house music, because in Germany I had already played the early stuff.

I went out to a few parties around Amsterdam and I just fell in love with the music.

I told my Mazzo bosses, Gerrard and Frans, that I had been

previously DJing in Germany for two years and asked if it would be possible to, occasionally, put on a few records. The owners were really cool and let me play from time to time.

Mazzo was, for me, *the* place to go, and especially the place for a DJ to play. I was really nervous because I knew this was where I wanted to DJ.

In 1989, clubs changed in Amsterdam. The Roxy started playing house music all night long, as did Mazzo from being an all-round type of club to more new-wave dance orientated. Steve Green was playing more experimental music and Soho Connection, featuring resident DJ and Soho Connection joint-founder Paul Jay, along with DJs Crazy Shaun and Edwin B, took over the Fridays, which in the beginning was called Choice and became very popular. They really created something special, with great decor too. It was those nights, along with the house nights at fellow club The Roxy, which cemented the house sound in Amsterdam.

Saturdays were not really going too well, which provided me with the opportunity to play more on a Saturday alongside other DJs, and I suggested we tried something new. I always enjoyed what Paul Jay and DJ Per were doing, but I thought Saturdays should be something different and so I took over.

We initially called it Unity, a collaboration of Paul Jay and me, with the idea of inviting DJs from different countries. It quickly became a very popular night. Paul came up with the idea to make a booklet as a flyer, which gave a description of the DJ. It didn't have to be a well-known or famous DJ. Carlijn then started to play as well and, like me, she was also working behind the bar. She was very musical, she played the piano and the guitar, and became inspired to DJ after hearing the music while behind the

489

bar. She soon joined, we went on to play for years together every Saturday and she always did a great job.

In those days we had a Dateq limiter in Mazzo, which was installed by the council, but it was horrible. The new wave music wasn't so much bass orientated, but with the house there were big bass lines. This was a problem for the limiter because it would go off if the red light was on. If the light was flashing it was okay, but you had to take a bit of the bass out. If the light stayed on for more than 20 seconds, it would be a problem and the music would suddenly cut out. You then had to press the reset button, while everybody on the dance floor was staring at you and wondering what was going on. Boos would quickly fill the room and the music would then suddenly restart to a loud cheer. But it was a constant battle with the limiter and it was really stressful. At one point we just bypassed the limiter, which meant it wouldn't cut out, despite the red light.

The sound in Mazzo was never really that great. The bass was the problem, because of the neighbours.

One of the nicest nights we had in Mazzo was with DJ Per and his Per's Paradise night, which was on Thursdays. Not every Thursday, but usually every month or two. It was awesome and I loved it, a really great night that I still remember fondly.

It's a pity that Per doesn't DJ anymore.

I usually always went to that night but I did miss one because I was too tired. On that particular Thursday, April 27th, 1995, I moved my record box earlier on from the DJ booth to avoid the possibility of it being stolen and put it upstairs in the light-booth because I wouldn't be there later.

Later that night, Mazzo was on fire! The blaze started downstairs but quickly worked its way up.

I don't know exactly who did it, except that it was one of the light guys, but they were smart enough to notice my record box and immediately threw it downstairs to the dance floor and away from danger just before everybody was ordered to leave and the club evacuated.

As soon as I heard there was a fire I went straight to the club. The fire brigade were there and had already put out the fire. I walked in and it was such a mess, but there was my record box completely unharmed. Thank God somebody was smart enough to throw it downstairs!

The insurance companies were involved and with no club something had to be sorted out. I remembered Zorba the Buddah, the club I went to in the 80s. It was on the Oudezijds Voorburgwal, in the Red Light District. It was no longer in use after Spider Willem had been doing his Mushroom parties there so I knew it was empty and available.

I called Henk de Vries from the Bulldog. He owned the building, he had an office on the same street and also his Bulldog coffeeshops. I didn't know him personally but I found his office number and picked up the phone. Together with Chris and Gerrard, from Mazzo, we had a meeting to ask if we could temporarily rent the place. Within a week of the fire we had found somewhere new.

Together with all Mazzo staff, we painted the entire club. Together with our sound engineers, Audio-Amsterdam, we moved the old sound system from the smouldering Mazzo into our new temporary home. The lights were also installed and
491

within a few days Mazzo was back!

Of course, the location was much larger than what we were used to on the Rozengracht. We had always wanted a chill-out room and finally we had one, plus two dance floors. We organised an ambient area, which was really lovely, and South African Ben, Frodo and Ambient Daan etc. would play.

Saturday was renamed Expect the Unexpected, and on both Friday, with Paul Jay, and Saturday it was really rammed. This new location was massive. We absolutely loved it!

I remember the all-nighter with Billy Nasty and The Advent. The floor and the walls were shaking. It didn't matter where you were, on the stairs, the dance floor, wherever, it was crazy!

I had to play after Billy but beforehand I was up in the office and took some MDMA. I was chatting with the others and couldn't remember if I had already poured a bit into my drink, so I poured some more in. I drank it, and within no time, I realised I *had* already put some in. I was fucked, completely off my face!

Billy was told he had to continue because I couldn't even stand up. I was sat in the corner with a wet towel over my head, trying to sober up. Eventually, I could stand, felt better and I took over from a much-relieved Billy Nasty.

That was a crazy night! Those times, back then, were heavy and hypnotic – and I loved it.

All the Brits would go there and we had many British DJs. We had Phil Perry, Paul Daley and Ireland's David Holmes, among others, playing regularly. I contacted David recently to see if he was interested in a Mazzo reunion but he said he had too many

492

commitments over in America, where he's based, especially movie soundtracks. Amsterdam resident MC Marxman, from England, also started his career at Mazzo back in the day. He was an English geezer with no money so we let him in. He would MC in return for a few beers and eventually he became the voice of Amsterdam, and especially Dance Valley, in the mid-90s.

There were lots of tourists every weekend, which meant an increase in the number of dealers, and we just had the old doormen from before. Our temporary home was much bigger and consequently it was a lot more difficult to control everyone.

Eventually we moved back to the Rozengracht. But I didn't like the new Mazzo; it was a sentimental thing. I thought the bar was too large, but the DJ booth was better. The bar was a concrete square and quite large compared to the club and the space we had.

We continued to rent the old place, we renamed it Club Red, and DJ Jorg took over the Saturday nights. We thought we could run two clubs, but it was tough. I was doing the bookings for both clubs, together with Jorg. After a while, we decided to shut Red, because it simply wasn't working out as we had intended.

That space eventually became Trance Buddah, before finally being transformed into The Bulldog Hotel it is today.

Back to the new Mazzo, where I continued on the Saturday alongside Carlijn.

Sex, Love et Motion was an immense night. It was every Saturday, together with Keith Fielder, Paul Tibbs and Russ Cox, who ran the London night under the same name at The Soundshaft.

493

Before the Mazzo fire I would often head over to London and go record shopping with Paul Jay. We would go to Intergroove, Tag Records and Zoom Records, where Billy Nasty was working. Keith Fielder was at Intergroove and that's how we all originally came in contact with each other.

Phil Perry was running Full Circle, an after-party every Sunday morning. That was very smart of him because he would invite all the guest DJs playing in London on the Saturday to come and play afterwards at his party. There wasn't big money involved, just love and passion. I played there twice, it was a really great place with a really nice garden too. It was Phil's wife, Fiona, if I remember correctly, who launched a DJ agency representing everybody.

It was Paul Jay who introduced me to the London scene and took me to The Gardening Club. It was there that I heard Billy play Underworld – Mmm Skyscraper I Love You, on white label. I had never heard it before, and I said: "Wow, what the fuck is this?" and Billy handed me the record to keep I thought that was really sweet of him and it wasn't long before Billy came over to Mazzo to play.

I met an American couple in Mazzo one weekend and they were having a great time. "Wow, this place, we love it,", they said. They were tourists and about a year later, I think 1995, I was contacted by the boyfriend, who he told me that his girlfriend, who I had met the previous year, had sadly passed away after being ill for a while. She really loved her time in Amsterdam, and especially Mazzo, and her friends had decided to organise a Mazzo rave, near Boston somewhere, in her memory. It was being held in an ice skating rink and he wanted me to play.

I went together with my girlfriend at the time, Nienke, but it was quite a heavy experience. There were large video screens projecting pictures of his girlfriend, which was very sad, and the crowd, about 1,000 in total, were really emotional.

In 1996 I decided to go travelling. It had been a heavy period in my life and I wanted to get away. I wasn't even planning on coming back but during my time away I received an email from Gerrard, who asked if I would come back to Mazzo. 'Why not?' I thought.

I totally miscalculated the impact that leaving Mazzo would have. It was a very personal experience for some and we had a really great group of friends going there too. It did begin to break up a bit and I left, but after I returned so did the friends and the vibe continued.

Soon after, Mazzo was raided after it re-opened on the Rozengracht, and was forced to close for three months. It re-opened on February 20th, 1997. Mazzo was now on probation.

Eventually, it all changed again. People moved on – new relationships, work, kids etc. – and the friendships suffered. There were no new friends coming to Mazzo anymore and no new scene developing. Mazzo had new ownership, the music changed and it was not for me. I didn't like it.

Another time in the States, this time near New Jersey, I was playing at a huge rave for, initially, 12,000 people. Carlijn was also playing alongside many others from Europe. Everybody was wearing elephant trunk gas marks and taking PCP. It wasn't a good look and I didn't like it.

Just before the rave started the local fire department shut down one of the areas, which dramatically reduced the size of the party from 12,000 to 6,000 people. The DJs were crammed together in one room so our set times were reduced to cater for the other DJs from the closed-down area and it was really ridiculous. Fortunately, I was paid in advance so it didn't bother me, but Carlijn had a problem and never received her fee. The sound technicians were staying at our hotel and they informed me that they were not paid either. The promoter was almost lynched and he locked himself in his hotel room for days afterwards!

One year I played on New Year's Eve in Boulder, Colorado. The night before, December 30th, I was asked to play at an illegal warehouse party. I said yes and the organiser had three or four venues ready in case of any issues. You had to call a phone number, which was on a small paper flyer, and you would receive directions to the party. Everyone was in a convoy, the sound system too. The first location was busted, so it was on to the second venue. That was also busted, so the convoy headed for the third venue. Everything seemed okay and the guys built the sound system. I was opening my record box, ready to play, when the police raided the venue. My main problem was that I was a foreigner and that wasn't really a smart move, while my girlfriend was under 21. We were smuggled out of the warehouse at the rear, just as the police came charging in the front. In charge of the sound system were Latinos, who were all armed with guns that they decided to throw over a fence. Despite the apparent danger, it was actually really exciting!

We escaped, no harm, but the party was busted. But the following night, New Year's Eve, I played in Bolder, which was really nice.

In Zaandam, near Amsterdam, there was a place called the Showboat and it was an after-hour location. One night, after
496

Mazzo, I had to play at the Silo, a warehouse in Amsterdam which had a huge basement for parties. After the Silo, it was time to leave for the Showboat.

When I arrived it was clear everybody was absolutely wasted. Everywhere you looked, just an absolute mess! I was playing, still amazed at what I was witnessing, and somebody put a line of cocaine on the spinning record I was about to play. I did it, but immediately the manager of the Showboat came running over to me and said "Oh, Cellie, you know that is not allowed here." I pointed to the mass of wasted people and said "What are you talking about, looooooooooook!" Anyway, I finished my set and everything was fine.

I was on holiday with my mate, Chris, in the south of France where my parents had an apartment. I was checking my diary and noticed that later that night, which was a Friday, I had to play in Haarlem, near Amsterdam. We were 12 hours away, and so we packed the car and drove straight to the club. We made it, but I was so tired from the journey.

I was playing and I asked Chris if there was anything that would wake me up a bit. He waved me over and we went to the toilet together. We both ignored the rules and went in a cubicle. The security guys were banging on the door and shouting "Open up, this is not allowed, open the doooooooor!" I was still actually DJing at the time and I had put on a long track whilst I went to the toilet.

The security staff were not happy and they told us we were being chucked out. But they didn't recognise me as the DJ. I told them that not only was I was the DJ, I was playing right there and then. "That's what they all say," he said, and we were actually about to be thrown out when the manager walked over. At this moment
497

the club felt silent. The record had stopped and the DJ was being thrown out mid-set. "You see, I am the DJ," I told them. "I'm so disappointed in you Cellie," said the manager. I apologised and explained why I was so tired. "Can I go back to the decks, please?" I asked. The manager agreed but the security guys were still far from happy. They were arguing with the manager as I embarrassingly re-entered the silent DJ booth.

Amsterdam had another after-hour spot back in the early 90s – the Subtopia boat, run by DJs Jeroen Flamman and Abraxas. It was an awesome place, behind Centraal Station by jetty 14, but was told it had to move. They moved to Amsterdam north and the parties were still happening, but why Paul Jay and I decided to get involved I will never know.

I was working behind the bar in Mazzo on Fridays and Paul was playing all night, but we still decided to DJ on the boat afterwards. We even dismantled the Mazzo sound system to take some speakers and amplifiers with us after the club had closed. Just thinking about it is really tiring and I can't explain why we even bothered. We usually went on until 12 the next afternoon and it was horrible. I was completely knackered and it was crazy.

I was really inspired by the Subtopia parties in the beginning, especially at the Kattengat squat in the centre of Amsterdam. It was always full of cool and crazy people.

I've played in Naples, Italy, a few times. One time, mid-90s, I was playing with Darren Emerson and he was accompanied by Karl Hyde, a fellow Underworld member at the time. The sound system was awful, something usually used for a reggae party. The sound technicians had even forgotten to bring needles for the turntables. Darren and I searched about and managed to find one needle so we just put on a record hoping we would find another
498

needle in time. We didn't and we ended up playing back-to-back on one turntable.

Despite the obvious issue, the crowd knew what was up and they went with it. They got so involved and made so much noise when the record started and finished, and kept cheering whilst we changed the record. Karl then grabbed the microphone and was doing his thing in between the records and it was actually a really great night. After about an hour of this, the second needle turned up and Darren and I started to play on two decks. Despite the problems, I still get goose bumps thinking about what was a truly awesome experience.

Another time in Naples, together with DJ Ashley from England, we found out that the promoter had done a runner during the party – with all the cash! All cash boxes and registers had been completely emptied, and the entire income was gone. The party was a sell-out, so a lot of money had been generated. Nobody was paid, not the barman, DJs, security – absolutely no one. We were furious and decided to take the turntables. We unplugged them, picked up one each and started to walk out of the club. But somebody from the club, who wasn't part of the promotion, screamed at us in Italian and gestured that we put the decks back. They were quite convincing so we complied with their request.

But one thing they didn't notice was that we had unscrewed the cartridges to which the needles were attached. We took them both, plus a third which was spare – anything to try to retrieve some of the cash we'd lost!

ADAMSKI

And finally, after all the revelations and madness you have just read, we conclude with a somewhat brief overview from another legend and pioneer of our beloved scene – Adamski.

After forming a band, The Stupid Babies, at the age of 11, with his five-year-old brother Dominic, Adam Paul Tinley would eventually go on to be a rave legend and give the world anthems such as N-R-G and Killer.

It was actually an earlier production that brought Adamski to promoters' attention, with a track entitled Liveandirect. Lenny D booked him and his career in the rave scene grew week by week. N-R-G is an acid house and rave crossover anthem that features a picture of a Lucozade bottle, with edited text, on its vinyl sleeve.

It didn't go unnoticed by the Beecham Group, who manufactured the popular fizzy drink back then. They demanded 2,500 pounds from Adamski for using the image without permission and his record company, MCA, paid the Nordoff Robbins music therapy charity the full amount, as requested.

Incidentally, in 1989 the Beecham Group merged to form SmithKline Beecham, which in 2000 merged to form GlaxoSmithKline, then in September 2013 GlaxoSmithKline sold Lucozade and another well-known soft drink, Ribena, to the Japanese conglomerate Suntory for 1.35 billion pounds.

It was the huge popularity of N-R-G that helped ignite Adamski's underground dance career, along with a more mainstream track,

Killer, which featured a young Seal on vocals.

Adamski had this to say...

My story is much like all the others...went to parties, made music, took too many drugs and ended up as a manic depressive has-been...that's it in a nutshell. Best regards.

THANK YOU

Many thanks to the following, because without your love, support and inspiration this book may never have been written...

My amazing son Louis, Mum, Dad, Tracy, Gary, Jacob, Francesca, Wendy, Big G, Stacey, Vicky, Marcus, Marceline & Dennis, Ian Hussey, Marnix, Dylan, Minnie, Wouter, Dr Peter Post, to all the artists, backstage hospitality, Awakenings, Cheeky Monday, Dance Valley, Paradiso, Melkweg, Pablo Discobar Soundsystem, Wooferland, Loveland, Dockyard, Dean Sadikot and the best team in the land and all the world – Manchester City Football Club.

For any future artwork or design needs, please contact Dean Sadikot at mindseyeful@gmail.com.

X

Printed in Great Britain
by Amazon